Cognition and Practice

SUNY series in Chinese Philosophy and Culture

Roger T. Ames, editor

Cognition and Practice

Li Zehou's Philosophical Aesthetics

Rafal Banka

Published by State University of New York Press, Albany

Printed in the United States of America

For information, contact State University of New York Press, Albany, NY
www.sunypress.edu

Library of Congress Cataloging-in-Publication Data

Name: Banka, Rafal, 1976– author.
Title: Cognition and practice : Li Zehou's philosophical aesthetics / Rafal Banka.
Description: Albany : State University of New York Press, [2022] | Series: SUNY series in Chinese philosophy and culture | Includes bibliographical references and index.
Identifiers: LCCN 2022005651 | ISBN 9781438489230 (hardcover : alk. paper) | ISBN 9781438489254 (ebook)
Subjects: LCSH: Li, Zehou. | Aesthetics, Chinese. | Cognition.
Classification: LCC B5234.L4874 B36 2022 | DDC 170.92—dc23/eng/20220323
LC record available at https://lccn.loc.gov/2022005651

10 9 8 7 6 5 4 3 2 1

Contents

Acknowledgments vii

Introduction 1

Chapter 1 Confucian Inspiration 7

Chapter 2 Marxist Framework 23

Chapter 3 Reinterpreting Kant 37

Chapter 4 Philosophy of Subjectality 69

Chapter 5 Situating Subjectality 95

Chapter 6 Beauty 111

Chapter 7 Aesthetic Experience 125

Chapter 8 An Alternative Account of Aesthetic Experience: John Dewey 161

Chapter 9 Contemporary Experience-Based Aesthetics 177

Afterword 191

Notes 195

Bibliography 217

Index 225

Acknowledgments

Nothing is born in vacuum. This book would not be published without help of many people. I would like to thank Roger Ames, editor of the SUNY Press series in Chinese Philosophy and Culture, James Peltz, SUNY Press associate director and editor in chief, as well as the anonymous reviewers who have made my project see the light of publication. I also convey my debt to the Charles Wei-hsun Fu Foundation and the International Society for Chinese Philosophy, who in 2015 jointly granted me a Junior Faculty Award for an article that was a prelude for a longer study completed as this very book. I offer my deep thanks to Jinhua Jia and, again, Roger Ames, who invited me to participate in the conference "Li Zehou and Confucian Philosophy," which took place at the University of Hawai'i at Mānoa in autumn 2015. It was an excellent exchange that led me to a comprehensive study of the liaisons of practice and cognition in Li Zehou's philosophical aesthetics. I am deeply thankful to Anna I. Wojcik, my former MA and PhD theses supervisor, for inspiring lectures in classical Chinese aesthetics, without which I might not have developed interest in this part of Chinese philosophy. I also express my regards to Szymon Szymczak, the most inspiring logician that I have met. Last but not least, I would like to thank my wife Jinli He for being a patient yet sincere critic and continuous supporter of what I do.

The project described in this book has been funded by the National Science Centre of Poland, funding scheme: Sonata 12 (project registration no. 2016/23/D/HS1/02451).

Introduction

This book aims to present Li Zehou's aesthetics as a form of cognition. There are two reasons for undertaking this project. The general motivation is to present the aesthetics of Li Zehou, one of the most influential living Chinese philosophers, to the Western audience. Li lived from 1930 to 2021. He studied philosophy at Peking University and was a former professor of the Chinese Academy of Social Sciences. He was active as a philosopher since the 1950s. His writings became particularly influential among Chinese intellectuals in the 1980s, a period often referred to as Chinese Cultural Fever (Zhongguo Wenhua Re 中國文化熱), when the monolithic discourse of social realism became replaced with cultural pluralism, which among others included qualitative changes in widely understood aesthetics.

Li is particularly known for proposing an original aesthetic theory founded on anthropological ontology, otherwise known as the philosophy of subjectality, but his work devoted to Kant's thought as well as the history of Chinese philosophy is no less important due to his specifically conceived approach to historical materialism. While Li's influence on contemporary Chinese philosophy, and more generally humanities in mainland China, is vast and can be counted in decades, he is hardly recognized beyond Chinese-speaking academia. It must be admitted that Li is not completely unknown among Western scholars. However, one should observe at the same time that in Western academia, Li's writings are known almost entirely among scholars who work in sinology or what may be broadly construed as Chinese studies. This shows that Li's philosophy practically passes unnoticed in the realm of academia that is unrelated to studies connected with Chinese civilization. This is also the case of Western philosophy scholars who, when they refer to the Chinese tradition, usually focus on Confucianism and Daoism. While the importance of these classical Chinese philosophy schools is undeniable, little attention is paid to contemporary Chinese thought, which can equally contribute to comparative or global philosophical research. In this respect, I believe Li's aesthetics to be one of the most important philosophical projects.

This elicits the second and main motivation for undertaking the project: to examine Li's aesthetics as a form of cognition. Although Li's multiple philosophical projects, including the one related to aesthetics, are discussed in a tremendously diverse fashion, as yet no consideration has been given to the idea that Li's aesthetic conception may be viewed from a cognitive perspective. I believe that the absence of a cognitive dimension in the discussion of Li's aesthetics cannot be dismissed on the grounds of being irrelevant or of minor importance in comparison with other issues. The cognitive aspect can be justified all the way from Li's philosophical inspirations to the final shape of his own aesthetic theory. First, considering the assumptions that Li shares with Confucian, Marxist, and Kantian philosophy, the need to explore the cognitive dimension of his philosophy is most apparent. It can be roughly stated that the philosophical context of Li's philosophy essentially contributes in a cognitive sense.

Second, the cognitive aspect does not reside solely in the foundations of Li's theory; Li's presentation of "subjectality," a subject that actively interacts with the world that concurrently shapes it psychologically, also testifies to the notion that Li's project is significantly underpinned by cognitive intuitions. In fact, the cognitive underlay provides the condition necessary for the coherence of the subject concept, as well as an indispensable heuristic element of Li's aesthetics.

Exploring and reconstructing the cognitive dimension of Li's aesthetics is of great importance for contemporary philosophical research. Not only does it enrich the perspective from which Li's research can be viewed, but, even more importantly, the cognitive dimension of Li's aesthetics situates it in proximity to contemporary aesthetics research in which great concern is given to the embodiment and embeddedness of the subject. This opens an interesting way of interpreting Li's project through the prism of situated cognition, but equally importantly it may offer global aesthetic research an alternative insight into how the cognitive structures responsible for the aesthetic apprehension of reality are developed. Considering additionally that a core characteristic of Li's aesthetic is practice, which is integrated with cognition, I believe and will argue that in this respect Li's theory can be viewed in terms of autopoietic enactivism, which allows the subject's action, cognition, and constitution to be integrated. Bearing in mind the fact that naturalized aesthetics can be described as in focus and progressive branch of research, the possible contribution of Li's aesthetics on this front deserves consideration.[1]

Li's aesthetics is compatible with the experience-oriented contemporary theories that redefine the discipline and contrast themselves with philosophy of art and axiological conceptualizations.[2] Importantly, this branch of aesthetic research also considers that, especially due to the advent of advanced technologies, the experiential world changes, which requires adjustment in theoretical approach. In this respect, Li's conception offers a comprehensive historical perspective, in which the world, as well as theoretical reflection upon it, are incessantly and progressively changing. According to Li, this change is best encapsulated in aesthetic theory. Considering this approach, one can even state that Li's aesthetics is metatheoretical in the sense of being inclusive of particular, temporal theories. It should also be mentioned that Li's aesthetics explains the sequence and character of particular, temporal aesthetic theoretical formations, which complements the comprehensive perspective with a fine-grained approach.

Apart from the possible contribution of the metatheoretical perspective, Li's aesthetics is also worth considering as an actual theory. It reveals high flexibility in configuring an interdisciplinary approach that includes diverse areas of study. As mentioned above, this compatibility makes Li's theory compatible with contemporary research into naturalized aesthetics, where the liaisons of the aesthetic, practice, and cognition may constitute a possible contribution.

Before proceeding to the interpretation of Li's aesthetics throughout the rest of the book, for the sake of avoiding ambiguity, I would like to explain the two terms, aesthetics and cognition, that constitute the framework of my discussion.

The most fundamental term is aesthetics. Jerrold Levinson generally defines aesthetics as "the branch of philosophy devoted to conceptual and theoretical inquiry into art and aesthetic experience," while also mentioning that it is especially focused on art, properties, and experience.[3] I believe that aesthetics is usually associated with three dominant elements, which are similar to those listed by Levinson: art, aesthetic values, and sensuousness. These associations lie at the foundations of particular aesthetic theories. As for the first one, it is usually mistakenly associated with aesthetics. In reality, it mostly overlaps with the philosophy of art, which as a philosophical reflection on art is a separate discipline. This fact does not mean that art is excluded from the aesthetic scope. Quite the contrary, art is included in investigation but it does not exhaust the entire discipline of aesthetics. As regards the axiological aesthetic theories, they are concerned with determining the aesthetic values of objects and events. Hence, theories of beauty, the sublime, ugliness, harmony, and other values fall into this category.

I will operate with the concept of aesthetics that converges with the third association, stemming from Alexander Gottlieb Baumgarten's understanding of aesthetics. Baumgarten coined the name *aesthetica*, from the Greek *aisthesis*, which means sense perception.[4] He defines aesthetics as a science of sensuous cognition.[5] In fact, Baumgarten's definition includes art, poetry in particular, but the main stress is put on how aesthetics matters in cognition. It bears an important implication for sensuousness as it is endowed with cognitive capacity. This connection between the aesthetic and the cognitive will prove significant in my further discussion of Li's aesthetic project.

Another important term that requires explanation is cognition. It is important that in the aesthetic apprehension of reality, cognitive processes usually do not lead to propositional knowledge, otherwise known as "knowledge that." The fact that aesthetic experiences are not aimed at this type of knowledge does not disqualify them from being cognitive. Experiencing the aesthetic can be, for instance, informative of a subject's successful adaptation to the environment or achieving harmony with it. Despite the fact that such states are not known but felt, they are also cognitive in character. For this reason, I describe Li's aesthetics as *a* form of cognition. This means that aesthetics is cognitive but should not be identified with cognition that culminates in propositional knowledge. Nor should it be ignored that according to some theories, as will be demonstrated in the book, cognitive processes that result in propositional knowledge must contain aesthetic components. Aesthetic cognition does not negate other forms of cognition. My reference to the cognitive processes will be in terms of how they are understood in aesthetics rather than the epistemology of knowledge.

As regards the book's structure, it is thematically arranged into three parts. The first three chapters introduce the philosophies that have significantly inspired Li's philosophical project. All are considerably formative with regard both to how Li conceptualizes aesthetics and to how this area is connected with cognition. In chapter 1, I discuss Confucianism, which has influenced Li's aesthetics in general and specific respects. Li's philosophical heuristics is deeply founded on a worldview that is present in almost all schools of classical Chinese philosophy, Confucianism being among them. The view assumes that the world is a dynamic reality, and humans as integral part of it intend to harmonize with the cosmos on multiple levels of their life. As for specific inspiration, it mainly consists in sharing the view that the aesthetic is inseparable from human life practice, and that primitive emotions have been cultivated to the aesthetic level. Confucianism also shows that emotions, apart from being responses, play an important role in cognition and moral knowledge.

Chapter 2 is devoted to Marxism, an inspiration that cannot be overestimated. In this chapter, I reveal the importance of Marx's *Economic and Philosophic Manuscripts* in Li's own formulation of historical materialism. By consistently following Marx in terms of the material practice consisting only in the manufacturing and use of tools, Li constructs his own theory of the humanization of nature and sedimentation, which underpin aesthetic practice and apprehension of reality. Although Li's project is by all means original, it can also be stated that the Marxist inspiration is decisive in determining its framework.

In chapter 3, I discuss another philosophical system that has crucially influenced Li—Kant's philosophy of subjectality. Whereas Marxism is responsible for forging the framework of Li's conception, Kant informs Li's account of aesthetic experience and how it is related to cognition. It should be noted that Li radically reinterprets Kant's apriorism and sets it on materialist foundations, by which it only reveals consistence with Li's anthropological ontology.

Chapter 4 opens the second thematic area, devoted to expounding and interpreting Li's philosophical project. My discussion is based on the ten statements and commentaries from Li's *The Outline of My Philosophy*, which can be considered as his philosophical credo. It presents in detail the conception of subjectality, a dynamic subject actively engaged in the world that concurrently molds the techno-social and psychological substances of which it is composed. I complement the discussion with material from experimental sciences that can examine Li's theory as well as address the issue of how the human mind is molded by human practice.

Considering that subjectality invites a perspective seen through the prism of situated cognition, in chapter 5 it is examined in embodied, embedded, extended, and enactive variants. I argue that the most compatible conceptualization is offered by autopoietic enactivism, mainly because of subjectality's inherent interactive character that can be interpreted as enactments. I also show that enactivism enables the emotional structures of subjectality to be viewed in terms of appraisal theory.

In chapter 6, I present the notion of beauty, which at face value may appear inconsistent with Li's experience-oriented aesthetics. However, it will be shown that beauty is not to be axiologically conceptualized. Instead, beauty emerges from subjective interaction with the objective world. It will also be explained in what sense beauty is tantamount to freedom and how it persists through time differently from aesthetic values.

Chapter 7 is devoted to a discussion of Li's account of aesthetic experience. Apart from discussing the stages and structure of aesthetic experience, I will also show how it can be interpreted in autopoietic enactivism terms.

Chapters 8 and 9 compare Li's aesthetics with other concepts. In chapter 8, I will discuss John Dewey's account of aesthetic experience. I believe and will try to demonstrate that it is an interesting alternative to Li's, which is informed by Kant's interplay of cognitive faculties. Dewey's aesthetic experience, apart from remaining consistent with the anthropological ontology framework, appears to offer more compatibility in extending aesthetic experience in naturalized aesthetics terms, which appears not to be so natural with the intellectual faculties inherited from Kant's philosophical system.

Chapter 9 presents a consideration of how Li's aesthetics can be referred to other contemporary experience-oriented conceptions. I refer Li's historical perspective to Bence Nanay's proposal that aesthetics may be viewed through the prism of philosophy of perception and Wolfgang Welsch's comprehensive and interdisciplinary approach. I also reveal how Li's conception can possibly contribute to the contemporary determination of aesthetics as a philosophical discipline.

Clearly, this book will not delve into the historical and biographical context of Li's philosophy. Nor does it aim to explore all the aspects of Li's aesthetics, for instance in relation to art, about which Li writes extensively. The aim of my project is far more modest and restricted to the cognitive dimension of Li's aesthetics, which I believe to be a most important linking point with contemporary aesthetic research, to which it may hopefully contribute.

Chapter 1

Confucian Inspiration

Introduction

Confucianism is one out of three main philosophical inspirations of Li Zehou, along with Kantian philosophy and Marxism. There are two reasons why one might refer to this particular tradition in the context of discussing Li's aesthetics as a form of cognition. The first is to show how Confucianism addresses the aesthetic and what role it plays in this particular philosophical school. The second, and more important, reason is how the aesthetic in Confucianism is connected with cognition. In fact, Li inclines more toward the belief that in Confucius's philosophy the aesthetic should not be associated with cognition on the grounds of it being experienced as a form of emotion.[1] However, this claim, by being underlaid with the assumption that the emotional is excluded from cognition, is arguable not only in light of the most recent research in, for instance affective science,[2] but also within the Confucian doctrine itself.

It would be very difficult to imagine Li's philosophical project in its current shape without the contribution of Confucianism. It has to be admitted that Li's theory of subjectality reflects more an amalgamation of Kantian and Marxist influences, but it is Confucianism that reveals itself in particular through the psychological intricacies of this philosophical construction.[3] It can be said that to some extent Li assumes the Confucian way of thinking in his project. For this reason, it will also be shown how Li perceives Confucian views related to the aesthetic, as represented by Confucius. Focusing on Confucius instead of the whole Confucianism tradition or some other representatives of this particular school is justified by Li's interest in Confucius as the first Chinese thinker who had proposed views clearly related to the aesthetic. In Confucianism, and generally in almost all other Chinese schools of thought, the human inner development and its manifestation of have never been of a religious or transcendent character. This area of human existence, according to Li, was accommodated by aesthetics, which was first directly discussed theoretically by Confucius. Li believes that the Confucian self-cultivation involved joy (*le* 樂), which crucially intersects it with the aesthetic.[4]

Another great achievement that Li ascribes to Confucius is showing the interrelation of ethics and aesthetics within his thought. According to Li, Confucius, although predominantly concerned with the matter of ethics, unlike some later Confucian philosophers, did not focus solely on ethical issues,[5] and accordingly did not downplay the role of beauty in his system. Moreover, beauty in Confucianism is not a separate field of investigation but is involved in mutual complementation with *ren*—the moral ideal. This complementation subject to the ethical objective, as good, particularly represented in Confucianism as *ren*, is more fundamental. Li supports it with the following fragment from the *Analects* 3.3:

> The Master said: "A man who is not good [*ren* 仁]—what has he to do with music?"[6]

Confucius seems to be very clear about the distribution of importance in his system, namely, by showing that good precedes beauty. It is also suggested what kind of beauty, expressed in this example by the musical medium, is regarded as valuable in the Confucian system—it has to comply with the ethical order. This interspersion of the ethical and aesthetic is very formative for Li's own philosophical project, where humans by means of proper practice bring beauty into existence.

Beyond any doubt, the influence of Confucius on Li is of great importance. Concurrently, it should be noted, however, that despite the above-mentioned important Confucian influence it would be considerably difficult, imprecise, and incorrect to place Li among philosophers with not only strong Confucian identity but also heritage, such as Mou Zongsan (牟宗三) or Xiong Shili (熊十力). These thinkers evidently remained under the influence of earlier Confucian philosophers—classical Confucian or neo-Confucian—and continued to philosophize in a Confucian spirit. Li clearly evades this category of thinkers. Although he refers to Confucianism more than any other Chinese philosophical tradition, he employs it while constructing his own philosophy and, accordingly, does not intend to convey the Confucian message. Li's profound inspiration from Confucian philosophy is merely a building block for his original project.

A Twofold Approach to Confucianism—General Interpretation

It also has to be mentioned that Li's interest in and inspiration from the Chinese philosophical tradition is not exclusively confined to the Confucian school. Li also values other schools in the Chinese philosophical tradition,[7] in particular Zhuangzi's Daoism. From a more general perspective, his choice of Confucianism as the main Chinese philosophical inspiration can be viewed as resorting to a representative of almost the whole Chinese philosophical tradition in terms of sharing some common assumptions that constitute the foundations of traditional Chinese thought. Admittedly, Confucianism has been one of the most important schools of thought throughout Chinese history of philosophy. Apart from developing a clearly distinct doctrine, it also shares with other philosophical schools some general, fundamental elements.

These shared elements can be described as metaphysical and ethical intuitions. The text that encapsulates the formative philosophical intuitions that are present in most classical Chinese philosophy, as well as the philosophical schools that follow it, is the *Book of Changes*, or the *Yijing* (易經). This text can be perceived as not belonging to philosophy on account of its original intention, which was a divination manual. However, its impact on and role in Chinese philosophy cannot be denied. It constitutes an early layer of Chinese thought that contains the intuitions that founded philosophical development in classical and later philosophies in China.

The philosophical intuitions from the *Book of Changes* that pervade into later Chinese thought are often referred to as cosmology or cosmological thinking. There are several aspects that constitute Chinese cosmological thinking, but for the sake of this discussion, I will limit myself to introducing only the relevant ones. They concern the holistic worldview, status of dualities, and the dynamic model of the universe.

The *Book of Changes* was written down over centuries, approximately from 900 BCE until 500 BCE, yet these rough framing dates remain uncertain. However, what is important is that the text was composed over a long period of time and it can be subdivided into three main chronological strata: trigrams, hexagrams, and commentaries. The oldest layer, is composed of eight trigrams that are all possible combinations of three lines, continuous and broken.[8] The trigrams correspond with natural phenomena that are thought to depict everything that happens in the universe. Importantly, they do not map a description of the universe that constantly changes, similarly to natural phenomena. This shows that the Chinese thinking already included the intuition of a dynamic universe. Consequently, one cannot describe such a universe as a static entity but as a process.

The second chronological layer that followed is the sixty-four hexagrams, which present all possible combinations of the eight trigrams. They were allegedly compiled by a historical figure—King Wen from the Zhou dynasty in the twelfth century BCE.[9] The hexagrams were accompanied by two types of commentaries—on the whole hexagram and on each line in it. Both types of commentaries bore a kind of moral advice introduced in situations. What is important here is that the behavior described in the situations is synchronized with the lines that illustrate the incessant changes in the universe. In this sense, human conduct is not set against the cosmological processes in the world but quite the contrary—it is paired with them, or, to be more exact, it is part of the processes that take place. This integration situates humans as integral part of nature that is influenced by the dynamic cosmos and tries to adjust to it with a prescribed conduct.

Finally, the hexagrams were followed by the final stratum of commentaries, some of which were allegedly written by Confucius, yet this authorship remains historically unclear.[10] The commentaries vary in kind. The one that contains a prominent philosophical message is the *Great Commentary* (*Dazhuan* 大傳), alternatively referred to as the *Commentary on the Appended Phrases* (*Xicizhuan* 繫辭傳). This work in particular aims to describe moral correlates of what happens in nature, more generally speaking the cosmos, represented by the hexagrams and the relations between the lines that constitute them. It can be observed that the world is dynamic and that human actions require proper configuration that is expected to bring correct behavior, and, more importantly, proper existence in the world.

Altogether, Karyn L. Lai distinguishes seven features of cosmological thinking.[11] However, for the sake of bringing necessary context to our discussion on Confucianism, I briefly focus only on two of them: holistic conception of the world and dynamics consisting in change.

In the first fragment from the *Great Commentary* we can read:

> As Heaven is high and noble and Earth is low and humble, so it is that Qian [Pure Yang, hexagram 1] and Kun [Pure Yin, hexagram 2] are defined. . . . The high and the low being

> thereby set out, the exalted and the mean have their places accordingly. . . . There are norms for action and repose, which are determined by whether hardness or softness is involved.[12]

The hexagrams from the passage denote the foundations of the world. We are confronted with a metaphysical universe composed of two opposite elements: *yang* (陽) and *yin* (陰). These elements exhaust the metaphysical universe, leaving no place for anything transcendent in relation to them. *Yin* and *yang* are not different substances, and together they form *qi* (氣), the "substance" of the whole universe.[13] For this reason, their opposition is complementary, not contradictory. They should be understood more in terms of aspects of *qi* that concurrently are the forces thanks to which the world is incessantly dynamic.

Further on, in the same fragment, we read:

> Those with regular tendencies gather according to kind, and things divide up according to group; so it is that good fortune and misfortune occur.[14]

This description is first of all of metaphysical character, but it should be noted that it concurrently applies to humans, who do not transcend the metaphysical laws of the universe. The cosmos is not only nature in the sense of background to human activity, as humans are an integral part of it and live in a dynamic world of changes. In this way, human actions are also part of the changes and they should constantly synchronize with the rest of the cosmos.

It is also stated that compliance with the cosmos is measured in terms of fortune or misfortune. Thus, valuation of human behavior, growing from the cosmic order, is provided. This shows the connection of the metaphysical and ethical orders, which, although not developed in a purely philosophical manner in the commentary, are clearly present as a potential form.

Considering that the whole universe is dynamic in nature, humans have to continuously adjust to the incessant processes of change. This requires an identification of the stage of change, or, from the perspective of the subject, where she/he is located in that process. Adequate, synchronized behavior also relies on making predictions with regard to what is the character of the future change—in nature, but also among humans. Therefore, it is impossible to act blindly according to principles, but only in response to the situation one finds oneself in.

To sum up, the *Book of Changes* contains intuitions of metaphysical and ethical nature. The hexagrams constitute the amalgamation of iconic and abstract representations of the situations that emerge in the process of changes in the world, conceptualized as the cosmos of multiple dynamic relations. The cosmos is the whole metaphysical universe. There is nothing that transcends the cosmos and everything is ordered and explainable within it. It is characterized by incessant transformations that also embrace humans, who as part of the dynamic whole have to accommodate the actions that are intertwined with the rest of the world, both human and nonhuman. It should also be observed that within this cosmological model there is no conflict between humans and nature, as they complement each other and should remain in harmonious relation.

These intuitions are present in Confucianism, especially in the sphere of human relations. As regards the social layer, Confucianism views the individual as part of the whole. Humans and the universe form a unity and they are involved in incessant interaction. On this view, Confucians build their specific system, where the self-cultivation of humans is viewed in terms of inner virtue transformation, and appropriate interactions with other humans in family and society. These interactions are also incessantly dynamic, and humans, through their behavior, have to constantly adapt to the situations. The social sphere is one of possible reflections of the holistic world view from the *Book of Changes* in the sense that it is part of the dense tissue subject to transformation. Therefore, the activity of humans is not only aimed at achieving social harmony. In fact, social harmony constitutes an integral part of cosmic harmony. As can be seen by the development of Chinese philosophy, the paradigm invites many different concretions, Confucian ethics being one of them.

Viewed from this angle, Confucianism serves as a pretty comprehensive epitome of the fundamental assumptions that determine the Chinese philosophical characteristics, in spite of the particular systems that are built upon them in many different schools.

A Twofold Approach to Confucianism—Particular Interpretation

However, these protophilosophical intuitions, in spite of being present and developed in Li's philosophy, are only of secondary benefit for him in turning to Confucianism. What matters much more for Li's aesthetics goes beyond the universal assumptions and is the particular development of the philosophical system erected on them. On a general level, Li admits that he values Confucius most of all classical Chinese philosophers because he was the first thinker to focus his philosophical attention exclusively on being (*you* 有)[15]—roughly speaking, what exists and is related to the existence of humans,[16] who are necessarily embedded in living in society and the natural world understood as the cosmos from the *Book of Changes*. This exclusive focus on being contrasts Confucians with some influential schools of their time that took a serious interest in experience-transcendent reality. A most representative of them was Laozi's metaphysically oriented Daoism, which mainly investigated nonbeing *wu* (無), by which the gravity of philosophical interest was shifted toward the other part of the ontic universe. Another example is Mohism, which stood in opposition to Confucianism. Although not extensively discussing transcendence, it assumed transcendent entities conceived in a quasi-religious fashion.

Confucius was focused on the existing world in many aspects, which, considering the holistic nature of reality, naturally included the social sphere as well as the study of the human mindset and the way in which these two are interrelated. As Li remarks, Confucius was probably the earliest Chinese thinker to have paid attention to the complex role that emotions play in humans. Li believes that emotion is situated in the center of Confucian philosophy.[17] In fact, he regards emotion as the key to understanding the overall Confucian moral, but also more generally, philosophical message. It can also be clearly seen that in his discussion of Confucian ethics, emotion is a composite of the human psyche and it can be molded under the influence of rationalization. This desired calibration of emotions is not seen by Li as a mechanism exclusively particular of Confucian philosophy—it actually is a most important process in Li's own conceptualization of the Marxist humanization of nature, which takes place in the history of the human species. But it is not only the ethical side of Confucianism that largely relies on emotions. They are equally important for understanding Confucian aesthetics, and, which is not difficult to expect, emotions are the linking point between good and beauty.

The most important aspect of Confucian philosophy that needs to be considered first for the sake of my interpretation of Li's aesthetics is practice. It should be viewed in two aspects: its external character in human interactions and the impact it exerts on the human being as a psychological subject. In order to view this issue in a systematic way, I will depart from the categorization of Confucianism as an ethical system. As mentioned above, Confucius was primarily concerned with interactions of humans with other humans and the world. His interest was almost entirely directed at the world of humans, with regard to both their individual and social identities. Considering this, on philosophical ground, his investigations almost naturally find development within the categories of ethics, where the aesthetic plays an important role, and, what is characteristic of Confucianism and some other Chinese philosophy schools, its natural extension—political philosophy.[18]

Ethical Foundation of Aesthetics

From the perspective of normative ethics categorization, the system developed by Confucius should be classified as a variety of virtue ethics. Normative ethics is mainly concerned with the principles "that govern the issues of how we should live and what we morally ought to do."[19] Thus, it is primarily concerned with how ethical valuation can be distributed with regard to the agent's actions and the ways in which they can be justified. Within normative ethics, we usually distinguish between the three types: deontological ethics (or deontology), consequentialism, and virtue ethics. As regards deontology, it is a normative theory that mostly concentrates on the principles that should be followed in order to attain an ethical goal. Consequentialism mainly consists in assessing the moral rightness of acts according to the consequences they produce (or are expected to produce).[20] In comparison with deontology, consequentialism shifts importance from principles to aims.

Comparatively speaking, virtue ethics in terms of behavioral repertoire is closer to consequentialism because its objective does not consist in what particular action should be taken (although it may initially appear to be the case, for instance in Confucianism). However, it also essentially differs from consequentialism in that the ethical goal is not identified as a consequence of the action taken.

Rosalind Hursthouse and Glen Pettigrove describe virtue ethics in contrast with consequentialism and deontology as "the one which emphasizes the virtues or moral character."[21] Therefore, it can be said that virtue ethics aims at constituting particular, regarded as good, character traits in a moral agent. It can be noticed that virtue ethics is substantially different from the other two types of normative ethics in that it is less external; the point of ethical gravity is shifted on the agent. The most important consideration is what moral personality she/he is, rather than whether her/his actions agree with some standards or lead to the desired moral goals that are understood as results of actions. To put virtue ethics into a more behaviorally oriented wording, we can understand virtues functionally, as stable dispositions that ensure a considerably permanent behavioral repertoire that testifies to the good moral personality of the agent. In this sense, the behavior confirms and builds the moral personhood equipped with proper character traits.

At this point, we can probably already notice that developing stable dispositions cannot be confined only to concentrating on building good character traits. Character traits should certainly be understood as constituting a certain mindset, but at the same time they are dispositions to "notice, feel, value, desire, choose act and react."[22] What can be noticed is that, although the moral goal of virtue ethics consists in achieving a certain moral mindset, the moral agent cannot close herself/himself in one's mind and refrain from extending her/his virtue in behavior. For instance, virtues cannot be achieved by self-reflection or a conceptual analysis of the value of good. It can be said that the virtuous mindset needs necessary confirmation or manifestation in practice.

Practice is indispensable for virtue ethics. Apart from the need to confirm or manifest virtues for the completeness of a moral personality, the need for practical extension of virtue can be even more important on the grounds of ontological dependence. Character traits may not be inherent or firmly and permanently established in the moral subject, and it is the moral practice that is necessary to keep them alive or to develop to a full potential. Such is the case of the Confucian virtue *ren*. In many fragments of the *Analects*, Confucius states that some persons are moral, that is, possess virtue, based on their conduct.[23] Statements of this kind are possible thanks to the assumption that practice is extension of virtue but also that practice ontologically "nourishes" the virtue.

Apart from extending virtue in practice, it is also important to ensure that the results of actions comply with the intentions, and therefore the moral agent also needs to take into consideration the particular circumstances in which the moral agent's action occurs. Virtue can be regarded as the central concept of virtue ethics, but because of practical extension, it requires an essential complement—practical wisdom. Character traits are necessary to act in a good way, but at the same time having good intentions rooted in them provides no guarantee that actions are always the correct extension. The moral agent can act with morally good intentions but the actions may prove to be shortcomings. For instance, assuming that being courageous is a virtue, we can imagine a situation in which a courageous act goes too far, as a result of which it is not moral at all. The agent when departing from good intentions concurrently needs to know how to implement them in a successful way.

Hursthouse and Pettigrove provide an example to illustrate the issue of practical wisdom. Children who possess good character traits are usually considered nice but at the same time not morally virtuous. Despite the fact that children may have good intentions, they often cannot effectively put them into practice.[24] On this example, we can see that the way from a good mindset to a good action is not straight. Being practically wise is tantamount to knowing what should be done in a specific, rather than general, situation. This shows that virtue ethics is strongly context-sensitive, for which reason it requires practical wisdom that would help in adjusting actions adequately to particular situations. Practical wisdom cannot be obtained from virtue; it gradually emerges during the process of implementing good intentions into actions. Virtue ethics is essentially different from deontology, where acting in accordance with principles downplays particular circumstances.

If referred to the above typology, the most natural category for Confucian ethics is virtue ethics. The Confucian counterpart of the objective virtue is *ren* (仁),[25] a particular form of sensitivity, which testifies to one's being a cultivated person, a genuine human being, or ethically speaking, one's being good. It is important to note that one's *ren* understood as ethical virtue requires special behavioral conditioning by means of the prescribed propriety (*li* 禮) in order to become advanced along the moral path as an exemplary person (*junzi* 君子) or someone even more advanced—a sage (*sheng* 聖). In other words, appropriate human practice, guided by practical wisdom, is essential in one's being well-disposed in different social interactions, but, first and foremost, it constitutes one's usually conceived "internal" sensitivity.

The ethics of Confucius and Mencius agree in assuming good human nature.[26] Mencius founds it on a special conception of the "four sprouts" (*siduan* 四端) that all humans are born with. There are two features of the four sprouts that are essential in this context. The first one is that the sprouts describe the functional aspects of the mind, showing its direct linkage with practice. Fragment 2A6 of the *Mencius* provides their corresponding features of behavior respectively: compassion (*ceyin* 惻隱), shame (*xiuwu* 羞惡), modesty (*cirang* 辭讓), and discrimination between right and wrong (*shifei* 是非). Whoever is deprived of them cannot be labeled a human.[27] The four sprouts are innate yet ontically dependent on their performative extension, which is most decisive in constituting human nature. In this way, practice does not only realize the potential, but it is a factor that introduces ethical (and in some sense generic) qualities in humans.[28]

Even if one entertained the idea that we could become morally knowledgeable by an exquisite conceptual analysis of the sprouts, it would merely stop at the explanation of the potential, which in Confucianism is not tantamount to being moral. Even the "epistemic" discrimination between right and wrong (*shifei*) refers to making this differentiation in our actions. Such practical wisdom is unlikely to become formalized as a theory. In fact, it has been confirmed in many fragments that practice, understood as knowledge, is prior to speculative learning. For instance, in fragment 1.7 of the *Analects*, Confucius's disciple Zixia describes a person of proper conduct in social relations to conclude:

> Even if you said of such a person, "Oh, but he is not learned (*xue*)," I would still insist that it is precisely such qualities that make one worthy of being "learned."[29]

The evaluation of someone's proper conduct and endowing her/him with the status of a knowledgeable person follows from the assumption that character traits and knowledge are manifested not only through practice but also *as* practice.[30]

Another feature of the four sprouts is that they are associated with emotional sensitivity *ren*. In realizing them in practice, the moral agent does not apply some rules indifferently (otherwise, it would be a variety of deontology), but the moral agent's actions are guided by sensitivity, which cannot emerge without action. It can be noticed that the emotional is necessarily entangled in practice, and does not merely constitute the internal equipment of the Confucian moral subject's mindset.[31]

The above remarks have important implications concerning the status of practice in the Confucian ethical project. Human behavior is perceived as a faculty that can forge the human mind, most importantly regarding *ren*, the central character trait in Confucianism. What can be noticed concurrently is that the molding of the human mind in Confucian ethics requires the presupposition of mind plasticity as far as character traits are concerned.[32]

Considering the nature of *ren* as described above, it can be inferred that the self-cultivation practice is not meant to achieve, and does not lead to, an "ethical robot" type of personality, characterized by impeccable conduct but leaving a moral subject who consciously and affectively participates in the community by means of her/his behavior. It can be said that the entrainment through practice constitutes the moral subject's cognitive architecture in the rational, but at least equally importantly, emotional aspect.[33]

In Confucianism, the prescribed practice is concrete not only in juxtaposition to the theoretical approach. The moral agent does not apply abstract rules but develops a pattern of behavior that is socially contextualized, proper to her/his position in a network of human relationships. The concreteness is founded on the fact that every human is involved in more than one type of relationship, such as family, friendship, or political ones. The moral agent's behavioral repertoire consists of several "moral roles" to realize as a family and society member. It can be said that such a particular lived existence is assumed to be the most fundamental. Thus, it is impossible to depart from constructing moral roles supervening on, for example, Sartre's existence preceding essence.[34] Furthermore, it can be stated that in Confucianism we proceed in a reverse direction compared with cogito-style approaches. For instance, Descartes in the Second Meditation places the subject in an "existential vacuum," thanks to which the subject mounts the level of abstraction that enables a question to be posed concerning her/his own existence.[35] The Cartesian subject is not only disembodied but logically prior to concrete existence. As such, it is virtually implausible in the Confucian context.[36]

The subject's embodiment entails practical knowledge that emerges both through practice and as practice. On the surface, art may appear to be a "special" area of human activity, but one has to bear in mind the anthropological underpinning of artistic practice[37] that does not allow it to be clearly distinguished, or it at least overlaps the "common" with what could be described as artistic rites to a degree that cannot be ignored. These blurred characteristics are perpetuated in a deeper structure of Confucian self-cultivation in terms of functionality. Being engaged in artistic activity serves the same purpose to furnish one's *ren* personality. This explains why several fragments from the *Analects* discuss music along with ceremonies.[38] Although it can be argued that the aesthetic is still reserved for a more refined activity—in this case music—the functional similarity cannot be denied.[39]

Confucius on Aesthetics

Similarly to ethical issues, Confucius does not approach aesthetics from an abstract level. He more inclines toward discussing what role art has in human life, specifically when it comes to cultivating *ren* in a Confucian person. However, this discussion does not stop at the level of art, or even philosophy of art; it reaches further, to the nature and function of the aesthetic.

Confucius sees the unique role of art in the molding of human mind. Out of all possible ways in Confucianism, the involvement of the aesthetic is superior. In fragment 8.8 of the *Analects* Confucius says:

> Find inspiration in the *Odes* [*shi* 詩], take your place through ritual [*li* 禮], and achieve perfection with music [*yue* 樂].[40]

Li remarks that the *Odes*, albeit poetry, played a slightly different role in the time of Confucius. The work was mainly used for educational purposes, in order to learn about politics, religion, and history. However, the *Odes* is at the same time a collection of poetry pieces. By this, the content is absorbed in an artistic form, which adds the emotion-molding dimension.[41]

Considering the artistic dimension of poetry, one might pose a question as to why Confucius intends to single out the final part of the fragment—perfection with music—and treats music separately. Also, we should not dismiss the fact that propriety can also mold one's *ren*, and is therefore functionally similar to music. A possible answer offered by Li is that it is only music that can bring the development of a Confucian personality to completion, thanks to its power to both mold as well as inspire humans.[42] In this respect, its difference from propriety and poetry is that music is most direct, in the sense of being unmediated, in influencing the human spirit/psyche. Being situated beyond mediation consists in bearing no traces of external rational standard. Propriety, mostly concentrated on morality, operates with overtly externally developed "behavioral models and standards," whereas poetry, despite being art, is still entangled in language—the discourse also used as vehicle for wisdom. Music transcends these two in being disentangled from external rationality and as such can bring the Confucian personality to completion.[43]

Li also refers to the *Analects* fragment 6.20, where he shows that Confucius refers to the same thing as in the previous fragment:[44]

> One who knows [*zhi* 知] it is not the equal of one who loves [*hao* 好] it, and one who loves it is not the equal of one who takes joy [*le* 樂] in it.[45]

In comparison with how propriety or music influence humans, this fragment is more focused on how one learns to become the Confucian exemplary person (*junzi*). It can be seen that "loving," which can also be understood in this context as the appreciation of what one does, is more valuable than simply acquiring knowledge about it, but at the same time not as efficient as taking joy, which can suggest additional pleasurable engagement in what is done.[46] This comparison, apart from showing the subsequent steps on the Confucian perfection path, indicates what kind of psychological state accompanies as well as facilitates the highest stage of Confucian learning.

Experiencing the aesthetic, for instance, as in fragment 8.8, provided by art is essential in building a Confucian moral personality. The exemplary person is thus someone who not only advances along a moral but also aesthetic path. The aesthetic, especially when experiencing pieces of art, can evoke pleasure and emotions in the subject, which is positively valued by Confucius. There is an important thing to be noticed here, namely, that experiencing the aesthetic is not only a form of positive reinforcement that co-occurs in positive self-cultivation practice. Confucius acknowledges that music also can mold human emotions, thanks to which *ren* can be improved and manifested through being appropriately sensitive toward others. Such mental states can be labeled as cognitive due to the fact that being *ren* consists in what Confucians regard as proper recognition of a situation (which usually involves interacting with others).

It is important that Confucius does not look for the pleasure and joy in participating in a transcendent world or entity. Humans can reach their full potential in the world in which they live as both individuals and society. Whereas it is quite intuitive that emotions form the mental content in individuals, Confucius also believed that they can become collectivized. This belief is based on the metaphysical intuitions common for almost all philosophical schools in China that the metaphysical universe is confined to one world and does not assume any transcendence. On this assumption, the sense of human existence cannot be exported to a variety of the Christian "heavenly" realm, for instance. Quite the opposite, human life seeks its fulfillment and sense in this very world and life that is actually lived by humans forming a community within which they interact with one another. This detachment from transcendental explanations in Chinese tradition redirects the meaning from religious transcendence to this-worldly aesthetics. Perhaps it would be going too far to say that this feature of Confucian philosophy has been a direct inspiration for Li's philosophical project, but such foundations provide compatibility for integrating some Confucian views in his sedimentation theory.

Li believes that in Confucianism this anthropological approach to locating the sense of life is particularly realized as "a historical becoming, that cannot be achieved apart from a relationship to the collective." The relationships are described by Li as "the interpersonal solicitude that has its basis in the emotions."[47] We can see that the emotions assume an explanatory function, but also, according to Li, they are regarded as substance that becomes humanized throughout history.[48] Thus, emotions are endowed with the ontic status of substance that becomes molded in time through human practice. This fact is very essential for Li's further steps in his own philosophical construction, especially in his conception of psychological substance, of which subjectality is composed.

As mentioned above, Confucius believed that emotions become collectivized. *Ren* as a type of sensitivity is essentially grounded in emotion. Importantly, it is no longer a "raw" emotion; *ren* undergoes the process of rationalization, as a result of which it is calibrated in order to, among other things, be implemented in human interaction, and reveals itself as the "communal emotions of interpersonal caring."[49] In this way, the emotions are socialized. In his *History of Chinese Aesthetics*, Li connects the socialization to the role of art, which, apart from molding the human mind, is also part of social practice and uses music as an example.[50] On the technical side, we can say that performing music consists in collective practice. In this way, music allows emotions to be channeled into social circulation in their proper form.

An example can be taken from fragment 17.9 of the *Analects*:

> The *Odes* [*shi* 詩] can be a source of inspiration [*xing* 興] and a basis for evaluation [*guan* 觀]: they can help you to come together with others [*qun* 群], as well as to properly express complaints [*yuan* 怨].[51]

Li explains, among other things, how this work, as a piece of poetry writing, can help properly express complaints or resentment. These emotions, although regarded as negative, should not be suppressed but expressed in their proper form. Art is naturally one of the possible ways in which it can be done.[52]

Conclusion

Confucian aesthetics works in two ways. We can say that it works within and without. When it comes to the former, it is assumed that the aesthetic has the power to forge individual inner psychological faculties. Human emotions can be also calibrated in a more external and rationalizing way, but experiencing the aesthetic is more direct and comprehensive, by which the moral development can be brought to completion.

As regards the latter, the aesthetic can bring humans together in a harmonious state.[53] Especially through the artistic medium, which encapsulates emotions in a proper form, humans can experience the aesthetic, which through evoking the mental states of aesthetic appreciation, puts humans in harmony with other humans, as well as the world.

Confucian aesthetics certainly shows the role of emotions, which do not only play an important part in aesthetic appreciation within art. Emotions constitute a substance that can be modified over time. The modification is achieved in a practical way. This psychological plasticity of humans is of great importance for Li, who departs in his philosophical construction from a very similar assumption.

Another very important aspect of Confucian aesthetics is that the aesthetic is not separated from the moral. These two aspects of Confucian philosophy are encapsulated in *ren*, which is moral sensitivity molded by the aesthetic. It is also where the aesthetic gains more importance than generating joy or pleasure to be cherished by the subject. The aesthetic gives the final and indispensable touch in calibrating emotions, by which it contributes to the subject's more natural functioning in relations with other humans and the world. This in fact results from correct and undistorted cognition of reality. In this sense, Confucian aesthetics is deeply integrated in cognitive activity. This extended function of aesthetics is utterly crucial for Li in building his own conception.

Chapter 2

Marxist Framework

Introduction

Contrarily to not being associated with philosophizing in the Confucian spirit, Li is quite often perceived as an inheritor of Marxist thought. Undisputedly, Marxism is an indispensable inspiration for Li's own philosophical project. Confucianism contributes to Li's philosophy mainly with the subject's psychological substance, especially with regard to its emotional structure. Considering this, one can say that Confucianism addresses the issues connected with the inner architecture of the subject. As regards Marxism, its contribution is most prevalent in a different area of Li's philosophy. Although also focused on the subject and her/his architecture, the main field of concern in Marxism is human existence in the world, particularly in society that humans actively create. Similarly to Confucianism, rather than viewed in terms of a "ready-made" entity that is subjected to a metaphysical dissection, the subject is viewed in the aspect of her/his becoming in the process of activities, both in the mental and material dimension. This process in Confucianism is mainly viewed in terms of the subject's proceeding along the path of moral self-cultivation. In Marxism, the perspective refers more to historical time, particularly the history of mankind, and therefore most attention is given to the subject as a representative of the transforming and active human immersed in society, rather than a moral personality.

In this chapter, I begin with locating Li in the context of aesthetic research in China in the mid-1950s, when the topic of subjectivity in Marxism began to gain importance. Next, I proceed to *Economic and Philosophic Manuscripts*, an early work by Marx that has exerted a strong influence on

Li not only as far as an understanding of Marxism is concerned, but also in his own philosophical construction. The next section will be devoted to how the foundations of Marx's philosophy, as tabled in the *Manuscripts*, are essential in Li's philosophical project, especially his anthropological ontology. Finally, I will discuss the aesthetic implications of Marx's philosophy that significantly inform Li's aesthetics.

Subjectivity in Marxist Aesthetics

Li's approach is rather selective with regard to the Marxist tradition, as his intention is to preserve Marx's most fundamental ideas and concurrently omit the ones that he regarded as inessential for his philosophical framework. In terms of particular Marxist influence, Li is mostly inspired by Marx's essay *Economic and Philosophic Manuscripts*.

Eva Kit Wah Man in her discussion of Marxist aesthetics in China views this particular text as a point of departure for different interpretations of the subject and object relation in aesthetic experience. The interest in this particular issue emerged in the People's Republic of China of the mid-1950s, was ardently discussed until approximately the mid-1960s, and has been revived in the past few decades. Man mentions Li as one of the most important representatives of the aesthetic theories that emerged from the different understandings of Marx based on this particular work. There were four major theories or "schools" of aesthetics, the most important representatives of which were Gao Ertai (高爾泰; b. 1935), Cai Yi (蔡儀; 1906–92), Zhu Guangqian (朱光潛; 1897–1986), and Li.[1]

These four schools essentially vary in explaining the nature of aesthetic experience. As regards Gao's views, he represents the subjective standpoint and claims that there is no objective beauty and that it is produced by the subject's mind that projects itself onto an object of experience. An opposite view, which agrees with objectivism, is presented by Cai, who claims that beauty is objective by virtue of being inherent in experienced objects that belong to the natural, material world and are independent of the subject.[2] Cai, therefore, understood that what is beautiful is simply what is typical in nature.[3]

As regards Zhu, he represents a "middle way" standpoint, supported by a more elaborate theory than Gao and Cai. His notion of beauty is relational and it is created by the mind in the aesthetic experience, where the self and matter are not discriminated (not metaphysically) as a result of the meeting of mind and matter, or the subject with the object. Zhu also believes that there is no possibility to have a clear-cut division of the subjective and the objective, as they are interdependent. In fact, these two form a unity (yet are not identical). It should be borne in mind that Zhu's distinction is not of a metaphysical but rather an epistemological character: the subject's mind is subjective, whereas the external world is objective.[4] This "integrated" solution leads Zhu to bold aesthetic statements that, inter alia, claim that beauty is a false concept. Considering the relational character of the subject and object, beauty should be conceptualized more in terms of being beautiful or aesthetic experience, by which the interaction of the subject and object would be brought to attention. Another statement converges very much with the Marxist message of fundamental character of practice. Following it, Zhu claims that aesthetics consists in a practice that leads to the unity of the subjective and objective.[5]

In comparison with the above-mentioned three schools representatives, Li appears to be more closely following Marxism in the sense of being more concerned with the origin of beauty. Similarly to Cai, Li postulated the objective status of beauty. However, Li concurrently essentially differs from Cai in that his objectivity of beauty is derived from the objectivity of social existence. Social existence is an objectively existing network of relations beyond human consciousness. Therefore, beauty, as a phenomenon belonging to this network, is also objective.[6] As can be seen, Li's objectivism consists not in that he locates beauty in the propensities of external world. He departs from the human practice that enables humans to understand the nature of reality.[7] The practice consists in the converting of the material world "according to human needs and human understanding of their nature."[8] This unification of the subjective and objective results in human freedom, which is especially expressed in artistic activity. Hence, beauty results from this merger. At the same time, Li assumes that humanizing nature takes place over the whole history on humankind, and beauty reflects these changes at different periods of time.[9] As can be seen, out of the four school representatives, Li's reference to Marxism appears to be most straightforward as well as highly compliant with its philosophical and anthropological foundations. Whereas labeling Li a Confucian would be an exaggeration, describing him as philosophizing in a Marxist spirit is a far more justified statement.

Impact of the *Manuscripts*

The *Economic and Philosophic Manuscripts* (sometimes also referred to as the *Paris Manuscripts*) was written by Karl Marx in 1844, when his philosophy only began to bud.[10] The text remained unfinished and, therefore, was not intended for publication.[11] It was finally published after over eighty years as an incomplete version in Moscow in 1927, and a complete version in Berlin in 1932.[12] The reception of the *Manuscripts* in Marxist scholarship varied. Western Marxists regarded it as one of the most important texts by Marx, whereas among their Soviet colleagues it was regarded as minor due to having been written by the young Marx, who had not yet developed his purely socialist line of thought. Chinese Marxists, similarly to Soviet ones, did not pay special attention to the text until as late as the mid-1950s.[13] More precisely, this date could coincide with Li's essay from 1956 "Regarding Aesthetic Experience, Beauty and the Arts" (*Lun Meigan, Mei yu Yishu*), in which he expressed the view that the *Manuscripts* was a very important work by Marx.[14]

According to Leszek Kołakowski, despite the fact that the work does not present Marx's ripe and complete thought, which he achieved in his later, monumental work *Capital*, and that the text is incomplete,[15] the *Manuscripts* is still important as a source of the evolution of Marx's views. A characteristic feature of this work is that here Marx views socialism from a broader perspective than a proposed social reform, and therefore he undertakes an analysis of the relationship between humans and nature, which leads him to investigations of a metaphysical and cognitive (and in some places epistemological) nature.[16] The fact that Marx shows a wider horizon for his social philosophy and reaches out to the fundamental questions concerning the existence of humans dovetails with Li's departure point for his aesthetics.

The character of the *Manuscripts*, with its emphasis on human alienation is also to some extent informative of what aspect of Marxism Li was particularly interested in—the history of alienation of humans as producers and the material practice or labor consisting in the humanization of nature. The latter theme will influence Li's own conception of the humanization of nature (*ziran de renhua* 自然的人化). Considering this, it can be said that Li's interests differ from the original version of dialectical materialism proposed by Marx and Engels mainly in this aspect—that he shifts the emphasis to the humanization. This redistribution in philosophical accentuation is important for his own philosophical construction, particularly for the sake of integrating Marxism with the psychological component of Confucian provenance.

At the same time, Li's selective approach is manifested by the fact that he is not particularly interested in the political economy dimension of Marxism, for instance, in what way private ownership becomes the outcome of estrangement. One should not exclude the possibility that this selectiveness is also related to the social and political context of Li's life. In Mao Zedong's China, the revolutionary aspect was prioritized in the sphere of politics as well as aesthetics, the latter being regarded as an ancillary theory to the communist ideology.[17] However, after the Cultural Revolution, especially closer to the beginning of the 1980s, the broadly understood culture became liberated from the obligation of expressing the revolutionary ideology.[18] Different aspects of Marxist ideology were abandoned, whereas others began to be accentuated, which can also be seen in Li's direct references to Marxism.

Human Practice

Li has been considerably inspired by the foundations of Marx's social philosophy expounded in the *Manuscripts*. As previously mentioned, Li sifts out what is important for aesthetics from other content, thus omitting the whole discussion connected with political philosophy and economics. Considering Li's philosophical objectives, which aim at constructing aesthetics rooted in human practice, as well as the indispensable conditioning from the particular historical, social, and political context, I limit my discussion to Marx's views as formulated in the *Manuscripts*.

Based on the *Manuscripts*, it can be stated that Marx offers two major things that inspire Li and result is in his own philosophical construction. The first is the conception of human practice in its internal aspect, consisting in molding the material substance, as showcased by the altered human sense organs, and subsequently perception, as well as consciousness and mental actions. The second is the historical perspective of human practice.

It is essential to know how Li particularly understands practice. The Chinese postwar aestheticians, for instance, Zhu Guangqian and Li, treat practice in terms of Marxist labor, that is, material production. They contrast with postwar Western Marxists, such as Louis Althusser or Raymond Williams, who, when they refer to practice, usually mean cultural practice.[19] Li adheres to historical materialism in seeing practice in a very defined shape, as material production and tool making and usage. He also follows Engels in that tool production is the distinctive feature of human beings. By this, Li concurrently remains critical of the Frankfurt School in that their conception of "praxis" is too broadly construed by including theoretical and cultural production. On the Chinese ground, Li similarly distances himself from Mao Zedong's views expressed in his essay "On Practice," where the original material practice is extended to, for instance, class struggle or political life.[20] Li also expresses his views that the Frankfurt school "praxis" and Mao's theory of practice diverge from the original Marxist conception.[21]

It might appear that the internal aspect of practice is equally psychology penetrating and thus presents the same focus as Confucianism. However, in discussing the mind-related issues, Marx is more concerned with labor than delving into the psychological meanders of the human mind. He is equally focused on human practice viewed externally, which stretches over the whole human history with different social relationships as its landmarks. These two aspects of human practice provide the foundations on which Li proceeds to create his own philosophical framework.

Marx opens the *Manuscripts* with the issue of the alienation or estrangement of labor (*die entfremdete Arbeit*), which is viewed in two aspects: the object of human production and the activity of production, which together lead to a comprehensive alienation. Marx regards labor as the fundamental characteristic of human beings. It is understood as "contact with nature in which man is both active and passive."[22] It is important to remark that labor is ontologically more fundamental than, and prior to, self-consciousness in humans. It is thanks to labor that the human being becomes a subject who experiences herself/himself in consciousness and is able to perform mental actions, not the reverse.

Humans self-create themselves through labor, which makes nature become "an object for humans, perceived in a human fashion, cognitively organized with human needs, and 'given' only in the context of the practical behaviour of the species." Also, it is only through labor that nature becomes humanized and self-acknowledged by self-consciousness, and, in this way, nature is the extension of humans. As Kołakowski remarks, there is no need and possibility of introducing creation to this world, as this would involve assuming the nonexistence of humans and nature.[23] Humans and nature form a world that is one, complete, and integrated. In Marxism, this worldview is explainable within itself. Similarly to the basic intuitions common to most of Chinese philosophy, there is no need to introduce transcendent reality or entities for explanatory purposes. In both cases, the metaphysical universe complies with the one-world view.

The assumption of labor as fundamental in the making of humans and nature reorients the cognition models that follow the Cartesian cogito-style approach. The cognitive conditions have to be shifted from a subject who is detached from nature and society to a situated one. One should also dismiss the situation in which we can cognize nature in itself and assume that humans with their "subjective equipment" are its product. In Marx's view, neither of these should be the starting point, due to labor being more fundamental.[24] Therefore, the cognition model should not involve the subject-object division in which knowledge about reality is obtained through, for instance, purely mental reflection or undisturbed perception. In fact, the character of mental actions and human perception are the products of the necessary and fundamental interaction of humans with nature. In terms of cognition, Marx clearly opposes isolating the subject from the world, and the cognitive act from the "totality of human behaviour."[25] In this sense, the cognitive act is concurrently also human activity in the world that she/he aims to cognize. Considering that this overlap is in fact an identity relation, human cognition is a form of human practice and as such should not be viewed in abstraction from human life.

Implications of Practice

In order to more precisely situate the aesthetic in Marx's philosophical project, it is also important to consider a wider framework of human practice, namely, what makes it possible for humans to be engaged in a practice that involves the aesthetic, as well as why it matters in labor-oriented activity.

Marx assumes that humans are essentially social. He writes that "society produces man as man" and that society is concurrently produced by humans. Humans and the aspect of their social existence are not separable, due to their being interdependent and conditioning each other. What subsequently follows from this relation is that human practice is intrinsically of a social character. It should also be considered that society is indispensable for humans in the sense that only in this particular environment does a human being's existence become human.[26] In other words, in order to realize their human essence, humans should lead a social existence.

There are two things that have to be considered with regard to social existence. First, it is not only the direct activity in a social space that can be qualified as social existence. It also includes mental activity in one's consciousness. Although mental operations do not manifest themselves directly, the one who performs them does so as a human being existing in society and therefore it is already her/his intellectual social existence.[27]

Second, it should also be considered that social existence is not some kind of abstraction built on the individual. Marx does not exclude individual life from a social one. Human as individuals and representatives of a species are in fact of no difference in terms of human essence; individual life and consciousness is an integral part of the life of the human species. Human consciousness of her/his existence as an individual does not extract the human being from the society; it is the awareness of social existence. Therefore, human thought and practice form a unity rather than disjunction.[28]

In their social existence, humans express themselves in a sensuous way, by which they objectify themselves. The expression should be understood more in terms of assimilation in a holistic way. This is possible thanks to human sense organs, which are perceptive, mental (including emotional), and social, which enter into relations with the object. In this way, they enable the objective appropriation of the human world.[29] Human sense organs are not raw in the sense that have become objectively and subjectively human(ized). For instance, the eye through the process of humanization enables an object to be perceived as a social object. Sense organs are directed at things, which are already things conceived as the objective relation to humans and themselves.[30] In this sense, the relation of humans to objects through their senses and objects to humans are both humanized. The modification of the sense organs also applies to confronting other humans in interactions, whereby the social organs develop and serve for both expressing and appropriating human life.[31]

The modification of the sense organs shows Marx's important views concerning the status of perception. It is part of the human relationship with the world, although its object is perceived as an already humanized object, conditioned by human needs and efforts.[32] From this perspective, perception is not simply a transparent, noninterfering, receptive cognitive tool. It is a "mode of life" of the subject, and therefore should not be understood solely an instrument for empirical cognition. Perception is concurrently human activity of constituting humanized objects. Considering this, the object of perception should not be treated as if in a "disconnected" cognitive situation of the subject and object. It is constituted in the interaction between them.[33]

Humans are not lost in their appropriation of reality thanks to the object becoming a social object and the humans becoming social beings for themselves. In this way, the object and the subject herself/himself become her/his objects. Accordingly, the objects become part of human reality, in which social human beings can find themselves by virtue of the objects being also the objectification of humans.[34]

Whether an object of human reality can become such for a given individual depends on her/his sensual "modality." For instance, one needs a "musical ear" for music appreciation. This shows that the world is mediated to the human subject through the sensory channels, where it can become humanized and only then cognized. Thus, the "subjective capacity" of the senses is the measure of someone's "social personality." The senses (including "mental" and social ones) can be originated or refined by the human's confrontation with humanized nature. This is an ongoing process that has lasted throughout all human history.[35] Therefore, it is very important to provide adequate conditions for humanizing the human sense organs. This can be confirmed by Marx's example dismissing instinct-motivated usage of senses. Starving, which motivates humans to satisfy one of the most basic physiological needs, does not lead to the humanization of the sense organs. Here food is not perceived as a humanized object. It is apprehended in a very animal-like way.[36]

As regards the estrangement of the object of human production, here Marx views the human being involved in labor as a reduced personality of a worker. Humans are involved in a mechanism of production in which the more they put into the produced object, the poorer they become. Marx compares it to religion, in which the more is that put into God, the less in left for humans, and consequently the estrangement between the two increases. Similarly, the production finally reaches the stage in which the product becomes an entity disconnected from the producer, also in terms of its existence, and thus becomes alienated[37].

In production, the human being needs nature as the material, and the sensuous external world, where her/his life is manifested. However, the worker becomes enslaved in this model of production, where her/his usage of nature is funneled into the sole production and maintenance of the worker's physical existence. In this model, the human being as a worker manufactures the product that does not form her/his extension in the sense of expressing the human essence. Considering this alienation of the object of production, as well as the "production bondage" of physical dependence, the human being reduces her/his existence to being a worker and a physical subject.[38] We can see that human practice is connected with altering the material reality. However, in the case of labor alienation, production constitutes an enormous infringement of one's freedom and results in deprivation of the human essence.

Apart from the estrangement of such labor products, the activity of production becomes alienated as well. Marx departs from the assumption that labor does not constitute the essence of the human being involved in labor as a worker; quite the contrary, it has become external to the human being. Consequently, labor cannot bring any satisfaction or other compensation for the mental and physical effort that the worker has put into it. This results in the fact that the worker cannot express or affirm herself/himself in the material reality that she/he modifies. Thus, not only the outcome of labor but the labor itself can be considered as not belonging to the human being. Also, assuming that the worker produces the estranged objects, the very process—by virtue of being aimed at such objects—can already be seen as alienation. Under such circumstances, the worker's labor is also not voluntary and spontaneous but enforced by the production.[39]

The above double estrangement leads to the observation that human alteration of the material substance and its expression in the sensuous world diverges from what is natural to humans. As Marx remarks, humans consider themselves as a living species that, like other animals, live in and are an integral part of the material world. This world is reflected in the human consciousness in terms of natural science or art. In the sphere of mind-external reality, nature is part of human life and activity (for instance as food or dwelling). In practice, humans as part of nature manifest themselves through the means of life and the "the material, the object, and the instrument" of their life activity. However, human practice is not only a means to maintain one's physical existence. As a conscious and free practice, it is what the life of the species consists in.[40] At this point, one can see that such a practice is not acquired but inherent in humans. As such, it seeks extension in labor, by which it confirms itself in "good life," understood as an expression of the whole human essence.

Also, on account of being a generic feature, practice is not separable from humans. We can view it in terms of anthropological ontology that defines humans not only biologically but also philosophically. Thus, diverging from the natural human practice remains in conflict with what is inherent in humans as a species. The true personality of humans becomes lost in this alienation. Labor in the circumstances of alienation resembles animal rather than human production, which is regardless of physical needs, and intended to be existentially meaningful for humans.[41]

As previously mentioned, human practice is conscious, which makes it distinct from other animals. Consciousness in a human being means that her/his life is an object for her/him. Kołakowski claims that consciousness described in the *Manuscripts* is "merely the expression in thought of a social relationship to nature, and must be considered as a product of the collective effort of the species."[42] It can be clearly seen that although consciousness is an important distinctive feature of the human species, it is not independent from practice. This can be viewed against the background of dialectical materialism, which is a variety of materialism that considers that mental phenomena are attributed to the body in the sense that what experiences thoughts or emotions is the human body, not any body-transcendent entity, such as, for instance, the soul. In this variety of materialism, mental phenomena are possible thanks to the development of matter in time, which has led to the development of living matter via physicochemical processes. Through these and biological processes, living matter developed consciousness. Mental life, which is the function of consciousness, cannot be reduced to the processes that developed it but depends on them.[43] Considering this metaphysical foundation of consciousness and mental processes that characterize it, we can state that humans are entirely part of nature. The basic understanding is that the bodily and psychological elements that comprise a human being do not entail dualism, and humans are entirely part of the material world. What also follows from dialectical materialist metaphysics with regard to human consciousness is that its actions are part of the materialistically conceived of world and, thus, they are integral part of human practice.[44]

Moreover, "deformations of consciousness are not to be as due to the aberrations or imperfections of consciousness itself: their sources are to be looked for in more original processes, and particularly, in the alienation of labour."[45] Kołakowski highlights here an important point—that consciousness is a product forged in human practice and its architecture should be explained in relation to it. It is also important to remark that consciousness conceived in such a fashion depends on practice and can be molded in time. This plasticity of the human mind invites conceptions that assume that certain behavioral entrainment influences human mindset. And this creates a potential linking point with Confucianism, which Li actually makes use of.

It is not only consciousness that differentiates humans from other animals; a more fundamental feature is the character of labor. Animals are also involved in a practice that consists in altering the material reality. However, in the case of animals, practice can be put down exclusively to the production for their immediate needs and according to the norms of their species. Humans, on the other hand, can produce when they are not in need, and therefore their practice is free. They also can produce "in accordance with the standard of every species, and know how to apply everywhere the inherent standard of the object." Humans in their production can transcend their needs and own species confinements, and, in this sense, they can produce "universally." For this reason, according to Marx, humans can also "form things in accordance with the laws of beauty."[46]

Aesthetic Implications

Marx does not bother to develop the aesthetic thought signaled in the previous sentence. The *Manuscripts* is a text concerned with completely different objectives. However, one can already discern that the aesthetic, although not elaborated on, is part of his human practice theory. Hence, there are several implications from human practice that refer to the aesthetic. First, there is some standard of beauty. Although not clearly formulated, producing things does not follow from one's subjective standards. These standards emerge in unconstrained (unalienated) human practice in accordance with the world. Importantly, a given beauty standard does not persist unchanged through time. Human sensory organs have evolved over human history, which entailed different conditions of perception and, what follows, producing and experiencing the object as beautiful.

Second, free human practice agrees with the standard of beauty. The importance of freedom from confinement of either labor estrangement or species-specific origin is a prerequisite for the production in which humans can forge material reality and meet the beauty standard. In fact, beauty is not an external ideal model, but it emerges in free production.

Third, although Marx does not develop his aesthetic statement and remains at a considerably general level with regard to this particular production, the practice of forming things according to beauty is not necessarily artistic. Considering this, the "aesthetic" practice should not be understood exclusively in terms of artistic activity. Nevertheless, going beyond art and opening the aesthetic to a wider spectrum of human activities makes it more integral with Marx's overall philosophical project.[47] Also, as we shall see, not confining aesthetics to art is also very important in Li's understanding of it as a completely different discipline than philosophy of art or an axiologically oriented study of beauty.

If we view Marx's philosophy of human practice through the prism of aesthetics, it can be stated that the estrangement of labor, due to the confinements it imposes on the free and conscious activity of a human being, leads the cessation of human activity that involves the aesthetic. Humans as species beings reveal themselves through practice. The object of labor is the reality produced by humans and thus it constitutes the objectification of the human species' life. Thanks to this, humans can contemplate themselves through their mind as well as the world they produce. Once estranged labor snatches this objectification from humans, they are bereft of their conscious and free creation.[48] Consequently, humans are no longer able to be involved in the molding of the material reality in accordance with beauty. In this way, human life is deprived of the aesthetic.

In this sense, the alienation can be also seen as turning a human into an alien being who cannot reflect on herself/himself through the aesthetic prism. From the point of view of the objective reality that humans create in accordance with beauty, the aesthetic can also be viewed as one of the cognitive channels for humans. In this regard, the aesthetic would cognitively matter in Marx's philosophical project. Indeed, as mentioned previously, Marx regards natural science and art as the two ways in which the world is reflected in the human subject's consciousness. In other words, the world is and should also be accommodated in a way other than conceptualization.

Although not overtly mentioned and developed by Marx, it can be seen that the aesthetic is integral with human practice and does not have to overlap with artistic activity. This fact opens the possibility of constructing aesthetics beyond art that is present in human material practice. This in turn allows aesthetics to be viewed more anthropologically, in terms of the importance of the aesthetic in material practice. It also enables aesthetics to be considered in accordance with its Greek etymology, from the perspective of human sensuousness, which through humanized sense actively constructs perception and constitutes a cognitive faculty. These issues, highly informed by Marx's *Manuscripts*, are discussed and developed in aesthetic theory by Li.

Chapter 3

Reinterpreting Kant

Introduction

Previous chapters were devoted to a presentation of the two philosophical traditions—Confucian and Marxist—that significantly influenced Li's own aesthetics. This discussion would be incomplete without including Immanuel Kant's philosophy contribution. It can be generally claimed that Kant's role in Li's philosophy is undeniably concerned with his focus on the subject and conditions of experience. This perspective made Li aware of the importance of this particular element in his own philosophy and finally led him to construct his own concept of subjectality as well as presenting his own understanding of the Marxist humanization of nature.

It can also be said that the Kantian influence, especially the "subjectivity subject," was to some extent conditioned by research in China from the mid-1950s to the 1980s. As mentioned in the previous chapter, some Chinese Marxist aestheticians—Zhu Guangqian and Li in particular—were deeply involved in the debate over subjectivity from the mid-1950s for approximately a decade. Importantly, that discussion coincided with the popularity of Marx's early *Economic and Philosophic Manuscripts*, where human practice was one of the main issues. This aspect of Marxist philosophy as well as the problem of subjectivity remained very important to Li and was crucial in his approach to Kant. Li referred to Kant in the 1970s, during the Cultural Revolution. The choice of this particular philosopher was not random. As Liu Kang remarks, Li regards Kant as the first philosopher to have been especially concerned with the issue of subjectivity, from which other philosophical problems were developed and discussed. One of the results was a very comprehensive exploration of the complexity of human rationality and mind.[1] Kant's extremely systematic approach to this matter gave Li the opportunity to focus on a very thoroughly constructed subject-oriented system and approach it from a Marxist perspective, particularly the one detailed in Marx's *Manuscripts*. This endeavor resulted in an original, strongly critical, and comprehensive study of Kant's thought—often translated in secondary sources as *Critique of the Critical Philosophy: A Study of Kant*, recently published in English as *A New Approach to Kant: A Confucian-Marxist's Viewpoint*.[2] This work, considered as one of Li's most important philosophical book publications, is not merely a new, critical interpretation of Kant's philosophy, although it certainly can also be viewed as such. Concurrently, and even more importantly, *A New Approach to Kant* marks a point of departure for Li's conception of subjectality that underpins his aesthetics, as well as the exposition of how he specifically understands historical materialism.

As already mentioned, there was a reason why Kant's philosophy particularly influenced Li—it makes the subject central for philosophical investigations. Indeed, it can be roughly claimed that all the philosophical problems that Kant tables, as well as the issues that he confronts in his three most important works—*Critique of Pure Reason*, *Critique of Practical Reason*, and *Critique of the Power of Judgment* (or *Critique of Judgment*), otherwise referred to as the three *Critiques*—are related to how the subject is constructed and how his/her cognitive faculties work.

Li's approach to Kant can be perceived as radical in the sense that he does not merely complement Kantian thought in the blank spaces or explicate some unclear passages that can be found in his writings (which is also done). Li's reinterpretation consists in situating Kantian philosophy in the context that Kant originally did not presuppose, and, even more importantly, is opposite to the character of Kantian thought, as historical materialism viewing humans in their inseparable natural and social habitat rather than in terms of purely rational mind can certainly be viewed in this way. As Li himself admits, his reinterpretation of Kant is in fact "Kant's philosophy turned upside down."[3] For this reason, Li approaches Kant comprehensively, especially by converting the idealist tenets of the Kantian system into established materialist practice.

In my discussion of Kant, I will only focus on the issues that are important for Li's conception of subjectality—the cognitive side of the subject as well as how the aesthetic and the cognitive are combined in cognition and experiencing beauty. My presentation of Kant's views in this respect will be based on his two works, *Critique of Pure Reason* and *Critique of the Power of Judgment*, to which I will hereafter refer by their alternative names—the first *Critique* and the third *Critique* respectively. These works are most relevant to the intersection of the cognitive and aesthetic dimensions of Kant's philosophy. As regards discussing these two *Critiques* together, an important remark should be made: there are some material discrepancies between these two works that bring inconsistency to Kant's philosophical system. It is likely that they stem from the development of Kant's views over time and one should read his earlier work through the prism of the last one. I adhere to this particular standpoint in my discussion, especially as regards the question of the autonomy of imagination in preparing the schemata for the understanding in theoretical judgments and judgments of taste.

I begin with the questions important for the conditions of experience, where Kant's model of experience and aesthetic will be discussed. This part of the chapter presents how Kant understands aesthetics and how it matters in constituting cognition. Next, the relation between the two cognitive faculties, the understanding and the imagination, will be discussed. It can be said that this relation, as well as "cognitive pleasure," sheds light on the cognitive aspect of aesthetic experience. Next, I proceed to aesthetics-focused issues, which include aesthetic judgment, the nature of beauty, and Kant's philosophy of art. Finally, these issues are shown in relation to human existence as the ultimate purpose of nature. Throughout the whole discussion of Kant's views, references to the cognitive implications and Li's critical approach are made. In fact, Li's reinterpretation of Kant in a Marxist way should be read as a formulation of his own anthropological ontology. Therefore, this chapter should be treated as a presentation of Li's own philosophical views built on the critique of Kant. The chapter ends with concluding remarks that underscore this particular issue.

Reinterpreting *A Priori*

The question of how a priori synthetic judgments are possible functions nearly as a signature feature of Kant's epistemology, and it is also one of the issues that show with clarity how Li reinterprets Kant's philosophical foundations. Apart from Kant's views and Li's interpretation of them, it will be shown why the reinterpretation of *a priori* is so material for developing Li's construction of his own philosophical framework.

Kant acknowledges that knowledge begins with experience, but he concurrently believes that knowledge is not identical with what takes place in sensibility. Knowledge is discursive and is expressed by judgments, which

Kant subdivides into analytic and synthetic. His main concern is to guarantee the necessity of judgments. A priori judgments are of universal necessity by deducing what is already contained in and not adding anything to what is included in the subject. This judgment is independent from experience. Kant's concern with necessity is focused on synthetic judgments, which pose a great challenge in this respect, as they add something to the subject, by which analytic deduction is impossible. These are a posteriori judgments, which are based on experience, that constitute empirical knowledge.[4] Empirical knowledge is subjected to inductive reasoning, which does not provide necessity. This fact bears very serious consequences for scientific knowledge, which is contingent because it is based on synthetic a posteriori judgments. To solve the problem of their contingency, the judgments constituting knowledge would have to be a priori synthetic, that is, not empirical and concurrently not contingent.[5]

As Li remarks, Kant believed that Euclidean geometry and Newtonian laws of mechanics were applicable to the whole world in experience, and, therefore, they were not only universal but also necessary and objective.[6] Given this, he had to prove that there are a priori synthetic judgments, which would bring necessity to these, as he held, universal laws.

In order to show the objective validity of science through the necessity of synthetic a priori, Kant departs from mathematics, which he does not regard to be analytic, but concurrently a priori. He refers to an equation example—7 + 5 = 12—and argues that the result cannot be analytically deduced from the three concepts of the numbers seven, five, and addition. Therefore, judgments of this kind must be synthetic. At the same time, such propositions are universally applicable in the world of experience, yet they have not been constituted through experience. The mathematical example is additionally relevant in Kant's argumentation as he believes that scientific knowledge must make use of mathematics, whose a priori synthetic judgments make it possible.[7] Consequently, whole natural science must contain a priori synthetic judgments.[8]

As can be seen, Kant resolves this question by adhering to human rationality, which seems to be the ultimate guarantee. Li approaches Kant from a completely different angle, assuming the Marxist conception of humanity, which cannot be simply reduced to the subject proposed by Kant and is countered by Marx's belief that "human essence is no abstraction inherent in each single individual. In its reality it is the ensemble of the social relations."[9] Li consistently follows Marx and Engels in that human essence is a "product of social practice in historical processes." It specifically consists in using and producing tools, which make humans distinct from other animals. The tools should be understood as material ones, for instance, axes or space shuttles, but they also include using energy, for instance, in nuclear fusion. Importantly, social practice expresses technological development. For instance, ancient land surveying was followed by Euclidean geometry, and later the advancement of industry with scientific experimenting was followed by non-Euclidean geometry and quantum mechanics.[10] Li shows that human conceptualizations do not permanently exist in a time- and anthropology-resistant vacuum; quite the contrary, they emerge together with human practice.

The impact of social practice should not be viewed only in terms of its external production, such as technology. It also significantly molds the human mind and, among other things, changes human perception. Kant's philosophy is also situated in a certain historical period of social practice, which is showcased by his a priori knowledge forms. According to Li, Kant's transcendental philosophy supplants empiricism and concentrates on subjectivity, especially with regard to perception and "inner psychology" experience.[11] His highly speculative philosophy may give the impression that it was conceived in an isolated abstract vacuum of philosophical investigations, but in fact it stems from a very basic level of tool usage and production.

The same applies to the universal and objective validity of Kantian a priori knowledge. Li believes that the question of judgment validity should be viewed in the same way as language. He converges with the later Wittgenstein from *Philosophical Investigations* in that language has been shaped by social life.[12] The universality of language as a system of signs is inherited from the universality of human practice.

Li also does not concede the absolute necessity of nature, which he attributes to a theoretical invention. On this view, Kant's alleged necessity for scientific knowledge, based on a priori, is universal only at a certain point of time in the history of human practice. He illustrates this temporary universality by the Newtonian laws of mechanics—regarded by Kant as absolutely universal—which were supplanted by Einstein's relativity theory and quantum mechanics.[13] It should not be understood that Li denies necessity. First, he recognizes the necessity of scientific laws in certain circumstances at a given time in social practice history. Second, the scientific laws gain another objectivity in exchange. It is derived from the objective human practice. This should not be mistaken with humans creating some coherent fictional narrations of reality. The objective reality exists independently from human practice and the laws that describe it are discovered in social practice. Therefore, they are objective by virtue of describing reality.

Li's reinterpretation of Kant consists in locating his philosophy in a certain period of social practice history. His a priori knowledge and subjectivity should not be viewed as an atemporal philosophical enterprise isolated from historical context that results in laws that are of absolute necessity. We can also see that although Li admits Kant's insightful transcendental philosophy encapsulation of the issue of knowledge, at the same time he cannot accept Kant's subject in such a disconnected condition. His situating of Kantian subjectivity in social practice precedes his conception of subjectality.

Sensibility

Kant's model of experience, although primarily explored in epistemological terms, matters no less for aesthetic reasons due to Kant's suggestion of a capacious, epistemologically inclined definition of aesthetics. For this reason, I will focus especially on the role of the aesthetic, which in Kant's philosophy is connected with sensuousness, to show how it matters in cognition.

In the first *Critique*, Kant expounds his epistemological views, which almost entirely center on the faculties of the subject's mind. The faculty that is responsible for producing knowledge is the understanding (*Verstand*). It presents the object in thought by means of concepts. The understanding is a discursive faculty of knowledge, as knowledge is necessarily conceptual and represented in the form of judgments.[14] To produce knowledge, the understanding relies on sensibility (*Sinnlichkeit*), which contains given representations—intuitions (*Anschauung*). Intuitions, or, more precisely, empirical intuitions, are related to objects through sensations (*Empfindung*), which result from the encounter of the object with the faculty of representation.[15]

Sensibility and the understanding are two mutually dependent faculties involved in cognition. This interdependence is necessary for constructing experience. Intuitions (representations in sensibility) cannot be comprehended alone in sensibility, and converting them into discursive knowledge is possible only thanks to the understanding, where concepts are applied to intuition. In the same way, no knowledge can be produced by the understanding if no intuition is provided by sensibility.[16]

At this point, it is appropriate to introduce Kant's definition of aesthetics. Kant defines his aesthetic, to which he refers as the "transcendental aesthetic," as "the science of all principles of *a priori* sensibility."[17] Therefore, Kant's aesthetic in terms of scope is conceived of as what takes place in sensibility. It investigates the sensations and how representations in sensibility are formed according to the principles already present in the mind.

It can be noticed that Kant uses the word "aesthetics" with no reference to what it usually refers to, namely, aesthetic values or aesthetic experience in the sense of experiencing, for instance, beauty or the sublime. Kant, as he himself admits in fragment A21/B35–36, is very close to Alexander Gottlieb Baumgarten's understanding of aesthetics as a discipline that includes art (poetry in particular) but at the same time the study of senses and perception.[18] Considering this overlap with Baumgarten's study of sensuousness, we can see that Kant's point of departure in his aesthetic investigations is at a cognition-oriented understanding of aesthetics. By this, as we shall see, Kant's discussion of aesthetic issues is naturally connected with cognitive issues. However, as will be demonstrated, it also includes the issue of beauty, connected with nature and art.

Here it can be seen that, from the perspective of Kant's epistemology, the aesthetic is an indispensable stage in constituting experience and, in turn, forming judgments, without which there would be no knowledge. One might form the impression that the faculty of sensibility is passive in cognitive terms by virtue of its receptiveness, whereas the active role is completely taken over by the understanding. Considering that Kant confines his aesthetic to sensibility, one could be led to the opinion that although his aesthetic matters in cognition, its importance can be simply attributed to receiving the material from the world and transferring it to the understanding. This impression can be viewed in a positive and a negative way.

Pure Intuitions

Apart from the empirical, Kant distinguishes between two pure intuitions: space and time. This conception of a priori pure intuitions is of vital importance for all experience, as they decide in what way our empirical intuitions are structured. Li reveals the context of Kant's discussion of pure intuitions in the conceptions of space and time. There were two paradigmatic views in this respect, represented by Isaac Newton and Gottfried Wilhelm Leibniz, which exerted an important influence on Kant's philosophy. It is even held that Kant wanted to integrate both Newton's absolutist and Leibniz's relationalist conceptions in his transcendental idealism.[19] Leaving aside the question of whether that intention was true, Kant certainly departs in his thinking from these two conceptions.[20]

Newton regarded space and time as actual and absolute, that is, ontically independent of consciousness and objects in nature. Leibniz believed that space and time have the status of relations or determinations that accommodate the coexistence of objects and their succession respectively. In comparison to Newton's conception, space and time do not enjoy an independent status. This relation is abstracted from experience and exists in the mind.[21]

Kant does not approve of either conception. With regard to Newton, he uses an argument of space and time perception. We can say that, in experience, time is not experienced separately. We rather perceive an event in time than time itself.[22] An analogous argument can be formed with regard to space. He also argues that space and time would have to exist without any objects, and would have to be God, who according to Newton has these two attributes. Despite arguing against Newton's view, Kant can see the practicality of space and time in informing science.[23] As regards Leibniz, Kant approves the fact that space and time determine things in experience. However, he cannot accept this conception due to the fact that geometry would be of an empirical origin, which would deny its universal necessity status.[24]

Kant proposes his alternative view of a priori, pure intuitions. As regards the possible confirmation of the passive character of sensibility, Kant makes an important claim about the relation of cognitive faculties to intuition by introducing pure a priori intuitions:

> Pure intuition . . . contains only the form under which something is intuited; the pure concept only the form of the thought of an object in general. Pure intuitions or pure concepts alone are possible *a priori*, empirical intuitions and empirical concepts only *a posteriori*.[25]

Accordingly, apart from the already introduced empirical intuition, there is also another type of intuition, which is not connected with sensations caused by objects. Such intuitions are composed only of the form that every intuition is given. They are also *a priori* in the sense that even without the object and sensation they are already present in the mind "as a mere form of sensibility."[26]

Pure intuitions determine how exactly sensibility is receptive in encountering the object—spatially or temporally. This shows that, before being adjusted to concepts by the understanding, the intuitions are already molded in a certain fashion, and are not so "raw" as it may seem from the overall division into sensibility and the understanding. This, however does not testify to the active character of the faculty of sensibility. On the contrary, a priori intuitions only determine that all intuitions have certain forms. In this way, sensibility can be viewed as receptive, in contrast to the spontaneous faculty of understanding.

Li sums up the importance of a priori pure intuitions of space and time in Kant's philosophy as three characteristics. First, they are nonempirical subjective conditions shared by all human beings. In psychological terms, time and space precede experience, whereas, logically speaking, time and space are independent from experience. Second, time and space are a priori intuitions, by which they are not concepts that belong to the understanding. And third, time and space are applicable only to sensible intuition.[27] This means that they are only the form in which the sensations resulting from our encounter with the outer world are received, by which the spatiotemporal description cannot be extended to the real world of things-in-themselves. This summary shortlists the characteristics of pure intuitions and the consequences that they bear, which Li regards as the most essential when addressed by his historical materialist approach. As one might expect, Li locates the origin of a priori intuitions in social practice. He points to Kant's distinction of time and space from color, sound, scent, taste, or temperature. The intuitions, unlike these representations, have not been developed in humans through passive perception, as this would not lead to the qualitative leap that transcends the sense-perception paradigm. The intuitions have developed through social practice, thanks to which they have become the "objective sociality of time and space."[28] However, as Li confesses, one should not regard the remaining characteristics as merely subjective. He provides an example of Locke's subdivision of qualities into primary and secondary ones. Locke's primary qualities are the ones that are inherent in object and independent from us, for instance, space occupancy, motion, or texture. Secondary qualities are caused by the interaction of sense organs with the primary qualities of the object.[29] For this reason, secondary qualities may appear to be subjective but, in fact, considering the context of social practice, they are, like primary qualities, objective, since they also refer to the object's qualities. We should be aware that the differentiation proposed by Locke results from a specific social practice in human history, and, therefore, the ultimate basis for this difference is historical rather than theoretical.[30]

Li argues for his historical materialism by resorting to Locke's and Galileo's view that extension, motion, or number are qualities that belong to physical bodies. These qualities did not stem from the development of sense organs, but emerged through human practice at some determined periods of human history. Li illustrates this with the age of mechanics, when humans discovered the above-mentioned qualities through relevant technological practice concerned with objects in space. The objective status of these qualities rests on their origin, which is the human practice of changing the world.[31] In other words, space and time have not been subjectively projected upon the world but the human practice has determined them. Li poses here a very important question laden with epistemological consequences. Epistemologies that build models that revolve around senses and perception ignore a wider horizon that shows how sense organs have come into being, and hence perception should also be viewed from a historical rather than a purely theoretical angle.

Li recalls Engels, according to whom space and time are essential forms for everything that exists. Thanks to human practice, these two forms constitute "sensible frames" for humans, whose practice is consequently located in a certain space along with a time sequence.[32] Here Li unfolds his own, at this point only Marxist-oriented, intuitions of anthropological ontology. He explains that representations of space are not a priori or transcendent but in fact they are sedimentations of objective human practice that have been internalized in subjective human consciousness.[33]

Sedimentation (*jidian* 積澱) is one of the crucial concepts in Li's anthropological ontology. It is a process that characterizes "the making of humans" through social practice. It departs from the assumption that the human practice of using and making tools develops a mindset whose character is determined by the accumulation of practice in human history. Sedimentation is unique to humans, as only they can be involved in "tool practice."[34] What can be seen here is that the architecture of the human mind, contrarily to many, including Kant's, conceptions, is not atemporal and it reveals plasticity that is conditioned by tool practice in a given historical period. This dependence of the mental on the practical draws Li's sedimentation toward the anthropological theories.

Because of its origin, space and time sedimented into humans are different than other sensations. For the same reason, space and time are not only internalized in the subject but also form an integral part of social existence. They have become homogenized and regulated, which has resulted in, for instance, the practice of timekeeping and mapping. Li also thinks that the replacement of old conceptions of space and time by new ones, which, for instance, was the case with the theory of relativity supplanting the Newtonian conception, testifies to the dynamic character of human practice that, through sedimentation, changes the way people define the physical reality from the very primitive stage of the human species until today.[35]

These historical dynamics underscore Li's anthropological approach to the development of theoretical constructions in science, as well as philosophy.

Considering the above historical and anthropological perspective represented by Li, Kant's a priori intuitions cannot enjoy the status of atemporal cognitive equipment independent from experience. What is regarded as a priori is in fact the effect of historically accumulated social practice that has been sedimented into humans. Kant is looking for the confirmation of necessity by showing that geometry as part mathematics is nonempirical, which makes it necessary. However, even such abstract systems as geometry and other branches of mathematics, are not reservoirs of a priori knowledge. Mathematics is in fact a symbolic representation of the primitive activities of counting and measuring. The practical foundation element is critical for this qualitative transformation, for, as Li holds, this cannot happen merely through passive observation or by just experiencing the world.[36] This can be achieved only by uniquely human tool making and using practice. It is also important to notice that human cognitive structures are not innate, by which is meant they are not the natural distinctive feature of the human species, contrarily to practice. Humans tend to only have an illusion of the mind being an inherent and certain distinctive taxonomic feature. In fact, the cognitive faculties are internalized and become transparent, for which reason one can misconceive them as items of a priori equipment.

Li's view of the mechanism of molding human subjectivity is that the laws of the objective world become "human's tools and means of cognition," by which practice apart from changing the material, objective world also changes the subjective human world. We can discern here a tacit assumption from Marx—that humans are an inseparable part of nature and their appropriations are also objective.[37]

The space and time of the human mind do not mold the sensations, but, historically speaking, experience through practice (or as practice) has furnished the human mind. The intuitions of space and time have been abstracted from reality, and their compatibility as part of a cognitive apparatus with the world is provided by appropriate sedimentation.

Li points to an interesting characteristic of Kant's cognition theory, which consists in identifying space and time with intuitions and locating them in the "lower" level of cognitive processing, the sensible aesthetic. Li assesses this location as correct, because space and time are not concepts of the understanding, but at the same time they cannot be labelled passive sensations. This makes even more sense in his reinterpretation of Kant, where sensible intuitions sediment social reason. Their location also determines the character of impact of social practice, namely, how they have been internalized. Li differentiates between ordinary internalization and sedimentation. The former consists in formalizing external practices, by which they become the structures of reason. This can be exemplified by symbolic logic. The latter one is more complex in that social reason is sedimented through perceptions. These processes can be and are often combined, which is the case of mathematics.[38]

The Imagination, Figurative Synthesis, and Schemata

The impression of pure receptivity of sensibility is dismissed by how empirical intuitions are made. On this front, Kant introduces the faculty of imagination (*Einbildungskraft*), responsible for figurative synthesis (*synthesis speciosa*), which seriously questions qualifying sensibility as passive. He describes it in the following way:

> What must first be given . . . is the *manifold* of pure intuition; the second factor involved is the *synthesis* of this manifold by means of the imagination. But even this does not yet yield knowledge.[39]

Kant holds that the imagination is a faculty not involved in producing knowledge, unlike the understanding, and belongs to sensibility. As for the nature of the synthesis for which the imagination is responsible, Kant describes it as follows:

> This synthesis of the manifold of sensible intuition, which is possible and necessary *a priori*, may be entitled *figurative* synthesis (*synthesis speciosa*), to distinguish it from the synthesis which is thought in the mere category in respect of the manifold of an intuition in general, and which is entitled combination through the understanding (*synthesis intellectualis*).[40]

The imagination constitutes another stage in processing intuition for concept adjustment in the understanding. Despite not being directly engaged in knowledge production, it is certain that, as a "lower level" faculty, the imagination makes knowledge possible. This in turn makes Kant's aesthetic even more cognitively meaningful. As for the activity of the imagination, Kant describes it as follows:

> Imagination is the faculty of representing in intuition an object that is not itself present. Now since all our intuition is sensible, the imagination, owing to the subjective condition under which alone it can give to the concepts of understanding a corresponding intuition, belongs to sensibility. . . . This synthesis is an action of the understanding on the sensibility.[41]

The imagination does perform the task of providing corresponding intuitions for concept adjustment. However, Kant seems to be persistent in generally associating the realm of sensibility with passivity. The character of figurative synthesis can indeed be viewed as an activity of the imagination, but, notwithstanding this, Kant subordinates it to the understanding, which seems to employ the imagination as its extension in sensibility. Nevertheless, disregarding the ascription of free agency, we can state that what takes place in sensibility in terms of constituting cognition cannot be described in terms of mere passivity.

Kant subjects figurative synthesis to further, detailed description. He points to the fact that represented objects have to be homogeneous with their assigned concepts in the way that concepts should contain "something which is represented in the object that is to be subsumed under it." This is met in both empirical and pure concepts. As for the former, for instance, it can be illustrated by Kant's example of the empirical concept of a plate, which is homogenous with the pure geometrical concept of a circle through its roundness. However, this homogeneity poses some difficulty when it comes to pure concepts (categories), which cannot be homogenous with intuitions in the same way as empirical concepts cannot "be intuited through sense and. . . . [are themselves] contained in appearance." To solve this problem of connecting pure concepts with appearances, Kant cannot insert intuitions, as they have "empirical content," and proposes the transcendental schema that "mediates the subsumption of the appearances under the category."[42] In other words, pure concepts must contain "conditions of sensibility [that] constitute the universal condition under which alone the category can be applied to any object,"[43] which are the schemata.

The historical materialist underpinning of Kant's philosophy is even more important for the emergence of Li's conception of subjectality when it comes to schemata than it is for the pure intuitions. Schemata are produced by the imagination. They are not "images of objects" as these would not be applicable to concepts of the understanding, because the former bear always some determinacy that would not match the universality of the latter. Looking from the side of images, schemata constitute the rules according to which images can be produced. From the side of the concepts, their universal status, as opposed to determined images, makes them compatible with the understanding.[44] Considering this, and bearing in mind that schemata are produced in sensibility, we can see that Kant does not simply see aesthetics as conditioning knowledge. The imagination has the capacity of adjusting what comes to sensibility in the way that it can be accommodated by the concepts of the understanding. In this way, the aesthetic (in the sense of processing intuition) as a stage in objective cognition makes it possible, but concurrently figurative synthesis cannot be interpreted as a characteristic of receptivity.

Li consistently maintains his historical materialist approach to the cognitive faculties and schemata. The production of rational knowledge by means of judgments with concepts is attributed to the development of language through practice. One might develop the misconception that concepts, judgments, and forms of reasoning enjoy the transcendental status as forms of the understanding that are processing sensible experience of the subject, which leads to knowledge production. According to Li, the origin of the transcendental lies in social practice and has been sedimented into the human mind in order to enhance cognitive faculties. In the long term, this particular sedimentation is meant to equip humans with rationality, by which humans can produce knowledge about the world, which increases their adaptation to it.[45]

The schemata constitute a very important element in cognition, as indispensable facilitators of knowledge production. According to Li, their function is even more important, as they decide on how knowledge will be conceptualized as theoretical models. Kant's direction of thinking views producing knowledge in terms of applying concepts of the understanding to sensibility through schemata. However, humans—through social practice—produce knowledge in the opposite direction, by internalizing categories. Analogously, schemata are not an activity of the imagination, but abstractions of sensibility.[46] This completely alters Kant's point of view, at least from the first *Critique*, where figurative synthesis is an ancillary action of the understanding, performed in sensibility by the imagination. This in turn also alters the question of the extent to which the imagination and the aesthetic in general is independent and active in constituting experience.

Purposiveness of Nature and Pleasure

Kant also introduces another important cognitive issue—the purposiveness of nature, that despite being located in the sensible aesthetic, bears consequences that go beyond it. In the first *Critique*, Kant explains that empirical intuitions are received in a certain form, but he does not justify the view that intuitions thus molded reflect the objective (sensible) world. This epistemological problem greatly involves the aesthetic at the same time. In the third *Critique*, Kant defines purposiveness of nature as follows:

> Now since the concept of an object insofar as it at the same time contains the ground of the reality of this object is called an end, and the correspondence of a thing with that constitution of things that is possible only in accordance with ends is called the purposiveness of its form, thus the principle of the power of judgment in regard to the form of things in nature under empirical laws in general is the purposiveness of nature in its multiplicity. I.e., nature is represented through this concept as if an understanding contained the ground of the unity of the manifold of its empirical laws.[47]

Kant is looking for confirmation of the concepts and, in turn, knowledge about the appearances (as sensibility cannot reach beyond the sensible world), which is based on there being some correspondence between judgments and the appearances that are aligned with them. Kant continues:

> The understanding is of course in possession *a priori* of universal laws of nature, without which nature could not be an object of experience at all; but still it requires in addition a certain order of nature in its particular rules, which can only be known to it empirically and which from its point of view are contingent.[48]

The a priori laws of the understanding are conditions of experience. However, empirical laws cannot be cognized a priori, and therefore the correspondence between the universal laws and the laws of the sensible world is not necessary. This contingency of objective knowledge constitutes a considerable problem in Kant's epistemological project. The adjustment of the manifold to the universal laws takes place before it reaches the understanding (because otherwise understanding would be unable to assign concepts and produce judgments), and therefore it belongs to the aesthetic, where it falls into the domain of figurative synthesis performed by the imagination. Even if we still adhere to Kant's belief from the first *Critique* that what takes place in the imagination is "an action of the understanding on the sensibility,"[49] it remains undeniable that the competences of the imagination are of a wider cognitive significance in the third *Critique*. The figurative synthesis is responsible for providing a "contingent guarantee" for cognition in the purposiveness of nature, thanks to which universal and empirical laws are matched, by which empirical epistemology is not art for art's sake.

The contingent status of Kant's epistemology, apart from location in sensibility, matters aesthetically also for another reason, which is the feeling of pleasure (*Lust*). Kant believes that "the attainment of every aim is combined with the feeling of pleasure,"[50] and this feeling does not omit the contingent adjustment of the manifold with the understanding.[51] It has to be borne in mind that this successful cognitive act takes place in the aesthetic, as a preparatory task for the understanding. Kant also mentions that pleasure does not have to necessarily occur in the adjustment that is attended to, which is showcased by "common experience," during which we are normally not aware of the contingent underpinning of our cognition, since it has become daily routine.[52] However, pleasure enters into focus when it comes to judgment of taste, based on the same sensibility hardware, which is a presumption for the identity of feelings of pleasure in these two types of experience.

Aesthetic Judgment

In the third *Critique*, Kant also considers in his philosophy the judgment of taste, which underlies beauty. The judgment of taste is the pure judgment, as opposed to aesthetic empirical, in that it "assert[s] beauty of an object or the way of representing it."[53] Pure judgments are of free beauty in the sense that, when something is judged by means of taste, "no concept of what the object ought to be" is presupposed.[54] Involving the concept of the judged object would inform us on what is the destination of the thing, which makes the pure judgment of taste impossible. Therefore, satisfaction in beauty is immediately connected with the representation in which the object is given, not thought.[55]

In terms of construction, Kant describes the pure aesthetic judgment as the free play of the two cognitive faculties—the imagination and the understanding, with a representation through which an object is given. It is very important that the faculties are involved in an interplay, as, otherwise, the sensible would be adjusted for the understanding to encapsulate it under a determinate concept. The interplay is free inasmuch as "no determinate concept restricts them to a particular rule of cognition."[56] Accordingly, it does not mean that the interplay is completely free. It is described several pages later, in fragment 5:256, with greater detail that "judging the beautiful relates the imagination in its free play to the understanding, in order to agree with its concepts in general (without determination of them)."[57] Kant does not specify the nature of this agreement (also translated as "harmony"), so we could assume it to be some kind of subsumption under concepts. Because an agreement with the concepts is established, the judgment should be labeled cognitive. However, when discussing the judgment of taste in detail, in fragment 5:209, Kant dismisses its cognitive status, and thus leaves this question imprecise rather than conspicuously resolved.[58]

Nevertheless, this limitation primarily concerns the imagination that is supposed to adapt the manifold for the understanding. Despite this fact, the interplay thus conceived assumes that imagination is an active rather than receptive faculty, as in the first *Critique*. It is also cognitive, regardless of whether the understanding subsumes or not the adapted representation under a determinate concept, as the interplay evidently leads to some kind of experience, and establishes the compatibility between the two faculties. From the perspective of contingency, this experience should also be considered as cognitively "successful," since, although not determinate in result, some proper match between the faculties has been configured, and so involves pleasure—similarly to other successful experiences.

It is important to notice that judgments of taste, due to not involving subsumption under determinate concepts, are excluded from being objectively valid. Despite judgments of taste being subjective, Kant wants to equip them with some alternative validity. He believes that there must be "a subjective principle, which determines what pleases or displeases only through feeling and not through concepts, but yet with universal validity."[59] He locates this principle in common sense (*sensus communis*), a term that contrarily to the common usage should be understood as sharing the same feeling of pleasure by all humans. Kant explains the universality it brings by describing the nature of taste by means of interaction of the cognitive faculties:

> I . . . say that taste can be called *sensus communis* with greater justice than can the healthy understanding, and that the aesthetic power of judgment rather than the intellectual can bear

> the name of a communal sense. . . . One could even define taste as the faculty for judging that which makes our feeling in a given representation universally communicable without the mediation of a concept.[60]

Kant departs here from the judgment of taste being proper to everyone, as the feeling of pleasure. Feeling supplants here the universal discursive communication. Kant importantly gives the condition for this feeling, the "communal sense" of which stems from the assumption that all humans possess the same cognitive equipment, which is indispensable for this feeling (as well any experience).

Common sense also has another important social feature:

> The beautiful interests empirically only in society; and if the drive to society is admitted to be natural to human beings, while the suitability and the tendency toward it, i.e., sociability, are admitted to be necessary for human beings as creatures destined for society, and thus as a property belonging to humanity, then it cannot fail that taste should also be regarded as a faculty for judging everything by means of which one can communicate even his feeling to everyone else.[61]

Later in the text, Kant provides an example of a person on a desert island who, deprived of possibility to communicatively share pleasure, would not, for instance, adorn herself/himself, as this activity is also a basis for being judged as a fellow person of sophistication who has the need and skills to communicate her/his pleasure.[62] This communicative inclination is part of human nature and affirms not only the expression of an individual refinement but expects an aesthetically refined community as well. This shows that experiencing beauty is also social, or even an anthropological realization of human needs.

Kant's Judgment of beauty can be defined as one in which taste is the faculty for judging and results in the beautiful under the four conditions: disinterestedness, universality, necessity, and representation without an end (otherwise referred to as being "final without an end" and "purposive without purpose"). Judgments of beauty have to comply with all these four conditions. First, the judgment is disinterested, which means that something is judged solely for the sake of finding it pleasurable.[63] Kant also remarks that, in the judgment of beauty, it is only the representation of the object, not its real existence, that is important.[64] In this context, Kant shows in fragment 5:207 that we should not take the judgment of beauty for a judgment that results in pleasure and elicits desire for similar objects, as it is object-based and clearly contradicts the disinterestedness.[65]

Kant describes the judgment of taste as "contemplative," which "merely connects its constitution together with the feeling of pleasure and displeasure."[66] He concurrently reminds us that this contemplation is also detached from concepts, which disqualifies the judgment from being cognitive. However, Kant operates with a considerably confined definition of cognition, where subsumption under determinate concepts is crucial. Additionally, considering his aforementioned remark that the interplay of the imagination and the understanding leads to agreement with concepts of the latter in general,[67] the cognitive aspect of the judgment of beauty should not be entirely excluded.

Second, the judgment of beauty has to be universal, which means that the judgments are agreed upon by everyone. Li points to pleasure arising from judgment and not vice versa. Only a judgment arousing pleasure universally in everyone is aesthetic. The universality can be extracted from judgment, not pleasure, which is a subjective feeling.[68]

On the basis of Kant's philosophy, the universality of this judgment is a very challenging condition. Kant cannot locate beauty in experienced objects, by which a judgment on the objective features would gain the universal dimension. However, at the same time, Kant obviously cannot agree to the "beauty is in the eye of the beholder" standpoint, as this would entail judging being bereft of any purpose and sense. The second condition has to be met by relying on the identity of human cognitive faculties to propose some alternative legitimation of judgment rather than universality. When judging, one must "believe himself to have grounds for expecting a similar pleasure of everyone."[69] Since humans share the same cognitive faculties, we should expect that everyone will have the same feelings.[70] Therefore, Kant believes that the free interplay of the imagination and the understanding "must be valid for everyone and consequently universally communicable."[71]

Third, the judgment of beauty is "purposive without purpose." By purposiveness, Kant means only possessing appearances of purpose in a hypothetical way.[72] There are two kinds of objective purpose: external, which is utility, or internal—perfection. Beauty cannot possess any of these, as they must be based on the relation of the manifold to the determinate end, which is concept. Although beauty is neither of these, it still requires a purposiveness that is indeterminate.

The fourth condition, that judgment of beauty has to be necessary, is interconnected with the condition of universality. Kant describes the alternative necessity as exemplary, which is "a necessity of the assent of all to a judgment that is regarded as an example of a universal rule that one cannot produce." For obvious reasons, this necessity cannot be provided by determinate concepts, and the universality of experience is also insufficient.[73] Kant resorts to the aforementioned principle of common sense, which he can only presuppose.

There is an important point that is revealed in Kant's discussion of common sense. The interaction between the understanding and the imagination does not result in any random adjustment between the two faculties. It is characterized as harmonious.[74] This shows that, although the interaction of the faculties does not culminate in the subsumption under determinate concepts, it is not discordant and leads to an agreement between them. Considering that some proper adjustment, or configuration, between the understanding and the imagination has been achieved, Kant proceeds to discuss the validity of judgment of taste:

> A presentation that . . . harmonizes with the conditions of the universality . . . brings the cognitive powers into that proportioned attunement which we require for all cognition and which, therefore, we also consider valid for everyone who is so constituted as to judge by means of understanding and the senses in combination (in other words, for all human beings).[75]

The harmony involved in judgment of taste, based on the harmony in which the cognitive faculties are properly configured, is qualified by Kant as the same type of requirement as in the case of the "common" cognition with determinate concepts. Considering that all humans share the same cognitive faculties by virtue of which their cognition of the things in the world should be the same, Kant believes that humans should also have the same common sense of harmony. According to Kant, this common sense allows the legitimization of the universality of judgment of taste, as well as its necessity.

It can be stated that Kant is mostly concerned with legitimizing judgment of taste, which must be achieved beyond objective validity. Thus, Kant's discussion of beauty, which is undoubtedly of aesthetic concern, runs in parallel and is equally cognition oriented.

Li approaches the aesthetic feeling of pleasure through the social practice in the aspect of gradual, historic separation of the nonbiological from the biological in humans. Through social practice, humans have managed to humanize nature (*ziran de renhua* 自然的人化). This mainly involves external nature being molded by practice to serve humans. However, limiting the humanization of nature to this sole process would be an unjustified confinement. In this process humans have concurrently transcended their biological existence and achieved a suprabiological form of social life. Aesthetics in the sense of aesthetic culture and aesthetic feeling have become part of it.[76]

However, it should not be misconceived that humans through their suprabiological mode of existence have been emancipated from nature and that there is some ontological discord between them, which inter alia would contradict the Marxist worldview, which Li does not abandon. Human nature, achieved through social practice, is constructed of these two components. The contribution of sedimentation in epistemology and morality has resulted in rational cognition and moral autonomy, both of which mirror the rationalization of the originally sensuous existence of humans. As regards the suprabiological dimension of the aesthetic culture, it has been likewise sedimented into humans. However, in contrast with the rationalization of humans, the aesthetic sedimentation can mainly be observed in the changes that have taken place in human sensuousness. Li illustrates aesthetic sedimentation by two examples. The first is food, which biologically serves the fundamental need of humans to satisfy hunger. However, on the sensuous, or, in other words, aesthetic, sedimentation, food has become a gourmet culture. Similarly, sex, which in terms of biological existence serves the genetic perpetuation of the species, has become a means to express love.[77]

The aesthetic matters in the liberation of humans. Li interprets Marx as saying that human liberation from alienation is mainly concerned but also confined to the spheres of economy, politics, or law, whereas humans are alienated far more comprehensively. According to Li, aesthetics and beauty seem to embrace alienation more holistically. The complete fulfillment of humans takes place in "aesthetic play," manifested by social practice and creative work.[78] If we return to Marx's *Manuscripts*, alienation is viewed in terms of the object and the very activity of production.[79] The aesthetic liberation by free play liberates humans in these two aspects. Humans are involved in the material production, where they freely create, by which they can express themselves and thus are not turned into the Marxian alienated worker. This unconstrained production by its products concurrently results in the humanization of nature, reflects Marx's understanding of "humans form[ing] things in accordance with the laws beauty."[80]

Marx also assumes that humans are part of nature,[81] for which reason their material production of molding nature is so essential, and the estrangement of labor so detrimental. The free expression of humans through labor brings harmony between them and nature. Depending on history, it is achieved by different tools. The humanization of nature is also realized through technologies, which allow humans to control nature and also internalize it through this labor.

It can be seen that Li in his historical materialist interpretation of Kant assumes a similar understanding of aesthetics. First, it is based on human sensuousness, similarly to Kant's sensibility. Therefore, the aspect of sedimentation that is most important to aesthetics is the one that results in the humanization of the sense organs. Second, Li also does not confine aesthetics to sensuousness. Quite the contrary, the humanized senses constitute the foundation for the feeling of beauty. The feeling in Kant's aesthetic is connected with the harmonious interplay of the cognitive faculties, whereas Li locates the aesthetic feeling as founded on free practice that entails beauty, which can also be understood as harmony between the human being and nature.

Philosophy of Art

Kant's aesthetics is extended in his views on art, more specifically, to the type of beauty present in it. His approach to this issue also consists in analyzing beauty from the position of the subject and the function of cognitive activities. Kant distinguishes between free beauty (*pulchritudo vaga*) and adherent beauty (*pulchritudo adhaerens*).

Free beauty does not include the purpose of the object, by means of which it fulfills Kant's required disinterested and purposiveness-without-purpose type of beauty as described above. The other, adherent beauty, otherwise, dependent beauty, is not free by virtue of dependence on the concept that determines the purpose of the object.[82] For instance, the beauty of the human body has dependent beauty as it presupposes the concept of its purpose and what follows the concept of its perfection (of what it ought to be). This combination of good (the way in which manifold is good for itself because of its end) and beauty nullifies the purity of the latter, which is in contradiction with free beauty conditions.[83] In Kant's view, whereas free beauty is present in nature, dependent beauty is exemplified in artworks, which have some purpose and have been made in accordance with it. In fact, the same object can be valued both in terms of free and dependent beauty, depending if the judgment involves the purpose.

Kant tries to determine the ideal of beauty. He dismisses the possibility of finding an objective rule for beauty in determinate concepts, as this would be self-contradictory by virtue of judgment of taste being based on feeling. Kant admits that we demonstrate taste through examples. However, examples solely serve to show that one can judge according to beauty, and beauty itself is not located in examples. Thus, the ideal of beauty is within humans, not the objects of nature or artifacts. The ideal of beauty cannot be taken from sensibility either, because, as Kant notices, these "norms" are determinate rules relative to people living in different communities.[84] Kant arrives at the conclusion that the ideal of beauty can only be presented as a rational idea, which cannot be sensibly represented into judgment, and it is exclusively in humans who are the only ones that can determine their ends through reason or can derive them from perception and compare them to the universal ends.[85] The judgment of dependent beauty is not purely aesthetic by virtue of having an intellectual component.

Kant's discussion on beauty in art starts with a remark that interest in the beautiful involves focusing not only on the form but also the very existence of the object. He exemplifies this with an aesthetic interest with flowers. The interest lasts as long as we think them to be natural, and disappears on learning that they in fact are artificial.[86] This according to Li testifies to the fact that the aesthetic pleasure from appreciation of nature is not confined to the form but also includes the presence of nature, and admiration of its purposiveness in particular. This is part of Kant's trying to show a link between the sensible nature and morality by way of judgment of taste.[87] He believes that moral ideas are reflected aesthetically and that taste underpins the judging of "the sensible rendering of moral ideas."[88] Accordingly, natural objects function as analogues of rational ideas and are received with a feeling of beauty.[89] Art realizes this paradigm by conveying rationality and showing beauty by expressing its formal purposiveness without purpose.

Kant's aesthetic ideas are representations of the imagination that cause thinking that cannot be subsumed under determinate concepts and linguistically conveyed. They are counterparts of the ideas of reason, which, conversely, have concept but no intuition.[90] In this way, aesthetic ideas express infinite thought within a finite representation, and it is only in this nondiscursive way that they can be expressed. They transcend the limits of experience and definiteness of concepts. In terms of construction, it combines the understanding and intuition, by which they are different from other rational ideas.[91] The task of aesthetic ideas is to represent the ideas that cannot be experienced. Kant believes that science, which operates by laws and principles, can be learnt.[92] On the contrary, in art there are no science-type laws, and an artist must follow her/his talent in order to find a way to represent a rational idea by an aesthetic idea. Thus, Kant does not regard artistic activity as cognition. It is done only because of aesthetic pleasure that results from the interplay of the cognitive faculties.[93]

Kant is very consistent in dismissing the activities of cognitive faculties that do not result in cognition in the form of propositional knowledge. However, the very nature of aesthetic appreciation that results in pleasure is the result of the interplay of the same faculties that take part in what Kant regards as cognition. One has to confess that the involvement of the same faculties does not prejudge their action to necessarily result in a cognitive act. However, one can also question the necessity of determinate concepts that are, in this case, the qualifying condition. Judgment of beauty results from a certain, although not prescribed or paradigmatic, representation of a rational idea that is a unique yet not unordered action. Moreover, considering that knowledge in the form of judgments composed of concepts is also representation, art, by virtue of representing achieved through cognitive faculties interplay is also a form of cognition. Importantly, in the case of dependent beauty, the purposiveness of the object is taken into consideration, and, as Kant admits, aesthetic appreciation is admiration of it. This requires the cognition of the purposiveness, in which context the feeling of pleasure can be seen as confirmation of this cognitive act. On one hand, one has to agree with Kant that art is not cognition in the same way as scientific knowledge, but, on the other hand, art can be regarded as possessing an indispensable cognitive component or being a form of cognition alternative to the discursive one.

Humans as the Ultimate Purpose

Purposiveness of nature is not an immediate part of Kant's aesthetics. Despite this, the implications of purposiveness allow Kant's aesthetics to be situated in a wider context, which is also important in Li's interpretation of Kant. In his discussion of nature, Kant highlights the internal purposiveness character of it, which cannot be explained by mechanical causation and consists in things being both cause and effect for themselves.[94] It applies to living organized beings in nature. These beings have three features. First, their parts only exist when forming a whole. Second, every part is cause and effect for each other. Third, they can reproduce themselves, which is unique to living beings.[95] It can be seen that the first two features show the organismic character of the beings themselves as well as in relation to all other beings. The third one is approximately restrictive to biological entities. All the three features show that organized beings form the part of nature that cannot be fully explored by mechanical causation.

Kant's analysis of organized beings leads him to a broader question concerning the purposiveness of nature. He considers the existence of some objective natural purpose that would explain the fundamental question concerning the reason for nature's existence. He situates humans in the center, as "the titular lord of nature, and, if nature is regarded as a teleological system, then it is his vocation to be the ultimate end of nature."[96] According to Kant, nature would otherwise be meaningless. Nature is bestowed with meaning not because humans can cognize the world or feel pleasure in what we think has a final end.[97] A human is the ultimate purpose as a cultural-moral being. Li describes the characteristics of a human being as the ultimate end of nature. A human transcends the limitations of nature (such as desires) and can "set voluntary ends for himself."[98] By this, nature is used in accordance with human free ends, as a result of which nature reaches the end beyond itself, and for this reason it is recognized as ultimate. This human activity is called culture. The prerequisite for this culture is to promote the will (morality).[99] It should be seen from a broader perspective that Kant regards science and art as ways that liberate humans from the confinements of sense perception and make them more cultivated in rationality and higher moral power.[100] In this way, humans realize themselves in freedom, liberated from the confinements of the sensible.

Kant's idea of nature evolving toward humans is essential in Li's reinterpretation of the ultimate purpose alone; in fact, this relation has important implications for philosophical aesthetics. Li interprets this "movement" of nature towards humanity as sedimentation achieved by social practice, which results in the humanization of nature as well as the naturalization of humans. The liberation from the confinements of sensibility and desires in motivation can be attributed to a change in sense organs, which, in Kantian terms applied to Marx, become more cultural. In this way, humans become more and more deprived of their animality and mold themselves as cultural beings whose ends are situated beyond their naturalistic needs. As humans express themselves freely through material practice and remain in harmonious relations with nature, Li's interpretation of the cultural development of humans does not lead to estrangement. Quite the opposite, cultural humans remain in unity with nature.[101] Considering this relation, aesthetics can be viewed as more than a mere method of dissecting artworks and creating them.

Both in Kant's and Li's systems, aesthetics is not defined as philosophy of art. It describes the humanization of nature that takes place on several levels of human life. From the perspective of time, the continuous sedimentation is recorded by changes in aesthetics at given historical moments. It is shown at the level of both sensibility and human cultural production, which includes, but is not limited to, art. In this way, aesthetics does not only demonstrate how rational ideas are differently expressed at different periods of sedimentation. Aesthetics is also the measure of how, in Kant's terms, nature evolves toward humans, or, in the Marxist perspective, the character of sedimentation. It has to be noticed that in the evolution of nature toward humans there is a division, owing to which humans, who are already equipped with rationality, have to act freely despite their animality. Therefore, there is an inherent division between humans and nature that requires unification. In Marxism, as well as Li's anthropological ontology that emerges from it, the humanization of nature departs from humans "in the making," whose rationality is sedimented into them through material practice. Accordingly, there is no original ontic foundation of this opposition. Aesthetics uncovers the harmonious relation in which humans change nature as part of it.

Conclusions

On the grounds of his whole philosophical project, Kant's aesthetics is inseparable from cognitive issues. Kant's aesthetic investigations literally emerge from making the subject the heart of all philosophical investigations, which, as will be seen in the next chapter, plays an important role in Li's construction of his own philosophical framework. It departs from subjectivity and consequently discusses its relation to the world, which must hinge upon cognitive issues. Remaining coherent with the whole philosophical system, Kant proposes a very capacious definition of aesthetics. It embraces what is usually studied within this discipline, beauty and other aesthetic values, as well as art, but, more importantly, it is also the study of sensuousness.

This comprehensive understanding of aesthetics in Kant's philosophy does not consist in simply combining what is usually covered by this discipline with some epistemological issues. Aesthetics thus construed provides a more detailed insight into how free and dependent beauty are founded in the subject and about the nature of their relation to cognitive structure. This, on one hand, enables a better understanding of both types of beauty and locates the judgment of taste and the aesthetic feeling in human subjectivity. On the other hand, aesthetics is not so discrete from other processes that involve the understanding and sensibility, especially cognition. Although Kant operates with a rather confined notion of cognition and therefore persistently refuses the cognitive status to the judgment of beauty, it can be said that, even if aesthetics does not lead to Kantian cognition, it is indispensable in it and can be treated as another form of cognition.

Kant's aesthetics is an integral part of his philosophy of subjectivity, predominantly concerned with the conditions of cognition. The aesthetic sensibility, which is responsible for receiving sensations and preparing representations for the discursive faculty of understanding, is an indispensable stage in experience that leads to knowledge production. Kant seems to be dismissive in endowing sensibility with an independent and active role in cognition. Even if his presentation of figurative synthesis in the first *Critique* establishes it in an ancillary role in relation to the understanding, the active character of the imagination in the third *Critique* provides reasons to reconsider this dependence. Nevertheless, whether the imagination depends on the understanding or not, its active character cannot be dismissed. Therefore, the aesthetic sensibility is not only an indispensable stage in cognition but also contributes to it actively.

The imagination as an aesthetic faculty also plays an important role in the purposiveness of nature, as it is through the reflective judgment that belongs to imagination that we can make the manifold suitable for the understanding. The contingency of this match and subsequently the applicability of universal laws to the empirical laws is made possible thanks to the aesthetic. Importantly, this cognitively essential matching is satisfied by the feeling of pleasure. As previously mentioned, pleasure does not have to be, and usually is not, attended to in common, nonaesthetic cognition. However, it is always conscious of the aesthetic experience of beauty. It is justifiable to assume the identical morphology of pleasure by virtue of being based on the interaction of the same cognitive faculties. The fact that the feeling of pleasure in both cases is a "confirmation" of the contingent match draws the aesthetic (not only in the strict meaning of the sensible aesthetic) and the cognitive very close to each other, possibly even merging. It ought to be borne in mind that the result of contemplating the form of an object (and, in the case of dependent beauty, also its end) is not random and results in subsumption under concepts in general, which can be interpreted as a form of cognition that is expressed differently than determinate concepts.

The general idea extracted from Kant's construction of philosophy from the subject, as well as the subjectivity-specific issues that involve the liaisons of cognition and the aesthetic, or even more specifically, beauty, will be considerably formative for Li's aesthetics which—similarly to Kant's project—grows from an original conception of subjectivity—subjectality.

Li's reinterpretation of Kant confirms what the author mentions at the beginning of *A New Approach to Kant*. Li sees his work moving in two directions, from Marx to Kant, and back again.[102] On one hand, there is no doubt that Kant's philosophy, by virtue of being concentrated on subjectivity and the cognitive issues that it entails, considerably sharpens the Marxist component of Li's philosophy. Through social practice, we obtain the subjectivity of a very intricate architecture, almost every aspect of which complies with the foundation of historical materialism. On the other hand, Kant's philosophy becomes complemented with historical and anthropological dimensions, as a result of which the a priori and atemporal character of the original Kantian subjectivity is dismissed. This in turn leads to several cognitive implications. First, the cognitive equipment is not inherent or ontically independent from the world but acquired through human practice. Another important feature of human cognitive structures is that they do not persist through time as an unchanging aspect of the human mind. The plasticity of cognitive structures is determined by the historic context of human practice. In this sense, mind plasticity can also be viewed as an adaptive function. The adaptation can be attributed to the biological level, but not necessarily confined to it. The tools of human practice are new technologies, by which humans produce but concurrently adapt to new forms of material production, which can be conceived of as broadly construed civilizational framework serving as a paradigm for particular cultures. It should be noticed that the persistence over time of changing cognitive structures questions Kant's common sense. In the weak version, we can consider the common sense based on the identity of all subjects holding in all time moments over the history of human practice. Human cognitive structures are subject to change but the character of change is universal and the necessity of common sense holds in all possible worlds formed of time slices. In the strong version, we can question the holding of common sense, which can appear to be necessary for some moment or moments of time, but it can turn out that there are some possible worlds where the cognitive equipment is not universal.

Second, following on from temporality, the subject and cognition are situated in their immediate social practice. As mentioned above, the cognitive equipment of the subject is molded by social practice. Its constitution and functions reflect the corresponding contemporary, accumulated historically practice, which makes not only the subject but also cognition situated in a given time in the development of humans.

Third, what also ensues is that Kant's speculative knowledge should not be viewed in isolation. Human cognitive structures have been sedimented into humans and they are not of a transcendent but anthropological ontology character. Accordingly, Li's reinterpretation invalidates the a priori status of knowledge, which, although firmly established in the subject, has been internalized through the universal human practice in the objective world. This anthropological interpretation is not confined to the genesis of knowledge; it also implies the temporal character of even very abstract knowledge, which has been showcased by the geometry example.

Fourth, what is of great importance to aesthetics is that not only the intellectual but also the sensuous is of a historical and anthropological nature. Human sense organs have been changing throughout the history of tool practice. Sensibility forms the "lower" level of human cognitive apparatus, yet it should not be downplayed in cognition as unchanging or transparent. Similarly to the discursive faculty, sensibility is characterized by plasticity. Pure intuitions, which belong to sensibility, create a most important example of how sensibility shapes not only sensations but also abstract thinking in, for instance, mathematics. Everything that comes through the senses is formatted in a spatial-temporal fashion but these pure intuitions have been sedimented into sensibility through human practice in the objective world, which testifies to the plasticity of human perception.

Fifth, a very interesting and important issue in Kant's cognition is contingency in matching the sensible manifold with the understanding, achieved thanks to the figurative synthesis that prepares the adapting schemata. This problem of knowledge validity is created by Kant's epistemology itself that starts from the subject that has laws that are not extracted from the world but have to be mapped onto it. In Li's interpretation, the problematic matching of universal laws and laws of the sensible world is dismissed, since our categories are sedimented through practice in the objective reality and thus the match is natural. However, it should be remembered that Li assumes that the human subject changes over time and our conceptualizations of reality are only temporally valid.

In the context of contingency, in the third *Critique*, Kant states that "the attainment of every aim is combined with the feeling of pleasure."[103] This refers to the successful matching of the universal and empirical laws in our cognition. Considering that an aesthetic feeling of beauty is achieved with the involvement of the understanding and the imagination, one can assume the possible identity of pleasure in both cognitive and—according to Kant—noncognitive situations. On this assumption, aesthetic pleasure is no longer reserved for the contemplation of an object's pure form in nature or the form and end in artworks. These two activities of the cognitive faculties also should not be viewed with strictness regarding the cognitive status. This aspect appears to be even more apt for discussion on the ground of Li's interpretation of Kant, since the unalienated, free humans are involved in practice in accordance with beauty by which they remain in harmony in nature as part of it. This harmony apart from being existential, can also be perceived as cognitive. Tool practice consists in using instruments, technologies, and being involved in artistic activity, all of which manifest human freedom. These actions are of a cognitive character or are at least of benefit as they affirm the free and proper adaptation of humans to the objective world, which is followed by the sedimentation of the cognitive structures, which include forms of rationality and emotion. Considering this, the Kantian pleasure resulting from a proper organization of either the sensible material of the object or its form can be understood as an attainment of a cognitive aim.

Sixth, in fragment 5:297 of the third *Critique*, Kant emphasizes human sociability in the sphere of communicating aesthetic feeling of pleasure to others. An individual human being needs community to feel pleasure in an appropriate way, which concurrently affirms her/his being a distinguished community member. As already mentioned, Kant believes that someone on a desert island would not indulge herself/himself in aesthetic refinement, and, therefore, community is essential not only for social appraisal but also developing an interest in beauty. Kant seems to think about aesthetic refinement in anthropological terms, by describing the development of aesthetic forms from primitive to sophisticated. This is also paired with reaching the point when the aesthetic feelings built on them are universally communicable.[104] This invites an anthropological interpretation, according to which communicating aesthetic feelings is an expression of belonging to the community of cultured humans who share the same taste for beauty.

Kant seems to identify it with the beginning of civilization. Li in *The Chinese Aesthetic Tradition* regards totemic dances as the most primitive layer of aesthetic constitution, where the expression of the "human instinctual emotion" of an individual becomes collective, and subsequently leads to the humanization of "sensuous pleasure and emotional expression."[105] Li understands the evolution of beauty appreciation like sedimentation. Social practice humanizes the original, purely based in the human biological existence, emotionality that at some point attains the stage of beauty appreciation. As regards Kant, he indicates civilizational development to the point when the possibility to communally share aesthetic pleasure with others becomes a validation of this very feeling. However, despite Kant's linking of human aesthetic refinement to civilizational advancement, it seems that the role of community is crucial for developing an interest in beauty appreciation. This leads to the assumption of a human being possessing the potential for beauty appreciation that has to be socially activated or cultivated. Similarly, as with other cognitive architecture of the subject, Kant does not presuppose the historical development of the disposition to feel pleasure in beauty. It has to be admitted that Kant's sociability of humans plays an important role in their refinement within and without. However, it is not so fundamental as Li's conception of social practice that not only aesthetically refines humans but also sediments into humans the possibility for this refinement.

Chapter 4

Philosophy of Subjectality

Introduction

As previously mentioned, Li's conception of subjectality was not born in a philosophical vacuum. This is especially visible in *A New Approach to Kant: A Confucian-Marxist's Viewpoint*, where Li, apart from reinterpreting Kant, also elaborates on how Kant's philosophy can be complemented by Marxist social practice, which sediments the alleged a priori equipment into the subject. This is undeniably important for interpretational purposes, but we can clearly see that Li also sketches the foundations of his philosophical aesthetics in the margins, based on this Kantian and Marxist amalgamation. The foundations do not end at the stage of scattered remarks on Kant and reach completeness as the philosophy of subjectality, more often referred to as anthropological or historical ontology. As Li himself admits, in Western academia, he refers to his philosophy as an ontology, as subjectality can be easily mistaken for subjectivity or subject concepts, which are not associated with human practice.[1] However, historical or anthropological ontology can evoke the connotations of a formal ontological study, which is certainly not the case of Li's philosophical project. Nevertheless, it has to be borne in mind that the terminology that Li applies to his philosophy may have different connotations or even denotations than in the Western tradition.

Subjectality (*zhutixing* 主體性) is the fundamental notion of anthropological ontology. There are several ways in which this originally Chinese word can be rendered into English, considering the philosophical context. It could be translated as "subject"; however, this word usually corresponds to the Chinese *zhuti* (主體). The suffix *-xing* (性) usually semantically modifies the word to show property, for instance, the adjective *kekao* (可靠), meaning "reliable," when suffixed with *-xing* becomes the noun *kekaoxing* (可靠性)—"reliability," or, analogously, the noun *kexue* (科學), meaning "science," becomes *kexuexing* (科學性), which can be translated as "scientific nature" or "scientific aspect."[2] Therefore, it would seem that the natural translation equivalence for *zhutixing* would be the semantically ambiguous "subjectivity." However, Li for the sake of his philosophical project decides to coin a new term in order to distinguish his conception of a subject from that present in Western philosophical theories. He justifies this choice as follows:

> Sometimes there is a kind of misunderstanding regarding my so-called *zhutixing*. It does not have the Western sense of "subjectivity" (*zhuguan*) [主觀]. I feel we should rather use a new term "subjectenity"[3]—even though there is no such word in the English dictionary—that means that a human person is the capacity of an active entity. *Zhutixing* is not a concept of epistemology; instead it implies that a human being is considered as a form of material, biological, and objective existence and as an active capability in relationship to the environment.[4]

As can be seen, Li insists on discriminating his "subjectenity," or "subjectality" in more recent English writings by Li and on Li,[5] from "subjectivity" not for solely linguistic reasons. By introducing this coinage, he wants to emphasize that "subjectality" denotes a significantly different type of subject from those which are theoretical and disembodied, as is in the case of Kant's philosophy as reinterpreted by Li.

Subjectality is essentially important in understanding the aesthetic part of Li's philosophy for three reasons. First, it provides an explanation of what types of processes underpin the aesthetic experience and the emergence of beauty. Li's notion of beauty is situated in aesthetic experience, which is embodied and, more importantly in Li's theory, historically situated. Consequently, beauty is explainable in terms of the processes that accompany aesthetic experience so conceived. Thus, the involvement of the subject experiencing beauty cannot be omitted or theoretically reduced to a passive receiver of sensations.

The second reason follows on from the preceding one regarding contextualizing Li's philosophical theory. In the perspective of Li's whole philosophical activity, subjectality is the focal point where the connection between his multiple philosophical inspirations and his own philosophical view is established and turned into the original conception. In this way, one can see the nature of Li's involvement in a creative dialogue with Confucianism, Marxism, and Kant's thought. By this one can also understand the particulars that decide on the originality of Li's theory that transcends the traditions that influence it, as well as see how this new approach is reflected on the ground of Li's aesthetic experience.

Last but not least, subjectality is indispensable in locating Li's aesthetics in the cognitive context. Admittedly, to some extent, it would be possible to discuss Li's aesthetic ideas in isolation from the experience and subject, in some specific aspects, for instance, concerning how beauty is encapsulated in art. However, isolating or reducing the role of subject would exclude exploring the cognitive dimension of Li's aesthetics. Subjectality is an active participant of the processes in which the cognitive and the aesthetic co-occur.

Apart from the objective of constructing his own project, Li's proposal of the subjectality conception can also be located historically. Bearing in mind that the debate over subjectivity in China in the 1950s and 1960s mainly gravitated toward Marxism, the area naturally sought was collective subjectivity that has not only philosophical but also political aims. The domination of the social concern that generated social philosophical perspective entailed the focus of investigations on human collective dimension, which concurrently downplayed the individual subjectivity. Li turned to Kant's philosophy during the Cultural Revolution, when stress was placed on the revolutionary ideology. Li's conception of subjectality can be viewed as a response to the need for a reinterpretation of Marxism in postrevolutionary China and the locating of a new human subject in the historical and cultural environment. Li's subjectality is importantly enriched by the traditional Chinese, especially Confucian, element that endows the construction with an emotional and cultural sensitivity. In this sense, the philosophical construction is given a historical and cultural location.

This chapter splits into several parts thematically related to subjectality. I will start from the definition of subjectality and its two composite substances, techno-social and psychological. Next, I will focus on the techno-social substance when discussing subjectality's ontic foundation as well as material practice within the historical context that constitutes it. This will allow me to proceed to the psychological substance, which will be discussed in terms of constituting cognitive structures and emotions. Next, it will be demonstrated how subjectality, constructed within a Marxist framework, is informed by the Chinese philosophical tradition. This will be followed by a presentation of how Li determines the horizon of subjectality, which is described in terms of utopias and destinies. In the concluding remarks, I will pay attention to one major downside of philosophy of subjectality, connected with the problem of explanatory gap.

My presentation and discussion of Li's philosophy of subjectality is mainly based on the fourth chapter of *The Outline of My Philosophy*, where Li's anthropological ontology tenets are tabled in the form of statements with appended commentaries. The reason for choosing this particular text as pivotal is that it is solely devoted to expounding Li's philosophy, in contrast with *A New Approach to Kant*, where Li introduces his anthropological ontology in the form of reinterpretation of Kant's philosophy. *The Outline of My Philosophy* can be also treated as Li's philosophical credo. It is the focal point where all the views meet and constitute a systematic and articulate account. The following presentation and discussion of the philosophy of subjectality is organized in accordance with the *The Outline of My Philosophy*, and supplemented with other works by Li.

Substances of Subjectality

Li subdivides his subjectality into two substances: techno-social (*gongjubenti* 工具本體) and psychological (*xinlibenti* 心裡本體). The techno-social substance is the practice of making and using tools, which is ontologically fundamental for human beings and constitutes the distinctive feature with regard to other species of animals.[6] It constitutes the external identity of humans. This is the objective aspect of subjectality by virtue of taking place in the objective world. Whereas the techno-social substance is connected with humans as the species, the psychological substance is related to the human subjectivity's social consciousness, and it constitutes the cultural-psychological structure. Among other things, it comprises intellectual capabilities and ethical consciousness, but also less rationality pervaded aesthetic feeling.[7] Not being merely a construction for explaining epistemological models, it is an embodied subject, living in her/his material and spiritual habitat, consisting of biological, anthropological, and individual-psychological elements, which show not only how human subjectivity is constructed but also how it has been constituted and in which aspects it incessantly develops. These composites do not only serve to offer a fine-grained, anthropological description of the relation between a human being and environment but are also highly relevant to cognition.

Clearly, subjectality is not only different from Kant's but also many concepts in the Western philosophical tradition. Constructing subjectality as a living being that actively interacts with the world entails distinct characteristics that will be discussed below.

How Li understands the ontic status of substance should also be mentioned. Li refers to its two composites—techno-social and psychological—as substances, *benti* (本體). This particular determination evokes an even stronger connotation in the Chinese language, where ontology literally means "the study of substance"—*bentilun* (本體論). The usage of "substance" is to describe subjectality as the ontic foundation of humans.[8] This is particularly evident in the techno-social substance, which is fundamental to the human species. However, apart from this ontological taxonomy, Li similarly understands cognitive structures and emotions, which are part of the psychological substance. Li analyzes separately the meanings of *ben* (本) and *ti* (體), and renders them into English as "root" and "body" respectively. Accordingly, "ontology" should be understood as the study of the root and body of human practice. Hence, *benti* comprises human "tool practice" and psychology, including emotions, which constitute subjectality.[9]

It should be remarked that Li's notion of substance ought not to be misconceived as atemporal in the sense of persisting over time without any changes. Quite the contrary, the substance that constitutes subjectality adapts over time due to sedimentation via incessant social practice. The dynamic character of sedimentation explains the plasticity of the psychological substance, which is constantly constituted by ongoing material practice.

Techno-social Substance

Techno-social substance determines the distinctive feature of subjectality as a human being. Li identifies it with the practice of tool making and use and shows how this generic human activity is situated in human existence. It is determined by the biological and collective aspect of existence from the historical perspective. Li starts from defining human existence with the following statement:[10]

> "Humans' living" is the first [fundamental] fact. "Humans' living" is a more fundamental fact than "why humans live" because it is an established fact.[11]

Li emphasizes that human existence has the same basis as that of animals. In other words, the ontic foundation of human existence is biological. This at the outset opposes subjectality to the conceptions that identify human subjectivity with the mind. Li admits that apart from living in the biological sense, humans are conscious of their existence and can reflect upon it. However, consciousness is not ontically prior to the biological foundation.[12] Human existence is the life of the human species and subjectality cannot be understood apart from this material foundation.

Li further explores the fundamental reality of human life by bringing to attention two important points. First, human life is not a matter of choice. Humans do not decide on their biological existence, but are thrown into it. The reason for this lack of choice between living or not living is attributed by Li to the instinctual continuation of the species.[13] It can be seen that Li consistently follows the materialist assumptions by locating subjectality's ontic status in biology, which, at least as far living is concerned, is independent from subjectality's decision.

The lack of choice by subjectality importantly extends to the second point, which determines subjectality's living as involving coexistence with other humans.[14] This is also not an optional feature of human existence that can be decided on or chosen by an individual. Human coexistence is also as fundamental as the very fact of living. This fact opposes subjectality to the theories that view society as established by human decision or consensus. An example of such a theory can be the establishment of society for the sake of individual safety that is guaranteed, for instance, in the form of social contract in Thomas Hobbes's philosophy.[15] It can also be exemplified with the Mohist conception, where pluralism of views resulting in chaos is prevented by establishing a society with one, shared standard.[16] Hence, the ontic status of subjectality cannot be constructed in abstraction either from biology or sociality. At this point, a tremendous difference is apparent between Kant's subjectivity that confronts the world and subjectality that is ontologically founded in it.

Li also further determines the existential character of subjectality as convergent with the later Wittgensteinian "everyday life," which belongs to Wittgenstein's conception of language,[17] and Heidegger's "everydayness" as a mode of existence in the world inhabited by others. This is to underscore that human collective life stems from the fundamental fact of coexistence rather than a theory imposed on it.[18]

More importantly for his philosophical project, Li also describes living as Marx's social existence (*shehui cunzai* 社會存在), in which humans cannot choose their own material production.[19] This is to show two things. First, subjectality is involved in Marx's material practice, and, second, more importantly, practice is not external to subjectality and determines her/his identity. In this sense, subjectality cannot be an entity abstracted from the world as subjectality's identity is existentially and behaviorally determined by the material reality. Considering additionally that material practice changes both the world and humans, Li also points to the dynamic aspect of subjectality. This clearly shows that subjectality is not a static, abstracted construction.

The fact that humans are situated in their social existence with others, and apart from that they are social by nature, bears an important philosophical implication: there is no abstract, void-of-any-qualities "I" that enters the world and in the course of life determines itself as a social human being. In fact, one cannot think about an individual in accordance with Sartre's view, on which we can separate a pure existence prior to essence.[20] Subjectality always lives some particular life, in a given time, place, and in a specific culture.

The material and dynamic aspect of human life is emphasized by Li also at the linguistic level. When Li describes human life, he uses the verb *huo* (活), which means "to live," instead of *cunzai* (存在), which means "to exist." Existence is a philosophical term, and we would find it more natural in describing abstract entities, in contrast to the usage of "living." Li wants to emphasize that the existence is lived by humans in the sense that it is not only some external necessary condition for life, but life itself. It should also be mentioned that Li uses the verb "live" in the continuous form *huozhe* (活著), by which his first statement literally means that "humans are living."

The socially situated and involved-in-practice subjectality's existence is juxtaposed with theorizing on it. Li unfolds it in the following way:

> It can be seen that the first implication of "humans' living" is how humans live in terms of eating and drinking, dwelling, and transporting.[21]

Li focuses here on the priority of life to its abstraction. Li's remark on the above implication is that the "how" of life precedes any questions concerning the meaning of human existence.[22] This confirms that theorizing about human life, which must involve abstraction into existence, is not appropriate for understanding subjectality. Instead, one should focus on the very fact that humans live and how they live their life. These two aspects are one in practice. The way in which humans live already determines them as humans. Humans do not require any abstract taxonomy, as their everyday life, apart from which they cannot exist, has already defined them. This view of human existence is most consistent with Li's Marxist assumptions, as what is fundamental for humanity is social practice, which encapsulates the very character of how life is lived. For this reason, Li does not abstain from mentioning eating and dwelling, as they already situate humans in their practice, which involves specific tools and technologies, and is manifested by some specific behavior. The techno-social substance is constituted by specific tool practice that takes place in social life. The techno-social substance as a distinctive feature of humans is pretheoretical.

Li notices a similar approach to life as prior to theory inter alia in Wittgenstein's philosophy. Wittgenstein is mostly concerned with language. When discussing language game, he admits that spoken language is "part of an activity, or of a form of life."[23] Wittgenstein, unlike Li, regards language to be part of practice. Thus, language game is based on practice and must be grasped therein because we cannot find the generalizations that are necessary to encapsulate language rules. Interpreting language practice takes place through the common behavior of its users. Wittgenstein illustrates this issue with different examples of games that seem to have something in common, but if we go through all of them, we finally do not find what all of them share but a sophisticated network of similarities. Uncovering them can take place only through practice.[24] In his discussion of language, Wittgenstein is more concerned with a methodological approach, but, similarly to Li, he assumes the fundamental aspect of practice and life.

Finally, the social and practical character of subjectality is complemented with the historical materialism interpretation, in that practice is of actual but also historical character:

> The limitless (*wuqiongjin* 無窮盡), permanent (*heng* 恆), and common (*gonggonghua* 公共化) time also appears to be of "the first implication." Its universal necessity (Kant) is actually social objectivity. . . . Considering this, only then do history (*lishi* 歷史) and being historical (*lishixing* 歷史性) matter in an objective and "necessary" way.[25]

Li alludes to his reinterpretation of Kant in that humans through their historical practice developed the ability to conceptualize their life in a temporal and spatial framework. The objective validity of this conceptualization is thanks to the fact that the laws of the objective world are sedimented through practice into humans. Importantly, the objective validity is not achieved in an abstract, logical way but through the historical accumulation of practice that has molded human cognitive structures.

To briefly conclude, the techno-social substance of subjectality constitutes the generic feature that is present in all humans defined by tool practice by humans who are social by nature.

Psychological Substance and Cognition

The above example of sedimenting the temporal and spatial framework of experience, apart from showing the necessity of the historical aspect on human practice in the dynamic constitution of subjectality, brings us to psychological substance, which involves psychological processes in humans, including cognitive and emotion-based structures.

Li believes that in comparison with the imprecision of other philosophical theories, his subjectality conception, thanks to the psychological substance has the advantage of attentiveness and sensitivity to the essential yet usually intangible composites of human essence. He particularly locates it in the emotional structure of the psychological substance.[26]

An important feature of psychological substance is its high level of plasticity, which enables the continuous sedimentation of new psychological structures by means of tool practice. How Li particularly understands it can be illustrated by Jean Piaget's theory of cognitive development, a theory that Li regards as highly explanatory of sedimenting psychological, especially cognitive, structures.[27]

Piaget claims that newborns' cognitive development is based on sensorimotor intelligence, which has permanent dispositions, named schemes, for simple sensorimotor actions. Thanks to schemes, children adapt to their environment without symbolic representations of reality. Along with performing more and more complicated sensorimotor actions, children gradually start mental operations. The cognitive development hinges on two main processes: assimilation, when children adjust sense data to their schemas, and accommodation, which consist in modifying schemas to accommodate new information. Piaget distinguishes among four stages of development: sensorimotor (newborns), preoperational (early childhood), concrete operational (late childhood), and formal operational (adolescence and later). Each of these stages consists in a different cognitive style.[28] What is relevant to Li's sedimentation can be found at the first stage, when children develop object permanence, which consists in objects' existence (persistence in time) independently from consciousness. This can be interpreted in favor of Li in the way that sensorimotor practice internalizes a cognitive structure (the temporal frame for experience) and also results in mental representations of objects existing in time.

One should remember that Piaget's theory of cognitive development is also inconsistent with Li's sedimentation. Piaget is concerned with the ontogenetic development of individual children, whereas sedimentation applies to the anthropologically and historically conceived humans. However, the importance of Piaget's developmental psychology for Li lies in the psychological plasticity of subjectality, who does not have inborn cognitive structures but acquires and expands them through motor interaction with the world, which is not reducible to being exposed to the world merely by sensuous receptiveness.

The plasticity of subjectality integrated with tool practice from a historical perspective allows Li to explain how highly complex cognitive structures responsible for knowledge production are sedimented. He claims that

> grammar (language), logic (thought) are also the needs, standards, and laws of "being with others" (that is, human collective existence) in this world. They are not related to nature.[29]

Li assumes the fundamental character of practice with regard to language and thinking. Now it can be seen where Li and Wittgenstein particularly differ when it comes to the status of language. Li believes that language and thought are not part of fundamental practice. In his commentary on the above statement, Li writes that ethic (*lunli* 倫理) is prior to cognition, which is discursive and therefore needs grammar and logic. These have evolved from the differentiations in ethical regulations.[30] Hence, Li regards ethic as more fundamental because it consists in the rules that are already present in material practice. This "code of conduct," as part of practice is sedimented into subjectality as cognitive laws.

An argument supporting Li's view of the development of language through practice instead of already being practice, can be found in evolutionary psychology. In the period ranging 40,000–50,000 years ago, the development of so-called modern human behavior took place. It is believed that one of the possibilities for speech replacing manual gesture was development in making and using tools that moved communication from hands to face, which gradually evolved from facial gestures into voice communication.[31] The advantage of speech was not only the possibility of performing manual operations while communicating but also using language in the dark or with intervening physical obstacles between interlocutors, as well as transmission of culture.[32] This theory can be interpreted in favor of Li's views, as it presupposes that practice necessitates a different medium of communication, and enables a better control over environment. However, this only shows the emergence of a new linguistic medium, not language itself, conceived of as a communication system. Before the emergence of speech, language had already existed in the manual gesture medium. As for the origin of language, there are theories that language and its syntactic structure emerged in the context of manual gestures, which can be argued for from different angles.[33] From the learning perspective, it has been found that teaching language to apes is more effective by means of gestures than speech. When it comes to neuroscientific argumentation, the homologue of Broca's area (a brain region responsible for speech production) in monkeys contains mirror neurons that respond to production and the perception of reaching and grasping movements. This suggests that language could develop from manual gestures. Another argument comes from studies of sign languages showing that they are constructed in the same way, including syntax-wise, as spoken languages. Finally, the left hemisphere in most humans is responsible for both speech and manual operations, including those in sign languages.[34] The hypothesis, as well as argumentation, dovetail with Li's in that language is preceded by human practice, which is structured, for instance, by ethic.

Li argues for the sedimentation of cognitive structures by resorting to Heidegger. He claims that cognition, human life, and reality are "ready to hand" rather than "present at hand."[35] Readiness-at-hand (*Zuhandenheit*) refers to the entities that we encounter in everyday practice and approach without pondering over their ontic status, but directly engage with by using. Importantly, when we use them, we are not conscious of them as tools and us as the subject of the activity. In contrast to readiness-at-hand, presence-at-hand (*Vorhandenheit*) consists in extracting entities from the everyday practice, by which they become objects independent from it. This also entails a change in the mode of being in *Dasein*, which becomes involved as the subject in the subject-object structure.[36] This implies that human life and the world do not entail cognitive subdivision into subject and object. Life and practice that includes cognition are prior to this subdivision. The theoretical framework of cognition is a product of sedimentation.

Li also presents the importance of practice in cognition and knowledge production in ontological perspective by referring to Vladimir Illich

Lenin, who underscores that practice is more important "than theoretical knowledge [cognition] for it has not only the dignity of universality but also of immediate actuality."[37] The human existence conforms to the universal natural law, and concurrently actualizing their purpose conforms to the universal law. Human thought and consciousness are an expression of this universality of the subject's practice in the material world.[38] The objective validity of knowledge comes from the practice that reflects it. It should also be taken into consideration that the cognitive structures of the subject that predetermine how the subject will respond to experience and think (conceptualize or have nonconceptual content) are also sedimented through practice, as has been showcased in detail by Li's reinterpretation of Kant. It can be seen that not only the content of knowledge but also its character depends on practice, and is therefore of a historical character, making the subject's rationality, sensuousness, and affectivity components relative to practice at a given time of human history.

The knowledge validity issue is also briefly discussed in a philosophical context in *A New Approach to Kant.* Li believes that only practice provides theory with both actuality and universality. He remarks that, on one hand, German idealist philosophers, such as Kant or Georg Wilhelm Friedrich Hegel started from reason, which brings universality without actuality. On the other hand, philosophers who start from the senses, such as John Locke or Ludwig Feuerbach concurrently begin with the individual, which brings actuality but not universality. Social practice overcomes these confinements by being grounded in objective reality. Particularly interesting in this respect is Li's remark on the natural sciences and philosophy. He refers to Marx's and Engels's view that these disciplines, despite their methodological rigor, focus on nature or thought, which are not constant by virtue of human practice that transforms nature and sediments as thought.[39] In this view, downplaying practice is not merely to ignore some aspect in account of reality but to misconceive the ontic status of both thought and nature.

The priority of practice to thought, symbolic operations, and language is temporal and logical in the sense that the psychological structure is the effect of practice that leads to the emergence of consciousness and thought, and that practice is necessary for consciousness and thought to come into existence and develop respectively. Therefore, subjectality dismisses the possibility of reflection that begins from the Cartesian cogito. Consciousness cannot be the point of departure that leads to proving the existence of the subject whose ontic status is less questionable than that of the world. Li's assumption is quite the reverse, namely, that without the world, there cannot be a subject who thinks and is conscious of doing so.

It can be clearly seen why Li decided to coin the term "subjectality." Li approaches the issue of human subjectivity in a completely different way than the Western tradition. Subjectality is not to be conceptualized as the subject of cognition, equipped with certain cognitive faculties. Subjectality is the human essence or nature that emerges in incessant practice. At the same time, one has to bear in mind that practice cannot be identified with solely subjective activity that is not objectively determined.[40] Therefore, subjectality is not constituted by, for instance, receptive sense perceptions. However, it should also be noticed that Li's definition of Western subjectivity does not seem to include other, situated conceptions of cognition. One such example is the conception of extended cognition, which considers the parts of the external world that are coupled with the human organism within cognitive processes.[41] Departing from such an approach to the subject and cognition would not make Li's subjectality entirely different.

Psychological Substance and Reflection on Life

Li also indicates that psychological substance, apart from cognizing the world is also responsible for reflection upon life.[42] This remark is key for Li's philosophy. It shows that psychological substance opens a new dimension in humans, which, although also founded on social practice, is not limited to the fundamental "how" of living. The questions related to the meaning of life are not connected with everyday practice but grow from reflection upon it. This remark brings us to another development of Li's thought, connected with emotions.

Emotionality is described by Li as "emotional substance" (*qinggan benti* 情感本體). These are sedimented emotional structures that constitute psychological substance.[43] Including emotionality in subjectality is a crucial complementation for Li's philosophical construction.

Li declares that Marxism—due to being mainly concerned with techno-social substance—does not devote appropriate attention to inner psychology.[44] As already mentioned in the chapter devoted to Confucianism, Li believes that Confucian psychology, where the self-cultivation consisting in calibrating primitive and instinctual emotional emotions is achieved through rational sedimentation, is based on specific practice.[45] It is important that emotions in this process are not eliminated or suppressed but given a proper form. Li takes over the emotional calibration from Confucianism and builds it into the psychological substance. Emotion inherent in psychological structures does not only function as response in interaction but also plays an important cognitive role. It is crucial in aesthetic apprehension of reality, which will be discussed in detail in the chapter on aesthetic experience.

Despite constituting inner life of subjectality, psychology is inseparable from practice. This psychological realm may initially appear as transcendent in relation to social practice, but it can only be found in collectivity manifested in everyday life and sedimented into the psychological substance. If humans were separated from the two substances, they would lose their distinctive feature and enjoy life merely on a biological level, like other animals, bereft of the consciousness of their own existence.[46] Li also remarks that, on the other hand, separating the meaning of life (*shengming yiyi* 生命意義) and the consciousness of human life (*renshengyishi* 人生意識) from life (*shengming* 生命) is nothing beyond a linguistic formulation, although at the same time life and human life are not the same as consciousness of human life or the meaning of life. This quasi-paradoxical statement conveys the inseparability of the psychological component from the base of practice in an ontological sense, but it simultaneously does not deny the difference between life and reflection upon it. This dovetails with the foundations of dialectical materialism, according to which consciousness and other aspects of mental life evolve from matter as a new quality.[47]

Subjectality and Adaptation

Li does not regard the consciousness of and reflection upon human existence as inherent in subject-independent products of the human mind. Their origin and character are situated in the material practice of living in nature. Humans, unlike beasts of prey or large animals, had to strive for survival in a different than physical way, which has led to the emergence of consciousness and meaning of life, as Li suggests.[48]

With regard to the human struggle to survive in nature, in *A New Approach to Kant*, Li points to human life being in this respect significantly different from animals by the practice of controlling nature and transforming it. Animal life is confined to survival activities that consist in a corresponding adaptive behavior. Thanks to social practice, humans do not have to adaptively conform in order to survive. They can control nature and make it serve their own purposes, which are different than those of nature. The social existence of humans has led to the emergence of symbolic systems, such as language, consciousness, and thought, which can transcend the purely adaptive survival strategy.[49] Because of this fundamental difference in entering relation with nature between humans and other animals, the subject-object division, on a Marxist view, does not apply to animals. It is only humans who enjoy subjectivity, thanks to which they are endowed with what Li refers to as the "spontaneity of cognition."[50]

Practice thus conceived from human survival, described as living, living with others, and living in one world, according to Li constitutes the foundation for more sophisticated psychological and cultural formations, such as human feeling (*renqingwei* 人情味) achieved through mutual care.[51] Li assumes an evolutionary perspective to explain the sedimentation of the psychological substance. Human psychology and culture are refined from the fundamental social practice. Their aims were determined by the "how" of living, in particular circumstances. This fact can be supported by research conducted in experimental sciences that trace some human cultural characteristics down to the practice that took place long before human beings became cultured in the modern sense. One such example can be provided by some human aesthetic preferences, for instance in facial attractiveness. Despite some differences in attractiveness assessment across different ethnic groups and cultures, there are also common features that are considered to be universally attractive. For instance, as regards the attractiveness of women's faces to men, high foreheads, big eyes, small noses, full lips, and small chins are universally considered as attractive. These features are associated with high estrogen level in women, and therefore signal their fertility. Similarly, as regards women's preferences in men's faces, those with big, square-shaped jaws, thin cheeks, and heavy brows were found most attractive. These facial features are associated with a high testosterone level.[52] These aesthetic preferences pattern in accordance with sexual dimorphism, and the attractiveness of faces is associated with possible human reproduction. We can interpret this aesthetic preference as rooted in Li's "how" of living, where the social practice is directed at the very fact of living, also in a biological and nonindividual sense, as the human species. In this context, the face preferences are dictated by improving the chances for reproduction. This aesthetic reference, through long practice has sedimented into the psychological substance and become cultural. The representations of faces in artistic photography or portrait painting are more considered beautiful than sexually attractive, which shows the shift of preferences from biological to aesthetic. The roots of this cultural formation are to be located in the social practice.

Another example that complies with Li's statement is aesthetic preference for landscape. It is rooted in the preferences for place, presumably from the Pleistocene era (1,600,000–10,000 BCE), a period with itinerant hunter-gatherer groups, who frequently had to determine the most suitable places for short-time residence. These sites had to provide safe shelter with food and water resources. In the case of Africa, one such area was the savannah, because of scattered flora that enabled good observation and fauna consisting of protein-rich mammals. It has been experimentally discovered that contemporary humans liked the savannah type of landscape, despite the fact that the participants in the experiment had never been to the real savannah and only saw it on slides.[53] This experiment was conducted with participants aged 8, 11, 15, 18, and 35. What is interesting, the appreciation for this type of landscape diminished with age, which, as is suggested, is due to cultural modification.[54] In comparison to the previous example, landscape preference is rooted in increased chances for survival. The human practice of frequently having to evaluate possible abodes has resulted in the sedimentation of landscape preferences, originally motivated by practical concerns, into the psychological substance, which results in our contemporary assessment of savannah landscapes according to aesthetic rather than survival standards.

Apart from the "receptive" aesthetic assessment, arguments supporting the sedimentation from social practice can also be found in the implementation of aesthetic features in an amplified way. In case of the face preference, plastic surgery and cosmetics are intended for beautification purposes, while at the same time enhancing the features with "reproductive signals." In the case of landscape preference, landscape gardening often amplifies the features of original places that were determined to be safe and rich in food resources.[55] The elements that are manipulated in the amplification process are evidence that the preferences become even more cultural than the previous examples, as the survival and reproductive signals are not merely reproduced but often amplified to a degree that is not encountered in nature. The relation between the aesthetically motivated practice and its origin complies with the statement that some psychological qualities in humans, although achieved through sedimentation, are already different from the fundamental level of living, which Li understands as social practice.

Subjectality and Individual Existence

In his exposition of the philosophy of subjectality, Li talks about humans in the collective sense. The everyday life activities, the social aspect of life, and psychological sedimentation are not identical with the life of a particular individual, which is an existence that is not repeatable and approaches death. Therefore, the propensities of the collective life of humans cannot determine or dominate the meaning of an individual (*geti de* 個體的) life. The origin of these questions does not lie in an individual existence, but grows from the collective practice. This could suggest that Li simply ignores or downplays the importance of individual life in his philosophical project. He addresses this possible doubt and clarifies that the historical sedimentation that results in cultural and psychological structure or psychological substance does not suppress or interfere with the dimension of individual life. The contingency of human living, which consists in making choices—as well as its impact on human reception and confrontation of, or attention to, the substance—is entirely different from the techno-social structure. Individual life comprises uncertainty, diversity, and challenge. The psychological substance informs humans culturally and psychologically but does not sediment into their individuality. Humans are always located in some particular context of life, yet their life is not reducible to strictly collective existence.[56] Hence, subjectality always describes a certain shape of individuality, in terms of, for instance, cognitive capacities or sensitivity. However, individual life is always idiosyncratic at the same time.

Subjectality and Chinese Philosophy

Apart from emotional substance, in terms of construction, subjectality may appear as not particularly informed by Chinese philosophical tradition. However, it can be found that the assumptions of subjectality are in fact extremely convergent with Chinese philosophical intuitions.

Li's interest in the Chinese philosophical tradition can be subdivided into two areas: historical and constructive. As regards the former, it consists in a study that can be located in history of philosophy. Li assumes his anthropological ontology perspective to examine the development of Chinese thought in time. The time perspective serves not as a temporal framework but as Chinese social and political history. Li undertakes situating philosophers and their views in their social and political context. One such study is, for instance, *A History of Classical Chinese Thought* recently published in English (originally published in Chinese in 1985).[57]

Although the historical study of Chinese thought can be regarded as an intellectual showcase of anthropological ontology, far more important is the fact that Li regards some part of Chinese philosophical intuitions, as well as some aspects of Confucianism, as a complement to his historical ontology project. In his preface to *A New Approach to Kant*, Li conspicuously underscores this question when he explains his philosophical approach to Kant. By far, his philosophical framework is Marxism-oriented, although Li also points to his Confucian inclination. Despite profoundly appreciating Marx's thought, Li admits that historical materialism mainly focuses on the material aspect of human existence in the social dimension.[58] This is complemented by Confucianism, which is concerned with human self-cultivation within and without. He refers this issue to the psychological substance and emotional-rational structure. Hence, Confucianism becomes integrated into the overall social practice paradigm and it affords a glimpse into how sedimentation molds the human mind. Li believes that one of the most important impacts of social practice on the psychological-cultural formation is the sedimentation of rationality within it. He particularly sees this aspect in Confucian psychology, where the self-cultivation consisting in calibrating (not suppressing or eliminating) emotions is achieved through rational sedimentation based on specific practice.

Li's generally expressed inspiration by Chinese philosophical intuitions, as well as selected aspects from the Confucian school are present in his philosophical construction as implicit particulars complementing the historical materialist framework. First, regardless of whether the world is conceptualized as the cosmos or nature, humans are an integral part of it. This is attributed to the assumption of a one-world view resulting in a conceptualization of the world that exhausts the whole metaphysical universe. Accordingly, it does not ontically depend on any transcendent reality or entity, nor is it governed by any extrinsic laws. In other words, the world is self-sufficient and self-explainable. This assumption is present in the whole of Chinese cosmology and cosmological thinking, which is present also in Confucianism. On this plane, Chinese thought is compatible with Li's materialism. Considering the focus on humans, human existence and life are subject only to the laws of a world thus conceived. Accordingly, the universe in Chinese cosmological thinking is conceptualized as an incessant transformation, which also applies to humans and their life. In *Four Essays on Aesthetics*, Li conspicuously admits this fact in the following way:

> My meaning of the *integration of human and the cosmos* differs from that of many people. I mean that all of society and all of humanity are living in a harmonious state with nature. . . . We cannot attain this integration . . . by virtue of individual's subjective consciousness, but rather by virtue of human material practice.[59]

Li's anthropological ontology conceptualizes the world as nature, and humans are an integral part of it. Similarly to the Chinese worldview, nature is constantly transformed by social practice that is unique to humans. Importantly and unlike later Marxism, this practice is always material.

The dynamic character of reality and humans as part of it brings the second characteristic, connected with human agency. The human engagement in transforming reality is concurrently an adaptation to it. In Confucianism, this is particularly visible on the moral level, and, although it could be perceived as confined to interaction with other people, it is in fact underpinned with a deeper pattern of cosmological changes. Humans aim not only at social but also cosmological harmony. Importantly, harmony is to be achieved by specific human behavior, which differs from one Chinese philosophical school to another. In anthropological ontology, humans are involved in material practice; the distinctive characteristic of humans is that humans can transform nature through manufacture and the use of tools. Tool practice also changes a whole network of relations, between humans and nature, as well as among humans themselves. On one hand, this activity can be labeled emancipation from the laws of nature rather than conforming to them. However, on the other hand, one ought to bear in mind that material production, when not alienated, as the free practice of humans, is how they express themselves in agreement with nature. Considering that humans are part of nature, the practice that aligns them in a harmonious relation with it can be perceived as a continuous effort to be integral with the whole.

Human practice should not solely be viewed on a macroscale. Both Confucianism and Li's philosophy of subjectality acknowledge the importance of human interaction with other humans as well as actions that constitute their relationship with the world. However, the confinement of practice to external activities would be missing the most important point for both philosophical projects—that is, the becoming of humans, or, more precisely, their humanity. The other direction in which practice works is human subjectivity. Its structure is dependent on practice in two ways. The psychological substance is molded by practice, and it could neither come into existence nor develop without human interaction with the environment. Confucianism meticulously describes propriety, which, if performed in an adequate way, will result in a specific sensitivity *ren*, a measure of humanity, particularly understood by Confucians as moral personhood. Li's subjectality is based on a very similar foundation, as he turns Kant's a priori upside down and claims the mindset, particular to humans, to be entirely sedimented. Also, how particularly the subject's mind is furnished is decided by the character of practice, which in contrast with Confucians is viewed historically. As can be seen, human agency is not only of an external character. In fact, it can be stated to be self-constituting.

Third, considering the constitutive aspect of practice, it can be also stated that cognition depends on behavior. Being *ren* equips a Confucian with a particular sensitivity that helps recognize a situation and act in a way that complies with propriety. The degree to which one's sensitivity allows one to take correct action depends on the propriety practice. Li's subjectality's psychological substance is constantly forged by practice. Human cognition depends on the cognitive faculties that have been sedimented into subjectality. It also has to be borne in mind that subjectality's cognitive structures change in the history of material practice, which shows the connection between accumulating behavior and cognition.

Fourth, one should not miss an important aspect of sedimentation with regard to emotion. The humanization of the human mindset, among other things, consists in the transformation of primitive emotions, as a result of which they are no longer originally raw but given a certain form in the process of rationality sedimentation. One should bear in mind that emotions in the philosophy of subjectality, similarly to Confucianism, are not dismissed or downplayed in cognition. Both philosophies assume that subjectivity is not to be conceptualized as detached from the world center of consciousness and cognition. The fact that subjectivity does not merely exist but is lived and cannot be conceived of beyond human life invites conceptions of subjectivity that interact with the world in more than just a rational way.

Fifth, the aesthetic is associated with freedom. According to fragment 8.8 of the *Analects*, Confucian self-cultivation relies on the *Odes*, propriety, and music.[60] As it has already been explained how these three components are essential in achieving the complete Confucian personhood, music comes as the last stage that molds the human mind in an unmediated way. In this sense, it is the most direct, unconfined way of cultivation as well as expression. It can be said that a Confucian can feel most freedom when engaged in art, which takes place both in reception of artwork and artistic production. Thus, the aesthetic can be associated with the realm of freedom. Li combines the aesthetic and freedom, which can be supported by Marx's *Manuscripts*, in which humans realize themselves through free production in accordance with the laws of beauty.[61]

Subjectality's Horizon

The inspiration with the Chinese philosophy can also be found in Li's determination of a twofold utopia as the horizon of his philosophical project. It is subdivided into external and internal. As regards the former, it is either the world of great harmony or communism. This confirms that Li does not regard traditional Chinese thought and Marxism as mutually exclusive in his philosophy. As regards the latter utopia, it is a complete psychological structure and emotional in particular. These utopias comply with both Marxism and Confucianism, which become integrated in Li's subjectality. The integration should not be mistaken for merely mapping Marxism onto Confucian philosophy. Li underscores this point by referring to the "sageness within, kingliness without" (*neisheng waiwang* 内圣外王) quotation from the last chapter of the *Zhuangzi*,[62] which, independently of its origin, in Chinese culture describes the ideal sage, who devotes herself/himself to self-cultivation both in terms of inner development and active participation in society.[63] He clearly sees that this aspect of Confucianism, unlike Marxism emphasizes the human becoming in a most comprehensive fashion, especially by paying attention to psychological traits that are not developed independently but are necessarily integrated with practice.

Li believes that human practice must be complemented with utopia. Humans need this ideal horizon in order not to lose one's way in their contemporary life, and lists God, Allah, and Being as possible concretions of internal utopia.[64] This shows that subjectality, although by far a practice-related construction, is flexible when it comes to what cultural content is sedimented within. Accordingly, humans can determine their utopia as, for instance philosophical or religious, with which the character of their practice will comply. At the same time, one must keep in mind that on the ground of Li's historical materialism, the utopian horizon is historically determined by the stage of human practice.

The subjectality's horizon is further determined by Li when he describes the philosophy of subjectality as destiny (*mingyun* 命運).[65] He believes that destiny is formed by three reflections on life: religious, artistic, and philosophical.

Religions believe in destiny, art expresses destiny, and philosophy reflects upon destiny. The reason for describing philosophy of subjectality as destiny becomes clearer when Li points to human nature, contingency, and destiny as the main subject of his philosophy. Considering that the philosophy of subjectality does not consist in analyzing abstract and unchanging entities, but quite the opposite, the dynamic aspects of humanity, Li's notions are also not fixed or complete. This concern with capturing the dynamic aspect of reality is as natural in Li's philosophy as it is in the *Book of Changes*, Daoism, and Confucianism. Therefore, the three main aspects of Li's philosophy are to be viewed in terms of their becoming rather than unchanging essence. Considering this, destiny is to be understood as a direction and horizon of the subjectality practice. Li succinctly views this aspect across three types of reflection.

As for religions, they offer an especially clear trajectory of human destiny, which stretches even beyond the end of material life. Hans Küng and Julia Ching distinguish between three great world religious "river systems": prophetic (of Semitic origin), mystical (of Indian origin), and wisdom (of Chinese origin).[66] Although the classification seems incomplete, it points to the heterogenous character of religious systems, which according to Li should manifest belief in destiny. Considering this subdivision, the most evident reference to destiny is formulated by the Abrahamic religions that schedule the entire history and future of mankind, and even extend to afterlife. However, the remaining religions, which stress different aspects, can also be viewed as offering destiny. Religions of Indian origin in their soteriologies usually emphasize liberation from the world of human existence and offer *moksha*—freeing oneself from the samsaric cycle of death rebirth or *nirvana* (for instance, in Buddhism, Hinduism, and Jainism). This liberation, although not located within a temporal framework, is also a clearly determined human destiny. In comparison with mystical and prophetic religions, Chinese wisdom religions are more focused on this-worldly relations with others and nature. They are probably the least explicit with regard to destiny, as, similarly to Chinese philosophy, they are more concentrated on the way rather than the end. However, the multifaceted scheme of life is part of a larger natural or cosmic process, which makes human life meaningful.

Religions can also be viewed as cultural phenomena that reflect human sedimentation by particular beliefs and destinies. This can be exemplified, for instance, by the Reformation in the sixteenth century, which can be contextualized in broader changes in social history. This also illustrates the important, temporal aspect of destinies.

As regards art, Li primarily associates it with expressing destiny.[67] Li's conception of aesthetics as well as art are not disconnected from human practice and hence mark the trajectory of cultural and psychological sedimentation in history. His *The Path of Beauty: A Study of Chinese Aesthetics* is the main work that, from an anthropological ontology perspective, traces the aesthetics development throughout Chinese literature and art history from the Neolithic period until the Qing dynasty.

Of the three ways of conveying destiny, philosophy presents the most discursive and systematic approach. On one hand, in comparison with art and religion, philosophy is by nature a distanced and disinterested reflection on the world and humans. On the other hand, however, when viewed from the perspective of Li's anthropological ontology, philosophy, similarly to other forms of reflection on reality, is also part of it. As manifested in *A New Approach to Kant*, philosophical constructions are intellectual sedimentations at a given time in history of human practice, and, as such, they present different conceptualizations of human destiny.

Conclusion

The philosophy of subjectality, albeit Li's original theoretical construction, clearly reflects the three philosophical inspirations. One might observe, both in terms of publications and constructing theory, that Li's thought has been inspired by Kant. An obvious, critical inspiration is provided by *A New Approach to Kant*, where the foundations of a priori philosophy become capsized. However, more importantly for Li's project, Kant's influence can be seen in focus on subjectivity, around which a complex philosophical system is built. This point of departure is transplanted to Li's philosophical project. This results in the philosophy of subjectality founded on the fundamental fact of living.

The foundations for the philosophy of subjectality are provided by historical materialism, as presented in Marx's *Manuscripts*, while also avoiding the Frankfurt school. It has been shown that, although historical materialism and the practice of tool manufacturing and use constitute the widest framework of Li's philosophical project, it does not dominate all aspects of Li's thought.

The psychological construction complies with the Chinese, especially Confucian, philosophical intuitions. On a general level, Li's philosophical thinking observably complies with the fundamental Chinese philosophical intuitions in terms of the interrelation between humans and a dynamic reality. On a more specific level, Li complements the Marxist aspect of humanity, which is mostly concerned with the historical and collective human, with the individual and intrinsic dimension, especially when it comes to the emotional structures in psychological substance.

Considering the above, subjectality is a complex philosophical construction that not only provides a profound insight into the internal construction of the subject. Subjectality cuts across intrinsic and extrinsic processes that describe the becoming of humans and their involvement in the world. It can be said that subjectality determines humans on social and anthropological levels. Although subjectality is mostly concerned with these two dimensions of humanity, it also addresses human individuality, by pointing to the idiosyncrasy that results from particular and specific modes of human living.

Although the philosophy of subjectality presents a comprehensive account of various strata of humanity, there are also some points that have not been specified in Li's project. It seems that the most important one is connected with how the practice of tool manufacturing and use has led to the emergence of subjectality. However important this question is, it must be admitted that the gap is to be filled by empirical sciences rather than philosophy. With regard to this, it should be noticed that Li himself admits that the psychological substance is to be further investigated beyond philosophy, by neurosciences, psychology, and pedagogy.[68] Li bases his psychological evidence on Piaget. However, it has to be remembered that Piaget's developmental psychology concerns the cognitive development in individual children. It is difficult to assess how the ontogenetic development model would work in historical materialism perspective, where the development concerns the human species rather than a particular representative of it in a specific historical time. More adequate evidence for examining Li's postulates is offered by evolutionary psychology. Research in this field has brought some hypotheses concerning particular aspects of human psychological development, for instance language. Evolutionary psychology also collaborates with neuroscience, which would be particularly appropriate to examine if material practice has involved changes on a neural level. It seems that the study of cultural neurocorrelates could form an adequate contribution.[69]

The problem of how mental faculties emerge from the biological foundation can also be located in the contemporary discussion present in the philosophy of mind. On assuming physicalism, the concern specifically consists in determining how it is possible for some complex physical entities to have conscious phenomenology. This ontological problem is referred to as the "explanatory gap."[70] The problem also includes the question why entities possess one particular phenomenology rather than another. Some theories try to answer the explanatory gap question by reference to evolutionary approaches. An approach in this vein is discussed by Martine Nida-Rümelin.

Rümelin describes the dualist version of emergentism. She departs from the theory that at some point in evolution, a change in conscious animals, including humans, took place. It consisted in some arrangement in their matter that led to the occurrence of consciousness. This fact can be interpreted in two ways. The first interpretation says that this change entails the origin of new individuals. The second interpretation does not involve new individuals but ascribes the occurrence of consciousness to qualitative changes that have taken place in previously unconscious individuals. In both cases, emergentism locates the change on the physical (broadly construed as biological, chemical, and functional) level, where a certain arrangement of matter takes place, which with nomological necessity leads to the occurrence of consciousness.[71] Dualist emergentism does not consist in the origination of a new substance in addition to matter, but holds that the conscious properties cannot be reduced to the physical properties, despite the fact that the former cannot occur and perdure without the latter. The sedimentation of Li's psychological substance can be viewed in terms of the explanatory gap problem whereby material practice causes the occurrence of conscious psychological qualities, which depend on a biological foundation but at the same time cannot be reduced to it, and an individual human subjectality is also irreducible to its material identity—the body. This tension between practice and human psychology on the ontological level also remains unsolved in Li's conception.

We can try to address the explanatory gap question by referring to the fact that subjectality is lived and therefore represents the dynamic paradigm of becoming. This shows that Li assumes the plasticity of mind, which gives rise to two interpretations of subjectality. According to the first one, subjectality is consistent with materialism in that the ontological basis of both substances is matter, which gives rise to the biological existence of humans. The mental qualities of humans also originate from matter, through the accumulation of practice. The origination of human mentality thus conceived remains consistent with the dialectical materialism law of the transformation of the quantitative changes into qualitative ones.[72] Concurrently, considering that the changes take place on the biological level, the sedimentation of human psychological faculties must have taken place at the neural level. For this reason, the plasticity of psychological substance should be viewed and further examined neuropsychologically.

According to the second interpretation, we have to depart from Li's definition of practice that is confined to tool manufacturing and use, and that assumes mental faculties to emerge through motor activities. This can be supported by Corballis's previously mentioned language emergence hypothesis, which tells us that speech developed from manual gestures. Considering also that sign languages are constructed in the same way as spoken, the development of language could have taken place in motor activities, where the articulated system of signs had already developed before it was transferred to the spoken medium. This also allows the possibility that thinking might have been sedimented even at the "motor stage" of language. Such a hypothesis is compliant with Li's belief that psychological qualities have their root in material practice.

As can be seen, although the explanatory gap problem can be addressed to some degree, based on the sole philosophy of the subjectality project, achieving a comprehensive answer is hardly possible. The solution to this fundamental problem of Li's philosophical construction may be solved by further developing his philosophical theory or reference to interdisciplinary research that includes evolutionary psychology.

Chapter 5

Situating Subjectality

Introduction

The philosophy of subjectivity draws a lesson from a profound and thorough study of Kant. The overturning of Kant displays an important feature of Li's general approach to philosophy in that philosophizing should not take place in a theoretical vacuum. This is, among other things, reflected with how differently Kant and Li conceptualize subjectivity. Kant assumes an a priori model, in which cognitive structures do not originate from the world or change as a result of interaction with it. Li does not accept such a theoretically constructed point of departure and builds his subjectality as necessarily and immediately connected to the world, not only by experiencing it but by the active involvement in material practice. This also entails determining the nature of cognition, which is unlikely to be performed by a computing, disembodied mind.

This necessary presence of subjectality in the world excludes the conceptualizations that clearly separate the subject and object. Li is highly skeptical about the Kantian cognitive model with the faculties of understanding and sensibility that process sensations and concurrently face the objective validation in knowledge production. Li is primarily concerned with the fact that Kant's subjectivity emerged from interaction with the world. The cognitive faculties were thoroughly molded by human activities and, equally important, they are of a historical nature. Therefore, Li's subjectality, which overcomes the shortcomings of Kant in this respect, is a conception in which the human cognitive apparatus cannot be viewed independently from human's environment that continuously molds it. Nor can the continuous adjustment of cognitive faculties through practice in objective reality be encapsulated by the subject equipped with the kind of computational cognitive structures that process experience and are responsible for producing a response to it. The interaction with the world is more direct, which invites the conceptualizations that consider the impact of environment on the psychological structures as well as extend the subjectality into the world so that it can be lived.

This chapter constitutes an attempt to address the issue of how particularly subjectality is involved in its interactions with the world. The discussion will locate this issue in the context of situated cognition. Although Li does not directly refer to this type of cognition paradigm, I assume it to be a natural direction that allows further exploration of the interaction between subjectality and the world. In my discussion, I will refer subjectality to the embodied, embedded, extended, and enacted—otherwise referred to as 4E—models of cognition. I will argue that autopoietic enactivism is the most likely framework in which subjectality can be optimally conceptualized. I will also show that, by supplementing with appraisal theory, autopoietic enactivism can comprehensively accommodate subjectality.

Situating Subjectality

Subjectality's involvement with the world can be viewed in terms of how it can be conceptualized in cognitive processes. The lived aspect of subjectality invites being viewed through the prism of situated cognition, where cognition is not only confined to the processes that take place in the brain but is influenced and coconstituted by external factors, which include the body as well as part of the environment that is relevant to it. Situated cognition varies in the degree and character of the cognitive involvement, which among others includes embodied, embedded, extended, and enacted varieties of cognition.

Embodied cognition does not delimit the subject's cognitive faculties to entirely mental activity located in the brain. Cognition is regarded as embodied when the cognitive agent's body, apart from the brain, plays an important part in cognitive processes. The proponents of embodied cognition hold that cognition would not be possible without embodiment. A popular example that tests this theory is a disembodied brain in the vat, which, as Daniel C. Dennett's version has it, is artificially stimulated by radio waves.[1] The brain, despite not being connected to the body, has exactly the same experiences. The depicted situation would suggest that brain embodiment plays no importance in cognition. However, this "experiment," as Shaun Gallagher and Dan Zahavi remark, is utterly theoretical, as humans are always embodied and their perceptions and actions rely on the embodiment. Even if one can entertain the possibility of a disembodied brain, it would still need some embodiment in the form of sensory information and life support in all biochemical and neural complexity that is particular of real embodiment.[2]

Embodiment plays an important role in human cognition, both in a phylogenetic and ontogenetic way. For instance, Edwin Straus's account of upright body posture enumerates some cognitive consequences that show the possibility of incorporating embodiment into Li's conception of subjectality. Bodies entail motor skills, which enable posture adjustment and other bodily movements. The manual operation repertoire, which is essential for manufacturing and using tools, is largely possible thanks to equilibrium maintenance on legs. As Straus remarks, this skillfulness in the long run has given rise to "abstract and rational capabilities of cognition," which include counting and more complex mathematical operations.[3] The very constitution of the human body, which can be included in the very fact of actual, biologically founded, human living, entails a specific repertoire of bodily operations, which include material practice. With regard to this, Li's subjectality cannot dismiss human embodiment on the level of material practice nor psychological substance because the practice is concurrently the basis for psychological substance.

Another example by Straus bears even more important implications for subjectality. Human upright posture determines how other humans and things are related to us as well as particular proprioception. This also determines the vision range and, in turn, the spatial framework for perception and action. Importantly, the standing position also prioritizes some senses with regard to others, for instance vision to olfaction. Embodiment shapes perceptual capacities, which naturally also have consequences for cognitive abilities.[4] This aspect of embodiment has a great explanatory potential concerning the character of sedimentation that takes place in cognitive structures. For instance, the mentioned spatial framework is indispensable for material practice and sediments into human visual processing. The prioritizing of vision over other senses is almost evident in psychological substance. It can be found in theoretical accounts of perception, which are also constructed for other senses in the visual paradigm. A large part of artistic production favors vision, causing touch, gustation, and olfaction to lag behind.

It should also be mentioned that, on the biological side, body is mortal. This fact, apart from determining temporally the life of individuals, organizes human practice of survival and life protection, which also sediments into the psychological substance as, for instance, eschatological thinking or longevity culture.

As can be seen, embodiment as part of human living is not only indispensable for material practice. The necessary condition for subjectality to be lived is conditioned by having a body, which is part of the material, biological underpinning from which other, psychological qualities emerge. It is not only the question of existence; the very character of how human body is constituted also bears important implications for psychological sedimentation.

Embodiment is very similar to another perspective of the subjectivity's involvement in cognition, embeddedness. Whereas embodied cognition is focused on the body, embedded cognition assumes a wider scope and also embraces the environment with which the body interacts. Rob Rupert formulates the embedded cognition hypothesis as follows:

> Cognitive processes depend *very* heavily, in hitherto unexpected ways, on organismically external props and devices and on the structure of the external environment in which cognition takes place.[5]

Accordingly, the cognitive process is no longer located in the embodied subjectivity but extends to the environment. Since Li's anthropological ontology assumes that subjectality lives the world and that the material practice leads to diverse internalization, it is likely that the character of individual cognitive processes is highly dependent on the environment. The link with, and influence of, the environment in cognitive processes performed by the embodied subjectality naturally follow from embodiment. For instance, some external changes, such as the amount of oxygen in inhaled air, cause internal changes in the subjectality. Embedded cognition can also be viewed in a historical perspective, where some environmental conditions persistent over time mold subjectality. This can take place on the adaptive level but also can lead to developing a different method for nonadaptive control of the environment, which alters cognitive processes.

Whereas embodied and embedded cognition locate cognitive system in the agent of cognition, extended cognition claims that "cognitive systems themselves extend beyond the boundary of the individual organism."[6] The nature of extended cognition is discussed in detail by Andy Clark and David Chalmers in "The Extended Mind." They follow David Kirsh and Paul Maglio in that some actions with environmental supports, such as using the rotation button for adjusting geometric shapes in the computer game Tetris, are "epistemic actions," which consist in altering the world in order to augment cognitive processes. They differ from pragmatic actions, which alter the world for its own sake.[7] Epistemic actions are believed by Clark and Chalmers to be part of the cognitive process. From this perspective, the subject in experience is no longer *the* place where cognition is located.[8] Accordingly, the human organism is linked to the environment, and, put together, they constitute a cognitive system. It ought to be noted that this cognitive model is different from embedded cognition, where the human organism remains an embodied subject to which cognitive processes are reserved.

Importantly, the external and relevant to human organism parts of the world are active and play a crucial role in cognition. They enjoy the same causal role as the internal features of the brain and any removal or change of them would alter actions of the human organism. This is referred to by Clark and Chalmers as external activism.[9]

One of the arguments supporting the extension of cognitive processes submitted by Clark and Chalmers is evolutionary. The brain has developed in the way that it uses the environment. One such evolutionary change is favoring in the brain the capacities that, for instance, help reduce memory load. The development of language can also be seen as a tool for exporting cognitive processes from the brain, for instance, to thinking in writing.[10] Such brain development can be accommodated by Li's sedimentation, since subjectality is inseparable from practice and the psychological substance is at least in some cases also molded in the fashion that favors the capabilities of optimal cognitive functioning in the environment through tool operation. In fact, it would seem very unlikely on the ground of Li's theory that sedimentation aims at the total emancipation and disconnection of cognitive structure from tool practice. First, this would lead to the disconnection of cognitive structures from being molded and eventually lead to their fossilization, which would be in contradiction with historical materialism. Second, in a historical perspective the unchanging cognitive structures would not comply with the transformation of reality through practice, which would not be able to sediment new structures whose cognitive validity rests on the objective world.

It should be borne in mind that the cognitive interwiring between the human organism and relevant elements of the environment—which evokes, for instance, thought in us—does not consist in the former acting upon the latter. In fact, the external operations also have cognitive status. If this view is applied to Li's anthropological ontology, subjectality is paired with the part of the world relevant to the material production in which someone is involved. The cognitive process is not exclusively based on the sedimented cognitive structures. The other part of cognition sits in the world involved in material practice. In light of the exterior activism postulated by Clark and Chalmers, the practice of making and using tools could be viewed as an indispensable cognitive composite in actual (nonhistorical) time. Thus, apart from the historical sedimentation effect, tool practice itself would constitute cognitive activity or part of it in two senses. First, it is a cognitive activity as perfecting skills of tool use, or devising completely new techniques or tools. Practice of this kind cannot be reduced to acting upon reality as it is not only done for the sake of the environment but contributes to using part of the world for the sake of the human organism. Second, in Li's theory, tool practice is interconnected with the mind by sedimentation, and considering this link (whose nature still remains to be explained in Li's theory) material operations are in continuity with the mental operations of subjectality.

What is particularly interesting in Li's conception is that the subjectality's cognitive structures are sedimented, which makes the cognitive system reliant upon the subject and environment even more interdependent and dynamic. The extended model of cognition that rests on subjectality and practice is characterized by modifications that act in two directions—the obvious sedimentation of the psychological substance through practice but also subjectality's modification of tool manufacturing and operation. This mutual modification can be illustrated by new technologies, for instance, widely understood Internet usage, which necessitates new operations within practice and entails a different emphasis on some brain capacities. This is turn results in a new configuration the cognitive system composed of both practice and cognitive structures in subjectality.

Enactivism

Finally, the philosophy of subjectality can also be viewed through the prism of enactivism, which involves the brain, the extracranial body, as well as environment. Francisco J. Varela, Evan Thompson, and Eleanor Rosch conceptualize enactivist cognition in terms of embodied action. Embodiment underscores two characteristics of cognition: that cognition depends on embodied experiences, which the authors mainly ascribe to the sensorimotor capacities, and that these capacities are embedded in biological, psychological, and cultural contexts. As for action, it is understood as the sensorimotor capacity of perception and action. The authors believe that these capacities evolved in an amalgamated form, instead of independently from each other.[11]

Varela, Thompson, and Rosch contrastively define the enactive approach in the following way:

> We propose as a name the term *enactive* to emphasize the growing conviction that cognition is not the representation of a pregiven world by a pregiven mind but is rather the enactment of a world and a mind on the basis of a history of the variety of actions that a being in the world performs.[12]

The enactive approach is first and foremost constructed in opposition to representationism and is action-focused. The embodiment and embeddedness of a cognitive agent is essential for her/him to enter interaction with environment without which cognition would not be possible. Importantly, enactivism does not involve the interaction within the model of subject cognizing object but claims that cognition is enactment in which both of them partake. Enactivism primarily differs from other situated cognition approaches in that it does not only show that it takes more than the brain for a cognitive process to occur but emphasizes, as the above definition says, that cognition is the interaction of all elements involved in cognitive process.

In my discussion of enactivism, I follow the approach by Varela, Thompson, and Rosch, who propose autopoietic enactivism. I will further argue that this variety of enactivism is the most compatible situation of subjectality. It ought to be mentioned here that enactivism is not a monolithic theory, and there are differing views on it, for instance with regard to autopoiesis.[13] This divergence especially applies to more recent conceptions of enactivism, which mainly focus on perceptual experience, consistent with the general enactivist assumption that does not involve inner, conscious, and reflective representations of the exterior environment.

Enactivism operates with a different type of representation, which is connected with bodily activity that transcends the simple reflexes of a living organism, and at the same time does not assume the form of conscious and reflective thought. Enactive representations involve bodily activities and, unlike conceptual ones, cannot be detached from enactments.[14] For instance, one can have a conceptual representation of a boxing bout without being engaged in it, whereas an enactive representation occurs only during this activity.

As regards autopoiesis, it is defined by Evan Thompson in the following way:

> Autopoiesis refers to an *organizational* property: An autopoietic system is one that is organized as a self-producing network of processes that also constitute the system as a topological unity.[15]

Thompson regards autopoiesis as necessary but not sufficient for the self-producing and self-maintaining of a living being. It lacks interaction with the environment. How organisms self-maintain themselves in the environment is achieved by adaptivity. Thompson resorts to Ezequiel Di Paolo's definition of adaptivity:[16]

> Adaptivity is being able to monitor and regulate the autopoietic process in relation to conditions registered as improving or deteriorating, viable or unviable.[17]

Thus, the living being reveals the plasticity of its internal processes to the environment. As these processes are meant to adjust to the environment, which is concurrently done for self-maintenance, the living being is intentional. The adaptive processes in autopoiesis are incessantly dynamic in the sense that the living organism constantly reorganizes itself (self-produces the inside) and concurrently specifies the outside. These two processes are not symmetrical in that the internal self-production regulates interaction with the environment.[18]

It is also important to be aware that in enactivism, life is not conceived in an abstract way, but as a concrete process in which living beings adaptively self-maintain themselves. Thompson understands life thus conceived as sense-making in precarious conditions. Precarious conditions are defined as ones in which autopoietic constituent processes cannot sustain themselves in the absence of the networks or physical conditions that enable them. Living as a process of sense-making cannot be conceived of without precarious conditions.[19] This aspect of life shows that living beings have to be confronted with situations that necessitate their adaptive behavior.

As for sense-making, the world of the living being is the sense that it makes of the environment. The world's sense consists in significance and valence, which result from the living being's actions. Importantly and consistently with enactivist assumptions, the significance and valence are not present in the world and wait to be cognized but they are constituted or enacted by a living being. Considering this, sense-making is cognition.[20] This shows that in enactivism cognition as a sense-making activity is integrated with sustaining adaptation. Sense-making characterizes the way in which living beings adapt themselves to the environment.

In light of the fundamental assumptions of autopoietic enactivism, as defined by Varela, Thompson, and Rosch, subjectality initially meets the enactive requirement in that it is viewed as becoming rather than as a complete entity. When interpreted from adaptive autopoiesis, subjectality interacts in such a way that it needs the environment for self-maintenance, which matters for the development of psychological structures, among other things. The type of interaction by means of tool practice is conditioned by the subjectality that transforms nature according to one's own purposiveness.

Varela, Thompson, and Rosch also view the constitution of cognitive structures in a similar way to Li. This is revealed in their description of perception:

> (1) Perception consists in perceptually guided action and (2) cognitive structures emerge from the recurrent sensorimotor patterns that enable action to be perceptually guided.[21]

As regards the first point, the authors develop the earlier cited contrastive definition that there is no pregiven cognitive framework. Perception is always a concrete action and changes during the perceiver's action. Therefore, what guides perception is the sensorimotor system. The emphasis in enactivism is not put on determining a perceiver-independent world but the sensorimotor characteristic of the embodied perceiver. The main concern of enactivism is, as the authors convey it, "to determine the common principles or lawful linkages between sensory and motor systems that explain how action can be perceptually guided in a perceiver-dependent world."[22] Enactivism does not follow the realist concern but instead it is focused on how to interact with the world in a sensorimotor fashion. It is important to notice that the world is determined as dependent on the perceiver, which excludes the interaction conceptualized as an exchange between the subject and the objective world. The world is enacted in perception and its meaning depends, among other things, on the enacting subject.

The conception of subjectality can comply with this claim by virtue of the fact that it cannot be viewed apart from interaction with the environment.

Li's subjectality is not a sedimented, passive receiver of sensations, but more part of an embodied perception process. Subjectality naturally entails that actions such as human involvement in the world constitute perceptions. It should also be mentioned that the world is continuously transformed by human practice, and hence subjectality does not aim at cognizing an objective world independent from her/him. Subjectality's concern is not a passive cognition of reality, but similarly to enactivism, cognition through harmonizing with the world by means of unconstrained practice. Hence, the world is not treated as a separate and indifferent sense, but endowed with subjectality-dependent sense.

As regards the second point, it is even more convergent with subjectality, especially as it relates to sedimentation. The pattern of recursive actions resembles how the cognitive aspect of the human mind is molded. Varela, Thompson, and Rosch, similarly to Li, refer to Piaget's genetic epistemology to illustrate this point (however, Piaget presupposes the "traditional" representationist model, with a pregiven, subject-independent world).[23] It should be noted that Varela, Thompson, and Rosch's reference to Piaget is more relevant than in the case of Li, as they view the emergence of cognitive structures in an ontogenetic sense. However, despite that sedimentation should be viewed in phylogenetic terms, it does not exclude the possibility that, historically speaking, the cognitive structures are internalized in the same way, through recurrent actions of material practice.

Implications for Subjectality and Appraisal Theory

Li does not stray too far beyond theoretical description to determine the particular character of subjectality's interaction with the environment. Hence, his theory should be interpreted particularly within a situated paradigm and approached in an interdisciplinary manner. It has to be noticed that the possible, empirically founded extension of subjectality is mentioned and advocated by Li as an examination of his theoretical construction.[24]

The compatibility of Li's conception of subjectality with the situated cognition paradigm bears important implications. First, considering that subjectality underpins Li's aesthetics, the fact that aesthetic experience is situated opens the possibility of viewing it as an embodied action within a nonrepresentationist paradigm. Also, the fact that other than aesthetic experiences can also be conceptualized in the same way prompts the question as to whether there is a significant qualitative difference between aesthetic and nonaesthetic experiences within this paradigm, and, if so, what it can particularly be attributed to.

Second, the embodiment and embeddedness of subjectality facilitates a proper examination of emotion, which is an important part of the psychological substance. The role of emotion matters in two contexts. The first is the psychological substance, which includes emotional substance. On this level, it is important to examine the role of emotion in cognition. This is not only important for the sake of complementing subjectality with a compatible conceptualization of the cognitive character of emotion. The characteristic of emotion is of great importance for the aesthetic context, where emotion is significantly involved in aesthetic experience.

The role of emotion, as well as its cognitive function, can be viewed in a wider framework of affectivity. The study of affectivity—affective science, focuses on broadly concerned affection, which includes emotions, feelings, moods, and mood disorders.[25] This study presents a multidisciplinary approach focused on affectivity in both human and nonhuman animals.

Affective science is largely preoccupied with investigating emotions in humans. The broader perspective of affectivity also reveals the role it plays in cognition. Giovanna Colombetti states that, by contingence and necessity, the embodied mind cannot be deprived of affective character. Affection is here conceived of in a less confining way, as sensitivity or interest in one's own existence. Nor does it have to be manifested as a particular mood or emotion but rather as being affected by something as meaningful or salient,[26] which seems to be a feature that comes naturally with situated cognition.

It is important to notice that affectivity, due to being broadly construed, apart from including emotions, also, and more importantly, makes them possible. It is a feature of living organisms that recognize their relation to the environment in an enacted way. Considering that this primitive form of affectivity (referred to by Colombetti as "primordial")[27] was the basis for constituting emotions in more complex organisms, we can map it onto subjectality, where humans are equipped with emotions that are historically developed and calibrated through sedimentation. It can be assumed that these emotions were originally the primordial affectivity, whose phylogenesis had taken place earlier, in less complex organisms, without fully evolved nervous systems and consciousness. Li claims that, similarly to other aspects of the psychological substance, human emotions have been molded from animalistic ones, which were of an instinctual character. It is reasonable to assume that these emotions were still very primitive in the sense of being unconscious, not to mention sublimated into some cultural format. Hence, the primordial affectivity was immediately connected with humans as living organisms in the environment, and was manifested as enactments.

Affectivity is importantly connected with the meaningfulness of the environment for all levels of living beings. Colombetti interprets it in an enactivist framework, with regard to sense-making, which takes place functionally, as an adaptive (re)organization of the living being.[28] If we considered living beings in mereological terms, their identity would be a composition, whose rules determine composition as a living being.[29] This particular composition is tantamount to the ontological foundation of the living being's autonomous identity with regard to the environment. Importantly, it also determines what sense-making involves for a particular living being. It can be said that the environment and the living being are ontically interdependent, and sense-making determines the character of interdependence for a particular living being.

Considering the characteristic of living beings, Colombetti follows Thompson's understanding of cognition as "behavior or conduct in relation to meaning and norms that the system itself enacts or brings forth on the basis of its autonomy."[30] She shows that cognition thus conceived is concurrently affective, which she characterizes in three interconnected points. First, the sense-making living being is intrinsically purposeful in that it aims at self-maintaining. This entails the affective interest in the environment. Second, for the purpose of self-maintaining, the living being is adaptive and affectively evaluates what contributes to the purpose in the environment. Finally, the environment is meaningfully enacted by the living being with regard to what the being is concerned with.[31] The cognitive character of primordial affectivity shows the basis for understanding the affective cognition for both simple and complex living organisms, the latter of which can be equipped with mind and complex emotions.

This enactivist characterization of sense-making in affectivity terms provides an important insight into subjectality, which, as has been shown, is situated in multiple ways. The primordial affectivity offers a paradigm for understanding the historical calibration of emotion in the psychological construction. Subjectality never remains indifferent to the world by being involved in material practice. It conveys a particular interest in the environment, which is manifested by the enactment of a meaningful world by the purposive transformation of nature. The sense-making enactment can be viewed as determined and motivated by complex adaptation (which should not be mistaken for conforming to nature), which constitutes the intrinsic self-maintaining purpose of subjectality. This self-maintaining of subjectality's autonomy is possible only thanks to remaining in a dynamic and harmonious relation with nature. In this way, the practice is twofold: it is motivated by autonomy self-maintenance and is an enactment consisting in transforming the world in a meaningful way.

Importantly, the sense-making involvement in the world engages the entire subjectality, which is due to its embodiment. It is manifested by dynamic self-maintenance, which includes different layers of sedimentation, ranging from neural to cultural. Considering that these sedimentation levels are interconnected by virtue of their originating from the same source—material practice (historically) and one organism constitution (actually), for instance, on a neuropsychological level (organismic interconnection)—the enactment is not reducible to some specific part of subjectality conceived as a living being. This can be seen as a reorganization of the living being, the literal organismic sense-making that, from a historical perspective, has led to the emergence of consciousness and complex cognitive emotions.

The enactive conceptualization of the sense making subjectality allows the cognitive aspect of emotion to be analyzed, which plays an important role in Li's conception of aesthetics. In affective science, the cognitive dimension of emotion is especially studied in affective appraisals. According to Klaus R. Scherer, appraisal theory holds that humans

> evaluate events in terms of the perceived relevance for their current needs or goals, including considerations of their ability to cope with the consequences and the compatibility of the underlying actions with social norms and self-ideals.[32]

Appraisals are situated, as they clearly result from the particular context in which the appraising agent finds herself/himself. They are also cognitively oriented; they are not simply impressions but also the recognition of the actual event. Finally, appraisals are practically oriented in the sense that they relate the event to both the short-term and long-term needs of the appraising agent. Given this, appraisal theory complies with the assumptions of the enactive approach in situated cognition, as it does not confine itself to merely considering the environment in cognition but essentially includes the enactment of the world, which is manifested by affectivity.

In affective science, emotions are essentially embodied, as they consist of perception patterns and have neurocorrelates. They are also fundamentally adaptive. When living beings interact with the environment, they do not collect information about it for its own sake but in order to simultaneously and particularly enact the world in an adaptive way. Emotion is one such interaction that occurs in complex living organisms. In comparison with simpler living beings, which usually respond to the environment in a fixed form of behavior, emotions motivate behavior but disconnect automatic behavioral reaction in the agent. Emotion provides the organism with an option of modifying the interpretation of the event and the response to it. It can be seen that in interaction with environment, emotions are not a kind of transparent link with behavior, which is the case in simple, enacted cognition. The involvement of emotion in interpreting perception results in a more complex action, which offers a reconsideration of perception and alternative behavioral reactions. This fact is regarded by Phoebe C. Ellsworth and Klaus R. Scherer as an important phylogenetic enrichment.[33] This evolutionary improvement of reactions also remains consistent with subjectality, whose emotional substance can be seen as resulting from a long process of sedimentation, which has led from determined, "emotionless" reflexes to a more complex enactment, as well as to further refinement of emotion thus achieved in aesthetic experience.

In terms of composition, the appraisal process is a link between the organism and the situation that produces emotion. Appraisals are usually viewed in processes during particular emotional episodes. An emotional episode consists of separate appraisals, which can occur subsequently, simultaneously, or in a configuration of both. Generally, appraisals are regarded as unconscious. One should bear in mind that the environment is not necessarily external, physical, or social, but appraisals can constitute emotion as a response to a mental event. If an emotional episode is viewed sequentially, it is reflected as changes at the level of emotional experience. The general framework of the emotional episode describes the first appraisal, referred to as "novelty," as arising from contact with the environment as a reaction to environmental change, which can be manifested by, for instance, attending to the change. The first appraisal is quite often followed by a very short-lived feeling of intrinsic pleasantness or unpleasantness. This appraisal, especially when the valence is negative, can be followed by other appraisals, which cause state changes and further alter emotion in the episode.[34] Such conceptualization shows the processual character of emotion, which underscores its embodied and embedded character.

The processual character of affective appraisals in emotional episodes leads to two implications concerning the structure and origin of emotions. Regarding the structure, it shows that emotions change dynamically according to the appraisals that constitute them,[35] by which one might assess them as highly adaptive to environmental changes. Accordingly, the emotional equipment enables a better adaptation than in the case of living organisms that operate with automatic behavioral reactions only. By the same token, the emotional equipment provides more fine-grained cognitive capabilities. Although appraisals are regarded as unconscious, their separate cognitive enactments are not completely nullified at the level of emotion, which differs over an emotional episode. In other words, the dynamic architecture of emotion is constructed by the episodes. The other implication from the anatomy of emotion leads to the question whether affective appraisals can explain the origin of emotion. The recursiveness and sequencing or other combining of the appraisals may have led to the emergence of some simple emotional episode formats, which in turn became more complex. This question remains under discussion.[36]

It is particularly important to focus on one of the composite appraisals—intrinsic pleasantness. It follows the first appraisal (novelty) and it consists of a short-lived, often unnoticed, intrinsic pleasantness or unpleasantness, which is a response to the environment that encourages or discourages further enactive engagement with environment. There is no unanimity as to what stimuli are evaluated in terms of pleasantness. There are theories that ascribe pleasure to the stimuli intensity and complexity, whereas other theories claim that intrinsic pleasantness or unpleasantness is evaluated by innate detection mechanisms. As regards the latter theoretical standpoints, they support their claim with empirical evidence, such as innate taste preference for sweet, and an aversion to bitter, tastes. Another example, concerning vision, shows preference for certain facial features and expressions. The intrinsic pleasantness also applies to responses that are not attributed to the sensorimotor levels. Appraisals of this kind are evaluated by preferences, which are ascribed to higher processing levels—schematic and conceptual. Hence, preference acquisition can take place through conditioning but also conceptually, through judgments. This results in some of the preferences being relative to culture. Importantly, pleasantness appraisal also applies to aesthetic emotions. Although pleasantness is varied in character, it is believed that the corresponding appraisal involves the same neurological system.[37] Attributing the pleasantness appraisal to aesthetic emotions bears important implications for both Li's subjectality and aesthetics. Considering that aesthetic emotion is constituted within the same model as other emotional responses, it implies that sedimentation has led to their refinement. In his discussion of aesthetic sedimentation, Li uses the examples of hunger and sex, which become refined into gourmet culture and love respectively.[38] Li's explanation remains mainly on the theoretical sedimentation level. This transition could be attributed to phylogenetic appraisals that, historically, have been refined from instinctive to aesthetic. The particular character of aesthetic preference is flexible and depends on particular acquisitions in different times and cultures, which remains consistent with Li's claim that aesthetics reflects stages of human practice.

Another important implication for Li's philosophy is that if aesthetic emotion is constructed in the same way as other emotions, the aesthetic should not be viewed as discrete from other aspects of human activity. This allows the aesthetic to be liberated from confinement to the realm of art, and, on the level of theories, from philosophy of art.

Aesthetic emotion can be also viewed in terms of a sequence of constitutive appraisals. Therefore, and significantly, one may consider the pleasantness appraisal evaluation on different processing levels, thus opening a wide spectrum for constructing aesthetic emotional episodes. This importantly determines the character of aesthetic experience and links it with contemporary naturalized aesthetic research.

Conclusion

Of all the above-mentioned situated cognition approaches, assuming autopoietic enactivism in conceptualizing Li's anthropological ontology seems to be optimal by virtue of the fact that it most comprehensively embraces all aspects of subjectality. Autopoietic enactivism offers an insight into the philosophy of subjectivity that remains consistent throughout the whole of Li's theoretical framework. It considers the crucial fact that subjectality is part of the natural and social world, and the character of this active involvement and belonging is decisive in how other aspects of Li's philosophy should be understood. Therefore, the lived engagement of subjectality should be considered at different levels of situation that are integrated within one approach.

Considering the compatibility of the situated and interactive subjectality, enactivism allows Li's theoretical construction to be extended with contemporary philosophical and interdisciplinary 4E approaches. Thereby, a door opens on how the processes of practice, sedimentation of psychological substance, and experiencing of the aesthetic can be further explained. Importantly, it offers the possibility of redefining experience from receptive and representational to a more direct, interactive model. This is especially important in the case of aesthetic experience, which evades not only passive but also typical cognitive accounts of experience.

Chapter 6

Beauty

Introduction

Before examining aesthetic experience, it is important to analyze how Li conceptualizes beauty. Considering the character of the philosophy of subjectality, it might be somewhat surprising that Li situates beauty in the center of his aesthetics. The historical and multiple becoming of humans, which includes the humanization of the sense organs as well as the psychological constitution of subjectality, would suggest a processual approach and focus on aesthetic experience rather than beauty, which has strong axiological connotations. This initial impression is misleading, however. It ought to be considered that Li implants in his philosophical framework some terms that have counterintuitive connotations. This is the case of subjectality, which in comparison to subjectivity-centered theories, including Kant's philosophy, so highly regarded by Li, is characterized by a strong reformulation. Li approaches beauty in a similar way, by constructing it within the framework of his anthropological ontology rather than adopting it from some already existing theory. Hence, since Li's philosophy is mainly concerned with the human becoming, his beauty-centered aesthetic remains consistent with the overall philosophical project.

In this chapter, after a brief etymological and theoretical introduction, I discuss how beauty remains consistent with anthropological ontology. Next, I present how beauty in Li's system is interpreted as objective, despite emerging in subjectality's interaction with the world. This interpretation will also be presented in enactivist terms. I will also demonstrate why beauty is tantamount to freedom as well how it persists through time.

Anthropological Roots of Beauty

In his attempt to define beauty, Li departs from the Chinese character 美 (*mei*), used to denote beauty or as an adjective "beautiful" in Chinese philosophy and philosophy-related writings since ancient times.

Li assumes an anthropological approach in interpreting the etymology of the character for *mei*. He refers to the earliest Chinese lexicographical source, *Explaining Graphs and Analyzing Characters* (*Shuowen Jiezi* 說文解字) from Eastern Han, compiled by Xu Shen (許慎; ca. 58–148 CE), a famous scholar of the time. The etymological explanation[1] departs from subdividing the character into the two composite parts: 羊 (*yang*) from top and 大 (*da*) from the bottom. These parts also function as independent characters. The character for *yang* means "goat" or "ram," whereas that for *da* means "big." Xu combines the semantics of the two composite parts to reach the explication "When a ram is large, it is beautiful." He further comments that "of the Six Domestic Animals, the ram is chiefly raised for food."[2] Xu most likely associated beauty with delicious taste, which points to pleasure felt through the senses. The dictionary also includes an analysis and definition of the character 善 (*shan*), which means "good." The definition of this character says that "beauty is synonymous with good." This, according to Li, connects the character meaning with earlier occurrences of the character for *mei* on the late Shang dynasty oracle bones and Zhou dynasty ritual bronze vessels. Li interprets their meaning by referring to the two composite elements *da* and *yang*. Accordingly, the first one originally depicted someone "standing facing forward," which suggests a kind of priest performing a totemic dance or shamanistic ritual. Li interprets the whole character as depicting a large man who is wearing a ram-like headdress, additionally decorated with ram motifs. The animal element in the character most possibly suggests the shamanistic totem.[3] This interpretation suggests that beauty is associated with social practices, and that initially it was not important for its own sake but rather embedded in rites expressing community identity and beliefs. In this sense, beauty was present in a society where rite participation was evaluated from a moral perspective. This idea of synonymy of beauty and good is better presented later, in Confucianism, where morally proper actions are also beautiful with regard to how they are performed in social interaction.

Li advances his anthropological interpretation by showing the role of shamanistic songs and dances back in primitive culture, which he regards to be the earliest form of culture in human history. The shamanistic collective activities were meant to consolidate the community and regulate relations on multiple levels between the community members. On the one hand, shamanistic activity, through endowing the community with, for instance, a moral or religious sense, contributed to its rational character. On the other, the ritual songs and dances engaged humans physically and psychologically, which gradually led to the expression of human sensuous nature in a symbolic medium.[4] It can be seen that Li views the social and cultural development of humans since primitive times as the humanization of nature, and regards totemic and shamanistic activities as the earliest layer of human practice. Beauty originated from these practices and has become more distinct through the progressing humanization.

The above anthropological glimpse of beauty implies its rapport with human life. First, considering the social practice paradigm, beauty is a product of human life. Importantly, it does not start with intellectual life but emerges earlier, in primitive communal activities. This origin can be supported by Li's remark on aesthetic sedimentation, which differs from the internalization of rationality in that it mainly concerns human senses and psychological structures, especially emotions. What is characteristic about sensuous pleasure is that it is directly given (instead of, for instance, being reflected upon) and transcends the utilitarian need (for instance, to satisfy hunger).[5] Second, the embeddedness of beauty in social practice and sensuousness suggests that, despite sedimentation, beauty still depends on human life. Hence, beauty as part of the historical life dynamic indicates the progress of humanity. This supervening on social practice also involves beauty's being twofold—it is aesthetic in bringing non-instinct-driven pleasure but also ethical in that it reflects some desired or proper order of the practice.

Beauty—Situating in Theory

Apart from situating beauty in anthropological and historical context, which complies with the historical materialist framework, Li also determines his understanding of beauty in terms of what theoretical approach it represents.

Li positions his notion of beauty with regard to aesthetic objectivism and subjectivism. He believes that the objective status of beauty in an object depends on its aesthetic qualities, although they must be complemented with a proper attitude on the part of the subject, without whom aesthetic feeling cannot be produced. Aesthetic objectivism claims that either the beauty of an object is attributed to some formal features (contemplative materialism) or that objects reflect or stem from some idea of beauty (objective idealism).[6] For instance, in Plato's realism, beauty is objective in the sense of being ontically founded in the realm of forms. From Diotima's speech in *Symposium*, we learn that beauty in itself is unchanging, everlasting, and beyond physical extension rules.[7] Hence, the beauty of objects, thanks to participation[8] in the form of beauty, is independent from "the eye of the beholder." The independence of beauty covers two meanings here. The first one is connected with the subject's cognition. Despite the subject's judgment of beauty being true or false, there is no influence on the beauty of an object. The second one allows formation of an even more radical statement that beauty is independent from the existence of the subject. Regardless of how strong a realist interpretation one assumes, it can be seen that beauty is independent from experience.

As regards the subjectivist approach to beauty, Li defines it as one in which the beauty of particular objects must depend on human subjective consciousness, which engages various faculties to constitute beauty. Therefore, the subjectivist approach is oriented at aesthetic experience and involves psychological processes of the subject. As regards the objects in subjectivist theories, according to Li, they are "carriers that convey, reveal, and embody subjective emotions and states of mind."[9] Thus, beauty is projected upon the object by the subject.

With regard to the above two approaches, Li admits that some subjective conditions, such as aesthetic attitude, experiential history, and background knowledge are required for experiencing beauty. However, he should not be too hastily qualified as an aesthetic subjectivist, since he concurrently ascribes aesthetic qualities to the object. Li's theory does not fit the strict subjectivist or objectivist qualification, although, as will be seen, Li finally falls into the objectivist category on his own terms. In his aesthetic theoretical founding, Li is more concerned with how some qualities in objects become aesthetic qualities.[10] This question can be viewed in a twofold way. From the subject's perspective, we can ask what psychological processes undertake the transformation of the objective into aesthetic. On the other end, we can formulate an equally important question concerning the object, namely, why some objective qualities, in contrast to others, are or can be aesthetic.

As regards the psychological processes, Li believes that aesthetic experience and the pleasure of beauty that accompanies it can be explained in terms of the isomorphic structures theory from gestalt psychology. As regards perception, gestalt psychology especially opposes psychological atomism and claims that perceptions should be studied holistically rather than analytically. In other words, perception as a whole is more important than its component sensory elements in that the whole determines the element properties. When we perceive objects, they appear as a whole, and only then can we distinguish between particular constituent sensory elements. This is explained by the fact that, in gestalt, constituting the object of perception does not consist in associating elements in space and time but identifying a figure—a more important element in a perception field, against the less significant background.[11] Li is particularly concerned with structural isomorphism in that the brain produces such holistic representations that are identical with the objects of perception. Disregarding the fact that the theory has not been empirically proven and is regarded as highly unlikely,[12] it would entail the structural identity of the psychological and physical objects, achieved by the interaction between external object and human physiological and psychological structures. This process is believed by Li to lead to the attainment of harmony, which produces aesthetic pleasure. The foundation of pleasure is the interaction of various corresponding structures such as, for instance, symmetry or rhythm.[13] This also shows the cognitive dimension of Li's aesthetics as pleasure occurs when the object and its representation are matched. The anatomy of pleasure that is discernible here reverberates the match of theoretical and natural laws in Kant's philosophy, described in the third *Critique*.[14]

Although the isomorphic structures theory is unlikely in light of neuropsychological processing, its overall idea of synchronizing the psychological state and the world reflects Li's aesthetic thinking. It seems to be influenced by the aforementioned fragment of Kant's third *Critique*. Li appears to have adopted the idea that cognitive accomplishment, which also takes place in aesthetic experience, is "gratified" by the feeling of pleasure. It would even tie in further with Kant's belief that, by way of habituation, in ordinary experiences the pleasure is no longer conscious. Aesthetic experiences are conscious and their character is different from other everyday experiences, which would confirm the Kant's "pleasant cognitive match." Regardless of how far the Kantian analogy goes, the gestalt model adapted by Li already situates aesthetics in the cognitive context.

Li's referring to the gestalt psychology approach is weak in an important aspect, which is the relation of the subject to the world. The approach seems to presuppose a clear subject-object cognitive model. The overall idea of the synchronicity between the subject and the world seems to better lend itself to being accommodated by the enactive approach. Enactivism importantly emphasizes the self-maintaining of the subject through sense-making enactment, which does not have to include representations. This type of adjustment complies more with Li's anthropological ontology, where the practical involvement molds the human mind. Hence, the adjustment between the subjectality and the world would be less a Kantian or gestalt "mirroring match" but more a sense-making enactment with the intrinsic pleasure appraisal.

The very idea of representations as viewed in isomorphic structures theory also seems not to be entirely compatible with perceptual processing. In fact, we can think about the aesthetic feeling of pleasure that does not carry any representation. Such a case would not be particularly suitable to be subsumed under an isomorphic structures paradigm. It seems to be more consistent with enactivism, where the direct involvement of the embodied subject involves pleasure. The enactive mechanism is even more direct as it does not involve the path from an object structure to representation, which produces pleasure upon matching. In enactivism, pleasure is part of the subject's enactment.

Despite the above-mentioned representation problem, the theory shows an important characteristic of Li's aesthetics thinking. Although not subjective, it is not constructed as a typical ontology of object-based beauty. This moves us to the other question about object qualities. It can be explained by distinguishing among aesthetic and nonaesthetic properties. The former ones are, for instance, beauty and ugliness, and they belong to objects. The latter ones, are the physical, sensory, or art-historical properties of the objects. Between these two groups of properties, there is a relation of aesthetic supervenience, where aesthetic properties supervene on the nonaesthetic properties of an object.[15] Li confesses that an aesthetic object has to possess the nonaesthetic properties, but they do not suffice for the object itself to transform them into aesthetic ones.[16] In this way, it can be seen that we cannot talk about aesthetic objectivism in a Platonic sense, where the object would already be aesthetic by virtue of reflecting some aesthetic form. Li believes that aesthetic properties come into being through aesthetic experience, which involves psychological and physiological processes. However, this type of experience does not qualify for aesthetic subjectivism, as the subject is not able to constitute the aesthetic object without the objective nonaesthetic properties that make it possible. Beauty emerges in human interaction with the world, in aesthetic experiences. Thus, on the ground of Li's philosophy, aesthetics is not regarded as an ontological analysis of properties or of "aesthetic operations of mind" but a study of human active involvement in the world, particularly realized as practice.

Objectivism through Practice

Li proposes a categorization of beauty, where he locates his own theory. He departs from outlining the semantic field covered by "beauty" in aesthetics, where three main meanings can be distinguished. The first one refers to the beauty of objects. It attempts to determine what objects are beautiful. The second approach is directed on ascertaining what properties make an object beautiful. Finally, the third meaning is more general and tries to determine the essence of beauty as well as its origin.[17] Li is particularly concerned with the third approach, which he regards as allowing the investigation of the fundamental facts about beauty. Quite expectedly, Li is inclined toward this particular approach, as it dovetails with his historical materialist perspective. Thus, the question of beauty is situated in practice, characterized as the humanization of nature. Li states that practice consists in endowing the "characteristics and forms of objective things with aesthetic qualities, which then become aesthetic objects."[18] It can be seen that Li believes that the answer to the fundamental question about beauty also embraces the remaining two meanings. This description also shows that, for the aesthetic properties to originate, the nonaesthetic objective properties that enable it are not the sufficient condition; it is practice that makes possible the transformation from the nonaesthetic to the aesthetic.

The indispensable participation of practice in the origin of beauty allows Li to determine the character of his aesthetics as objectivist. To explicate this, he takes a philological departure from the Chinese *zhu* (主) and *ke* (客), which stand for subjectivism and objectivism respectively.[19] Li points to the fact that *zhu* usually has a subjectivist denotation connected with mental actions and processes. However, if the subject's activity is understood differently, as practice, which is material and objective, its unity with the objective world, although composed of *zhu* and *ke*, should not be encapsulated within a subjectivist but rather objective theoretical framework.[20] The fact that the subject's practice takes place in objective reality, historically conceived as the practice of humankind, leads Li to the claim that his philosophy of beauty is of an objectivist character.

Beauty emerges in, as Li writes, "the interplay of subjective practice and objective reality, not of subjective consciousness and objective nature."[21] First, it confirms that Li's beauty is not subjectivist. Second, the character of involvement of the subject is active not in the sense of, say, active perceptual processing, but material practice. The emergence of beauty complies with the enactivist approach, where the living being (here the subject) is part of the objective reality in which it is involved in sense-making.

Li explains how his aesthetic objectivism should be particularly understood. It consists in the unity of subject and object, which should not be interpreted in Zhu Guangqian's subjectivist spirit, as previously mentioned in the Marxism chapter. Quite the opposite, the unity is "a material existence of sensuous reality, which is social and objective, independent of a person's subjective consciousness and individual state of mind." The social character consists in practice being essential in making the life of humans in nature meaningful to them.[22] Thus, practice is not only an involvement of humans in the world that observes the laws of nature, but constitutes sense-making, which includes beauty among others. The objective character of the subject-object unity is characterized by the idea that a purely subjective practice that does not conform to the laws of nature would be confined in subjectivism, bereft of material and sensuous existence, which are indispensable for beauty. Li endows the subject's practice with a Marxist dimension, according to which humans are involved in production in accordance with the laws of nature, and, consequently, their own species.[23] For this reason, as Marx claims in the *Manuscripts*, humans produce in accordance with the laws of beauty.[24] Hence, beauty is achieved through objective practice, that is, the humanization of nature. It emerges in this objective process in the form of a transformed world.

Li also makes a remark concerning objective beauty with regard to beauty in objects. Beauty's origin is explained by the humanization of nature, and some natural laws of form have analogously become aesthetic. Thus, some natural properties of objects, such as movement or development, as well as their forms, for instance, symmetry or rhythm, have become aesthetic. Importantly, these properties are not independently aesthetic, nor do they become aesthetic through being perceived. Their beauty comes from the isomorphic correspondence, assumed by Li, between the properties of objects and human practice.[25] They are nonaesthetic properties that can become aesthetic in active experience. Thus, they cannot be treated as a sufficient condition for beauty.

Li's explanation and attributing the objective character of beauty to social practice indicates an important feature of his aesthetic thinking. In constructing his aesthetics, Li does not delve into the processes in human consciousness that are sufficient for experiencing beauty. He proposes an objectivism on his own terms, which is not limited to the discussion of what particular nonaesthetic objective properties enable, or how they necessitate, the supervenience of aesthetic properties. His objectivism is focused on practice that combines, or even merges humans and the world. As mentioned in the first and second statements of *The Outline of My Philosophy*, practice is as fundamental as the existence of the objective world, and hence it constitutes the distinctive property of the human species.[26] Li departs from this fundamental level, and to a considerable degree his aesthetic is "thought" in terms of practice. This theoretical construction also complies with the enactivist approach, where enactment is mostly in focus in comparison to the living being or environment.

The free human practice ensures a full expression of humans, who actively remain in agreement with nature. Beauty as a form of such practice reflects this harmonious state. In enactivist terms, beauty, and the feeling of pleasure that it involves, reflects the living being's sense-making enactment, which is aimed at self-maintenance. Concurrently, this autopoietic enactment is made possible thanks to the adaptive enactment in the environment. Thus, beauty and the intrinsic pleasure appraisal reflect in these terms the homeostatic state of the living being and the environment. This interpretation denies that beauty can come into being within the boundaries of the subject. Neither is it merely an exchange between the subject and environment, as the former actively engages with the latter and, as integral part of it, contributes to the changes that lead to homeostasis.

The enactive approach situates beauty deeply in the human physiological and psychological processes that are involved in active involvement in the environment. This fact also converges with Li's understanding of aesthetic objectivism. Subjectivism should be dismissed, as beauty is the form of the living being enactment and thus it cannot be enclosed by self-sufficient operations of this system. Also, aesthetic pleasure as part of enactment cannot be interpreted as internally and independently generated. As regards the objective character of beauty, it cannot be defined solely in terms of the environment (minus the living being), as it is not an intrinsic aesthetic property existing apart from the enactive living being. Thus, the objective status of beauty hinges upon the enactment that stretches it between the living being and the environment rather than locating in one of them. The adaptive enactment is the objective foundation of beauty, as it takes place in the external environment in accordance with the laws that apply to both the being and environment.

Beauty as Practice of Freedom

Apart from the strictly aesthetic dimension, Li describes beauty as a form of freedom. In the anthropological ontology framework, freedom is the process of active comprehension and acting in accordance with objective laws. Hence, beauty as a form of freedom is understood as a process characterized by purposiveness and regularity.[27] Beauty is a form that emerges in the active transformation of nature. Li illustrates it with an oft-quoted fragment about cook Ding from the Daoist text *Zhuangzi*. The cook cuts oxen without really thinking about the technique involved. His skillfulness consists in the direct and concrete practice that harmonizes his action of cutting the oxen with the material he is working in.[28] Thus, Ding acts individually in accordance with his *dao* (道) of a cook, and concurrently puts himself in agreement with the world, which in this particular reading of Li is the accordance with objective laws. Ding's freedom is realized by accordance with his own *dao*, which is concurrently the way to harmonize with the *dao* of the world. In classical Chinese philosophy terms, an individual as part of the cosmos harmonizes with it in her/his idiosyncratic way. This form of freedom should not be interpreted as conforming to external laws as an individual is part of the whole and can only bring her/him to complete fulfillment within the cosmic order, the laws of which are in agreement with individual laws. Thus, the individual harmonization with the world is an act of freedom, not conformism. Li's thinking about beauty as a form of freedom exactly follows this pattern. Humans as part of nature realize themselves in accordance with objective laws, but in an individuated, subjective way, which is tantamount to freedom. Such free expression of humanity has embedded beauty that emerges as an agreement between the individual and the objective.

Beauty's Persistence through Time and Extension over Technology

Li refers to nature with the epistemic term "truth" by virtue of nature's objective laws. In a similar way, he applies the ethical term goodness to humans, due to their subjective purposiveness, as the power to transform nature. The unity of truth and goodness thus understood, as introduced above, in the fragment from the *Zhuangzi*, constitutes the foundation of beauty. Li constructs these two important epistemological and ethical notions by departing from practice. He proceeds in the same way as when reinterpreting Kant's a priori. In the case of truth, the laws of nature have been abstracted and generalized by social practice. The fact that they emerged through practice does not put human subjective purposiveness in conflict with them. The beauty of society manifests itself as the human practice aimed at the control over nature, followed by other social activities. In historical perspective, the human endeavor to control nature has been gradual and consists in a subjective purposiveness that led to transforming the undefined and formless nature into the regularity of objects. This has resulted in the achievements of, for instance, technology, architecture, and art, where the form of goodness has been given to the content of truth.[29]

The historical aspect of the human purposive transformation entails that beauty does not persist in the same form over time. The human transformation of nature, led by subjective purposiveness, changes in history, and the beauty that characterizes this endeavor of a temporal character changes as well. It can be stated that beauty persists through time in different forms, subsumed to different aesthetic standards. Such a characteristic of beauty does not merely comply with Li's anthropological ontology framework, where the world is incessantly transformed by human practice. The temporality of beauty standards has an important philosophical and cultural implication. The philosophical implication confirms that beauty cannot be ontologically treated as a permanent Platonic value, insensitive to the changes that take place in the material world. Quite the opposite, the ontic foundation and character of beauty is conditioned by the human activity of transforming the material world. Thus, aesthetics does not discuss beauty in a vacuum but looks into the anthropological processes from a historical perspective. This in turn leads to the cultural implication. Beauty can be discussed in terms of some artifacts, natural objects, or phenomena beyond the historical context. However, in addition to it, beauty is the measure of how humans culturally progress in history. Hence, aesthetics is also a historical study of the development of humans through their material practice. It is important to remember that beauty and aesthetics do not solely apply to the study of art, which is only part of human activity. In terms of art studies, aesthetics complements history of art in that it provides a wider anthropological context. A very similar statement can be formed with regard to social phenomena and technologies. In fact, since the second half of the twentieth century, technology has changed human material practice even more conspicuously. The digital technologies have led to a completely new character of beauty, which stretches over both the analog world and virtual reality.

Distributing aesthetic features among different activities, not only artistic practice, is justified by some forms of objects or phenomena, initially, nonaesthetic properties, having been extracted from nature through practice. They initially became part of human cognitive structures. For instance, rhythm derives from observations of repetitiveness in time, whereas symmetry derives from discovering and determining spatial relations. These properties enable humans to cognize and improve their life in nature. The initially nonaesthetic world propensities in turn have become aesthetic properties that determine beauty.[30] Aesthetic properties and beauty were not born in a separated realm of artistic reflection on the world, but they are the effect of a long accumulation of purposive practice. The common source of material practice shows that beauty is not reserved for the artistic realm and can be found in many aspects of human activity.

In this vein, Li believes that aesthetics should devote more attention to beauty in technology, conceived of as human activity that manifests freedom. Technology is a form of practice that enables humans to transform the material world on a large scale. It also contributes to human equality in participating in beauty. This can be best showcased by digital media, which, for instance provide a widespread access to audio-visual art, making it no longer reserved to a narrow portion of society. Technologies are also contemporary tools in Li's conception of practice. They are powerful instruments used in the humanization of nature. Importantly, Li also remarks that the part of nature that has not been transformed by humans should also be qualified as humanized, as technology and science have conquered the whole of nature in the sense that the relation of the whole universe to the human being has changed. This reveals Li's adherence to the Chinese cosmological intuitions in that human activity, although indisputably local, is at the same time an interaction with the whole cosmos. This agency of interconnection can be rendered into the language of relations, as accomplished by Li. A change in the relation of humans to uncultivated parts of nature can be exemplified by, for instance desolate landscapes or violent storms, which nowadays, thanks to technologies do not pose a threat to human existence and can be approached differently—for instance, aesthetically. At the same time, one might well note that humanization of nature has to reach a certain threshold for an aesthetic approach to nature. The primitive humans, who had insufficient control over the natural environment and had to confront it to survive, were at too early a stage to enter aesthetic relation with nature.[31] The beauty of nature contrasts with beauty of society in the opposite content and form distribution. Li claims that in natural beauty, the content of goodness is transparent, and what is more observable is the formal aspect of nature's structure that agrees with regularity.[32]

Conclusion

Li's conception of beauty is firmly founded upon his anthropological ontology. Beauty cannot be conceptualized in objective, ontological terms, although it is connected with object propensities. Nor can it be seen entirely through the subjectivist prism, although it relies on subjectality's psychological processes. Historically speaking, beauty has originated from primitive social practices that were followed by gradual refinement. It emerges in subjectality's interaction with the world, which can be understood in ethical, adaptive, and cognitive terms. This reveals the inseparability of Li's philosophy of beauty from life characterized by practice, and makes his aesthetic project experience oriented.

Chapter 7

Aesthetic Experience

Introduction

Aesthetic experience, similarly to beauty, is another concept whose determination reveals the character of Li's philosophical aesthetics. Although Li's aesthetics operates with the concept of beauty, one has to consider its character. Beauty is dynamic and it emerges in human engagement in the world rather than in a detached and purely mental contemplation. It is inseparable from the psychological processes of subjectality, and thus the nature of beauty should be understood through experience.

In this chapter, I will first introduce how aesthetic experience is conceptualized and what tendency in defining it can be observed. Next, I will discuss the psychological inspirations for Li's aesthetic experience and assess to what degree they are consistent with anthropological ontology. Subsequently, the fundamental conditions for aesthetic experience will be presented on the basis of Li's theory, which can be attributed to "new sensuousness." The next step will consist in discussing the stages and constitutive elements of aesthetic experience, as well as types of aesthetic pleasure. The discussion will be focused on the cognitive aspect of aesthetic experience, which can be interpreted within enactivism.

Conceptualizing Aesthetic Experience

One can distinguish among different kinds of theories of aesthetic experience. James Shelley distinguishes between internalist and externalist theories.

The internalist aesthetic theories are concerned with intrinsic features of experience, mainly phenomenological, whereas the externalist ones focus on what is extrinsic in experience, especially features of experienced objects.[1] This subdivision largely overlaps with Gary Iseminger's distinction of the accounts of aesthetic experience between phenomenological and epistemic. The phenomenological approach focuses on the "what it is like" of aesthetic experience, drawing on the phenomenology of the experience. The epistemic approach tends to determine the conditions of aesthetic experience.[2] It can be said that the crux of contemporary debate concerning aesthetic experience is mapped by this division. Generally speaking, the internal or phenomenological theories cover a wider range of possible objects of aesthetic experience in comparison to the external or epistemic standpoints, which usually gravitate toward philosophy of art.

Richard Shusterman offers a diagnosis of aesthetic experience, ranging person-wise from John Dewey to Arthur Danto. This period can be characterized as a transition from focusing on to questioning the sense of aesthetic experience. It is, among other things, connected with the scope of aesthetic experience, which stretches from quite broadly construed to exclusively art centered.

Shusterman diagnoses aesthetic experience by enumerating four dimensions. This depiction, and concurrently a sort of diagnosis of contemporary aesthetic experience, divides the aspects that are apparently intuitive in this type of experience into what should be treated as indispensable and what ought to be carefully questioned. The first, the evaluative dimension, describes aesthetic experience as enjoyable and valuable. The second, the phenomenological dimension, includes feeling, affective engrossment, and attention, which distinguish aesthetic experience from other, "common" experiences. The third, the semantic dimension, claims that it is not merely a sensation but a meaningful experience. The fourth, the demarcational-definitional dimension, consists in identifying aesthetic experience as distinctive, whereby it is connected with fine art. These dimensions, as Shusterman remarks, reflect the theoretical tensions and differences between approaches to aesthetic experience, some of which even question existence of experiences of this sort.[3]

With regard to these four dimensions, Shusterman presents the critique of aesthetic experience. It is represented by continental philosophy, which Shusterman particularly identifies with Theodor Adorno, Roland Barthes, Walter Benjamin, Pierre Bourdieu, Jacques Derrida, and Hans-Georg Gadamer. Continental philosophy dismisses aesthetic experience due to the fact that it is not conceived as an independent reception of artworks. The argument states that the pure phenomenology of immediate experience does not include the hermeneutical setting, which is indispensable for a proper reception and response to artworks.[4] This critical standpoint presupposes that the aesthetic is reserved for the realm of art, which practically defines the postulated autonomous reception of artworks and provides a cultural interpretational context. In one sense, the continental approach described by Shusterman would see aesthetic experience as more complex, but concurrently this experience would be reserved to a narrow portion of reality.

Shusterman refers this critique to the Anglo-American tradition to show that the aesthetic experience concept as conceived by John Dewey as phenomenological, evaluative, and transformational (in the sense of redefining rather than describing the existing aesthetics) has become more descriptive, semantic, and demarcational. This tendency can be landmarked by Monroe Beardsley's confining aesthetic experience to art.[5] Beardsley regards artworks as distinctive in that they can produce aesthetic experience, characterized by focus, intensity, and unity.[6] These features serve as a comparison of value between artworks. Thus, although Beardsley retains the phenomenological and evaluative dimensions, his narrowing of the aesthetic experience scope to art practically makes his philosophical project belong to philosophy of art rather than aesthetics. Beardsley's concept of aesthetic experience was further criticized. A most important critique comes from George Dickie, who believes that the term "aesthetic experience" does not denote anything in reality. Therefore, the description of aesthetic experience is in fact an account of aesthetic objects as experienced. He also remarks that aesthetic experience does not always have any affective content.[7] Thus, Dickie further strips aesthetic experience of phenomenology and evaluative dimensions. Both Beardsley's philosophy of art approach and Dickie's critique show not only that aesthetic experience loses its broad scope but that its very existence may be redundant on account of reducibility to descriptive approaches.

Based on the four dimensions and a brief critique of some of them, two observations can be drawn. First, the dimensions proposed by Shusterman show that the points of tension in the discussion about aesthetic experience are negotiable. We can talk about aesthetic experience only with regard to art or even determine the generic feature of aesthetic experience as exclusively applying to artworks. Similarly, the experience can be defined in, for instance, phenomenological or evaluative terms, and complemented with other dimensions. This reflects not only radical divisions in approaches to aesthetic experience but also its rather weakly determined core properties, which do not remain rigid in all approaches. Instead, the proposed concepts can be related by the Wittgensteinian family resemblance. This can suggest that aesthetic experience may not have a clear common denominator, which results in considerably varied points of view in this matter.

Second, the undetermined and varied character of approaches, as well as flexibility in understanding aesthetic experience, reveals some gap in contemporary research that has to be filled. The reductionist tendencies, although being relatively detailed accounts, may not be the only option. Perhaps one should take into consideration the family resemblance character of aesthetic experience and retain a certain level of indeterminacy, which would allow it to be accommodated within different particular theories.

Considering that it seems problematic to achieve a clear and unanimous conceptualization of aesthetic experience, one should also consider the question concerning the existence of aesthetic experience. Perhaps aesthetic experience should not be differentiated from other types of experience in phenomenological or epistemic, or both, terms, as the alleged difference cannot be attributed to the experiential characteristics. An interesting standpoint in this respect is proposed by Bence Nanay, who admits that aesthetics is essentially about experiences, although not only the experiences that are usually regarded as aesthetic. Aesthetic experience can be generally conceived of as "any strong (or intense, or emotionally significant) experience that we have in an aesthetic context 'aesthetic experience [*sic*].' " However, as Nanay admits, this can include experiences that significantly vary in type, and there are no principled reasons to distinguish between them.[8] Therefore, it is difficult to propose a clear-cut and monolithic definition of aesthetic experience, as it is unlikely that there is such a thing.

The postulated nonexistence of aesthetic experience is, paradoxically, also conducive for the discussion of experiences that are usually described as aesthetic. Abandoning aesthetic experience entails abandoning the definitions and classifications of it, which provides a wider perspective from which to approach aesthetics anew. It allows aesthetics to be set in a wider philosophical context and treated as more integrated with other philosophical disciplines that investigate experience and cognition.

The above spectrum of approaches, some of which are very pessimistic toward the issue of aesthetic experience, should not instantly dissuade us from looking into this particular issue. Although it is extraordinarily difficult, or even impossible, to capture aesthetic experience in a clear-cut and comprehensive definition, this evasive issue can provide coordinates that approximate the description of what processes and phenomenology accompany the experiences that are usually regarded as aesthetic. This wide and unconfined approach, rather than comparing specific definitions, appears to be more appropriate in discussing Li's concept of aesthetic experience, which goes beyond the artistic but also narrowly conceptualized aesthetic definitions.

Psychology in Aesthetic Experience

Li believes that the experience of beauty is first and foremost a psychological process and therefore it should be explained in psychological terms. However, this process can also be analyzed from a philosophical point of view, especially considering the anthropologically and historically constructed beauty already presented by Li. One should also not dismiss the fact that the psychological dimension of practice and cognition is incorporated as subjectality's psychological substance, where it is especially connected with emotions. The strong linkage between Li's philosophy and psychology is also confirmed by the fact that subjectality is necessarily situated, which requires the cognitive and evaluative actions to be embedded and processed in a psychological fashion. In this sense, psychology can be regarded as material in aesthetic experience, including on a philosophical level.

Li believes that psychology in aesthetics plays an important explanatory role with regard to the transition from philosophically conceived beauty to aesthetic phenomena and objects.[9] Psychology constitutes the link between the theoretical construction and the world in which the aesthetic is concretized. Although not conspicuously stated, this belief presupposes the embodied and embedded subject, thanks to which the psychological involvement of subjectality is possible.

The involvement of psychology in aesthetics generates a methodological issue concerning the status of empirical knowledge in comparison to other, more formal sciences, such as logic, which appear to more naturally integrate with philosophy. However, one should remember that we are standing on the ground of historical materialism, where practice is the common origin of all knowledge. Both abstract and empirical knowledge stem from social practice, as has been shown in Li's reinterpretation of Kant, and it describes the objective laws of nature. This opens a promising avenue of integrating Li's aesthetics with empirical sciences, especially psychology. Although Li expresses some doubt with regard to whether results from empirical sciences can comprehensively capture aesthetic experience,[10] it has to be admitted that, among other things, psychological evidence can contribute to explaining the character of some part of theoretical formation.

For instance, the quantitative research concerning nonaesthetic properties of objects can verify whether some preferences can be accepted as universal. It must be admitted that experimental research is fragmentary due to having been conducted during a period that generally does not fit the historical framework of Li's theory. However, it can at least examine some aspects of aesthetic experience during a given time of tool practice, while also possibly offering confirmation concerning the sedimentation of aesthetic preferences. For instance, the previously discussed experiments concerning landscape and face preferences constitute possible evidence for how some adaptations sedimented into psychological substance and became aesthetic preferences.[11] Other experimental research can show how human aesthetic preferences can change with regard to other, apparently unrelated factors. This can be illustrated by Frédéric Brochet's experiment that examines taste preferences of wine in connection with the bottles in which it is served. The experiment consisted in comparing the same low-quality wine poured into table wine and grand cru bottles. The experiment has shown that the aesthetic preferences and the feelings of aesthetic pleasure are not solely based on the sense of taste but on familiarity with wine brands. Thus, aesthetic judgments can depend on factors other than purely sensuous, which may be situational and social.[12] Experiments of this kind can be conducive to the aesthetic theory by suggesting that, for instance, aesthetic experiences should not necessarily be viewed as confined to their particular sensuous character and that they can be significantly influenced by other senses, prior knowledge, or unconscious epistemic factors. This in turn questions the theories that advocate autonomous experiences of objects as they believe to have identified sufficient propensities for evoking aesthetic experience. Conceding that experimental evidence may not comprehensively explore the nature of aesthetic experience, one can still state that it sheds some light on some particular aspects of theoretical construction.

Among psychological conceptions that could be compatible in explaining aesthetic experience, Li regards gestaltism and psychoanalysis as most suitable approaches. The main aspect of gestalt psychology that Li finds attractive is structural isomorphism, which fills the explanatory gap of how humans respond to objects. However, as previously mentioned, the isomorphic mechanism, which assumes that the phenomenological account of perception and the neurophysiological description structurally correspond, has not been confirmed. Nevertheless, whatever neuropsychological process underlies the holistic perception, humans have the capacity to empathize with the environment, which is understood by Li as particular emotional responses to particular stimuli from the environment. For instance, the swaying of willows evokes sadness as the swaying rhythm is similar to the "rhythm of human sorrowful feelings." This formal structure present in nature can also be employed in, for instance, art or design to evoke similar feelings.[13]

Apart from gestalt isomorphism, this mechanism of response can be alternatively accommodated by enactivism. Considering that perception must be situated, the response can be interpreted as affectively enacted. Following Li in that particular sensory stimuli cause particular, corresponding responses, they can be conceptualized as emotional episodes triggered by affective appraisals. Li also tacitly assumes that emotional responses are typically recursive. Thanks to this, they can be "manipulated" by, for instance, artists or industrial designers, who can intentionally implant some formal features from nature into their products to elicit a desired perception-based emotion. This repetitive pattern in responses of emotional episodes can be explained by phylogenetic adaptations, which, owing to the change of human life, illustrated by, among other things, growing advancement in tool practice, have at some point been disconnected from the very adaptive function. Consequently, the responses have achieved the feasibility of occurring in cultural contexts with similar or identical emotion-evoking capacity.

The main advantage of the enactive approach over gestaltism is that affective appraisals do not require the structural analogy between experience phenomenology and neuropsychological processing for triggering emotional episodes. The emotional response is of an adaptive (in an enactive sense) nature and it can resort to emotional responses from the hard-wired sensorimotor as well as schematic or conceptual processing levels. The latter offers the explanatory potential for modality in responses, for instance, in, say, culture-relative taste for art. In this way, Li's description of artistic creation as the intentional employment of certain formal features and their reception can be explained by this highest level of processing.[14] Importantly, the affective enactment underscores the fact that the reactions depend on both the object and the subject, who brings a complex interactive idiosyncrasy.

Li also complements gestaltist isomorphic structures with Carl Gustav Jung's concept of the collective unconscious, which includes instincts and archetypes. Jung claims that psychological processes in humans should be attributed to the development of phylogenetic brain structures. These structures function in the same way as long ago in the life of primitive humans. They are unconscious and genetically inherited by all humans. These unconscious structures are strictly related with consciousness. They are a continuous process that can be manifested in consciousness, which works discontinuously. Whereas the unconscious structures remain unchanging, they are manifested at the consciousness level in a varied and idiosyncratic way. The structures are repositories of archetypes shared by all humans, which reveal themselves as the same pancultural motifs concretized differently across cultures. Jung importantly remarks that archetypes are "the matrix of all conscious psychic occurrences," which implies that what is manifested on the conscious level is not acquired but conditioned by the unconscious.[15]

Li regards Jung's theory of collective unconscious as convergent with the concept of sedimentation. This comparison seems to be rather superficial, though. We can admit that Jung is similar to Li in that the archetypes stem from collective experiences in the remote past, and they have been genetically transferred until now. However, in Jung's theory, the inherited structures are not influenced by personal experience. This may initially appear to remain consistent with Li's theory, in that subjectality applies to the collective humanity engaged in practice rather than an individual human being, by which it downplays the personal furnishing of mind. However, Li also claims that human psychological substance is subject to incessant molding by the progressing practice of manufacturing and using tools. In this view, the psychological substance would be plastic rather than resistant to any changes in practice, were it to include the collective unconscious. Jung's theory does not seem to presuppose plasticity at a deep, unconscious level. On the philosophical level, although the archetypes can create various configurations, this is all attributed to some unalterable psychological repository. Thus, Jung's subject with regard to psychological structures persists through time as unchanged and is ontologically independent from the environment. On the contrary, Li's subjectality is an open system, which changes her/his structures over time through being involved in tool practice.

New Sensuousness

Although Li values the general insights of both gestaltism and Jungian psychoanalysis, he also discerns the shortcomings that make them particularly compatible with his aesthetic concept. Despite some convergence, the two theories do not consider the historical dimension of human psychological development. It should be admitted that Jung's collective unconscious is phylogenetic but it lacks dynamics. This does not give credit to the contemporary practice in molding the human psychological substance. For this reason, and that Li is ultimately concerned with the aesthetic issues in his philosophy, he proposes the term "new sensuousness" (*xin ganxing* 新感性), which encapsulates the molding of human sensuousness in historical perspective. He also draws attention to the issue that the historical transformation and constitution of this aspect of humanity has led to the emergence of its universal character, which he compares with Kant's third *Critique* common sense.[16] Apart from the fact that common sense enables the communicability of feelings among people, its convergent aspect involves it being indispensably developed in human interaction.[17] Although humans possess this disposition, it cannot be manifested in solitary life.[18] Counterintuitive as it may seem that collective life and practice are needed to develop aesthetic feelings, Li agrees with Kant in that they originate thanks to the practice particular of group and social life.

New sensuousness is particularly identified by Li with the psychological and emotional dimension of humans. Similarly to other features of subjectality, it has been sedimented into humans through the practice of tool production and use, as well as social interactions, including shamanist rituals, which are viewed by Li as the earliest layer of aesthetic beginnings. From the perspective of humanization of nature, new sensuousness results from the inner humanization, as opposed to the outer transformation, of the world. This realm is concerned with the origination of beauty, whereas the internal one deals with aesthetic experience. The inner humanization is particularly connected with human needs, desires, feelings, perception, and sense organs. The character of humanization presupposes that the psychological substance is embodied as the humanizing processes are physiologically founded. These processes have led humans to transcend their solely physiological existence and become social.[19] The physiologically grounded changes resulted in the humanized, more sophisticated, and less adaptively motivated perceptual responses. As the practice of tool manufacturing and use is an indispensable element of humanization, the physiological qualitative changes were induced by human activities. This interrelation between the practical and physiological can be interpreted as adaptive enactment that transcends the short-time perspective of adaptations of a certain living being and historically leads to developing better adaptive structures that can be genetically transferred and constantly modified by qualitatively new, recursive enactments.

Li believes that the humanization of inner nature that leads to the emergence of new psychological, emotional structures, as well as broadly understood cultural structures, can be subdivided into three ways. The first one concerns "human recognition," which is connected with the evolution of such cognitive structures as logic and thinking patterns. The second one covers "human ethics," and it includes morality and volition. The last one is "human emotion," which includes the aesthetic sense of taste.[20] This subdivision reveals Li's inspiration with Kant's philosophical system subdivided into the three *Critiques*, which, roughly speaking, are thematically arranged into epistemological, ethical, and aesthetic parts that retain a high level of consistency with one another. Kant's influence continues over the third way of psychological substance development, where the aesthetic is understood in terms of a proper emotional response.

Such an approach to aesthetics also converges with Confucianism. The Confucian involvement in feeling constitutes an essential part of self-cultivation, which leads to the emergence of psychological structures that, apart from aesthetic sensuousness, can also be viewed in terms of the other two dimensions. Appropriate sensitivity allows a human being to fulfill herself/himself internally and externally, in social space as complete Confucian moral personhood by means of proper, compassionate, and caring interactions with others. The disposition of such psychological structures also constitutes cognitive equipment that enables the accurate recognition of situations (mostly related with human interactions).

Li claims that the changes in aesthetic psychological construction result from two processes: phylogenetic and ontogenetic. Phylogenesis complies with the overall framework of Li's philosophical project and is particularly explained by social practice. The ontogenesis of the aesthetic psychological construction takes place in a way that is very similarly described by Piaget's cognitive development.[21] At this point, Li's philosophical project becomes more diverse by not only adhering to the historical materialist practice.

These two processes provide a comprehensive molding of the human aesthetic sensitivity. Importantly, they are integrated and dependent on each other. Li remarks that human practice is the fundamental process that precedes personal development. From a historical perspective, humans were involved in performing totemic dances, which gradually led to developing the aesthetic structures. This pattern can also be detected in ontogenetic development, as children are initially engaged in performing activities such as dancing, singing, or other forms of artistic playing prior to contemplating fine arts.[22] It can be noticed that this practical-contemplative sequence in learning roughly overlaps with developmental psychology theories. Thus, practice is an indispensable stage for further, more reflective and even intellectual, cultivation of aesthetic sensitivity.

Analogously with the two channels of dynamic molding, the aesthetic structures are plastic. From a historical perspective, incessant practice makes the structures change. On the individual level, the dynamic is conditioned more by individual experience history, which includes both practical and contemplative engagement. The plastic character of aesthetic structures is not only confined to historical-ontological implications. The sedimentation of aesthetic psychological structures can be viewed in strata that correspond to specific times in the history of human practice.[23] In this way, one can trace the development of aesthetic structures as part of psychological substance in subjectality. This is manifested as a phenomenon that can be described as an aesthetic culture of a given time, characterized by the account of aesthetic taste and production. However, instead of this narrow account, Li sees the aesthetic psychological construction of a given time as reflecting more what he refers to as "historical traces," which include "concrete social, national, epochal, and class features." This characteristic of the aesthetic structure shows Li's strongly historical materialism-informed perspective, which takes into consideration multiple aspects of collective life reflected in the aesthetic. This not only draws attention to the historical aspect of the aesthetic structures. Human aesthetic sensibility is not pancultural but depends on specific practice, which may shape human aesthetic taste differently. For this reason, aesthetics is not only studied diachronically but we can also distinguish various aesthetic categories across temporally coexisting cultures.

The structural humanization of the psychological substance results in an aesthetic sensibility that enables the appreciation of beauty. Li distinguishes two aspects of how this is achieved through the humanization of the human interior nature. The first concerns human hardware and humanizes the human sense organs. Li adopted this idea from Marx's *Manuscripts*. The senses become social in human interaction and make the world an object related to the human being.[24] The relation of the world to humans and humans to each other is highly complex and includes aesthetic appreciation, among other things. Li believes that the humanization of senses developed at a particular stage of the practice of manufacturing and using tools, when humans realized and recognized the relation of form and function of the objects. This drew humans' attention to these two aspects of objects, which in turn entailed a change in the sense organs. This not only enabled a more finely tuned perception of these features but also provided greater responsiveness to them on the sensory level. Li exemplifies this with the sense of touch, which transformed from receptive to more kinetic.[25]

To emphasize that humans are unique thanks to tool practice, Li alludes to *The Outline of My Philosophy*, where he points out that humans are not strictly adaptive as animals and they can act in accordance with their own purposes.[26] This capability does not rely on senses, which in the cases of many species of nonhuman animals provide very detailed perception. These perceptions, however, cannot be humanized and develop a new, nonphysiologically adaptive relation of the world to humans. Human beings, thanks to the use of tools, have developed a distinctively human relation to the world, which is realized externally by transforming nature in accordance with human purposes, and internally as the humanization of the embodied subjectality. The character of the qualitative transformation of sense organs is also unique to humans. It cannot be attributed to making the senses more perceptually precise. The humanization of the sense organs leads to a new sensuousness in terms of emerging new perceptual qualities. For instance, if applied to the auditory sense, humanization does not consist in hearing a wider sound frequency range but in hearing in a qualitatively different, perhaps musical, way, which is underpinned by the uniquely human meaningful relation to objects.

Li holds that this qualitative change in human sense organs has led to the differentiation with other animals. Whereas nonhuman animals' organs are "utilitarian," the humanization of the senses has liberated humans from this very aspect. Although human sensuousness is still influenced by desires, it is no longer entirely utilitarian. This means that the senses are no longer governed by human physical needs, for instance, the need for food or reproduction. Instead, sensuousness has become social in that the senses can be used in accordance with human purposes, which include aesthetic ones. Interestingly, Li observes that some of the senses have become more social than others. Touch, smell, and taste have not been as strongly humanized as others due to the fact that they are more directly linked with physical needs. On the contrary, vision and hearing, as they are less entangled in directly satisfying biological needs, became more social and, subsequently, more aesthetic.[27]

Aesthetic experience is possible thanks to the process in which the senses have been liberated from purely biologically motivated perception. It can be said that aesthetic experience is highly individual in the sense of being nonrational, intuitive, and nonsocial in character. However, considering the humanization of senses, it is social, which is revealed by the uniquely human disinterested approach.[28] This twofold aspect can be mapped onto the division of a first- and third-person account of experience. The individual one is phenomenological and hence not universally communicable and evades rational, intersubjective discourse. The social one pays attention to the objective conditions of experience, a most important feature that is free from the biological-instinctive confinements.

The second aspect of humanizing the psychological substance involves emotion and desire. Originally human emotions were reducible to the biological level as physiological passion related to instinctive desire. One of them was the sex drive, which was to assure the reproduction for genetic transfer. This biologically founded and functional passion has been altered by rational sedimentation, which contributed to qualitative changes. The changes have led to human emotionality, which transcends the biological level. Hence, the mentioned reproductive desire has evolved into love, which, although having a biological foundation, is not completely reducible to it.[29] Li also discusses this particular sedimentation in *A New Approach to Kant*, where by showing the development of sexual desire into an expression of love, he describes a transition from the natural to the aesthetic.[30] Not only do the sense organs become capable of aesthetic experience, but the instinctive desires, after being detached from their original motivation and function, become aesthetic feelings. It can be noticed that aesthetic feelings are not disconnected from sensuousness itself but its initial functions. This illustrates the qualitative change, which consists in not intensifying, suppressing, or abandoning sensuousness. Aesthetic feeling is based on the senses, but the nature of the experience is suprabiological. In this sense, the new sensuousness brings the aesthetic dimension to human life and becomes the measure of how far humans have progressed in humanizing their nature.

Li regards this progress as analogical to epistemic and ethical development. In their pursuit of knowledge, humans have to develop adequate tools (or manual skills), language, and cognition, whereas in ethics rules of conduct must reach the suprabiological level to become moral. However, these two realms of humanization are different from aesthetics with regard to the role of sensuousness. In knowledge and ethics, rationality, exerts control over the senses. It can be said that in neither of them has rationality become part of sensuousness, as is the case with aesthetics. Aesthetic feeling, and consequently aesthetic experience, must be embedded in sensuousness and, unlike thought or will, it cannot be felt beyond it.[31] The framework of aesthetic experience based on new sensuousness presents a model in which rationality is built into sensuousness. It is not engineered in a Kantian way, as the controlling unit over sensuousness. Unlike in epistemology or ethics, it seems to collaborate rather than dominate the senses. The rational composite has led to a certain calibration of emotions, which enable a humanized, suprabiological response to the environment. Although Li separates aesthetics from knowledge production and labels it as disinterested, one could entertain a cognitive interpretation. First, Li operates with an understanding of knowledge that has to be discursively formulated. But discursive knowledge does not exhaust other levels, or other forms, of cognition. The emotional response to the environment is a subject's enacted cognitive act that considers the character of an event, which marks a change in the environment, and adjusts in the way that leads to aesthetic pleasure, which can be viewed as constructed of affective appraisals.

Second, it should be considered that even in ethics, emotions play a cognitive role, present in moral sentimentalism. Confucianism can serve as an example where practical knowledge, mainly moral in nature, relies on a proper emotional calibration that enables one to recognize the social interaction and act accordingly. Here emotion cannot be reduced to merely one of its functions, which is feeling. It concurrently provides an evaluating feedback that is supposed to lead to a moral act, that is, one that is appropriate to the cognized situation. This can be supported by Jesse J. Prinz's argument that moral judgments are based on sentiments that dispose humans to approving or disapproving emotions, which constitute moral judgments.[32]

Stages of Aesthetic Experience

The new sensuousness constitutes the framework for experiencing beauty. Li proposes his own analysis of how the experience is particularly processed as well as what stages constitute it. Li subdivides aesthetic experience into three subsequent phases: aesthetic attitude, aesthetic attention, and sense of beauty.

Aesthetic experience commences with aesthetic attitude (*shenmei taidu* 審美態度). It is the first response during the aesthetic appreciation of an object. Li explains that the aesthetic attitude consists in distancing oneself from daily life and approaching the object in a nonutilitarian way. He concurrently remarks that this stage is short-lived and cannot be maintained.[33] It is more a kind of initial moment when one enters the "aesthetic mode." Considering this, if referred to appraisals, the attitude as a short-lived response can be understood as the first element of an emotional episode, referred to as "novelty." It is caused by a change in the environment, and the function of this occurrence is to orient the subject. As novelty appraisals are reactions to both physical and mental changes, they also apply in aesthetic appreciation underpinned solely by a mental event.[34] The short-lived, triggering character of the novelty appraisal complies with Li's aesthetic attitude in that it initiates the conscious aesthetic appreciation. Li describes the attitude as "the preliminary stage of aesthetic consciousness."[35] As for whether this initial and instant stage itself is conscious, Phoebe C. Ellsworth and Klaus R. Scherer describe the novelty appraisal as preparation for further emotional response and fueling the organism's attention. It has to be considered that, in Li's account, attitude is followed by attention, which could suggest that the subject is aesthetically conscious prior to evaluating the object.

There is not one, clear-cut approach for determining the role of attention in conscious states. Prinz proposes that attention is necessary and sufficient for consciousness. Among other things, he provides evidence from behavioral research. He provides three examples. The first one is the motion-induced blindness; where when one pays attention to the moving cross hairs grid, the fixed spots that are over it are not perceived continuously.[36] The second one is a case of the attentional blink, which occurs when the subject is asked to detect two target stimuli in a series of rapidly displayed stimuli, at a rate of ten per second. The first one that captures attention is detected, but the second comes too quickly to be attended to and is not consciously perceived.[37] The third example is inattentional blindness. It is encountered in divided attention experiments, where many subjects are unconscious of a stimulus that is plainly visible as they are asked to attend to something else.[38] Inattentional blindness can also occur with stimuli presented for a long time, as in the oft-quoted experiment by Daniel C. Simons and Christopher F. Chabris,[39] in which the subjects are asked to count passes in a basketball game and do not notice, for instance, a person clad in a gorilla suit walking among the players.[40]

If we accepted Prinz's view that attention is necessary in consciousness, aesthetic attitude would have to be the unconscious, short-lived stage that gives rise to a stage with attention, which entails the conscious part of aesthetic experience. Then one might assume that some part of aesthetic valuation, or some determination of it, is already included in aesthetic attitude. Unconscious experiences can influence valuation in aesthetic experiences. This is the case of subliminal priming in visual perception. It can be illustrated by, for instance, an experiment by Piotr Winkielman, Kent C. Berridge, and Julia J. Wilbarger,[41] in which the subjects were shown angry, happy, and neutral faces for 16 milliseconds. Afterward, the subjects were asked to assess the quality of drinks. Their evaluation was influenced by the valence of the prime.[42] The experiment shows that unconscious experiences can at least influence our other sensory valuations.

As regards the second stage, aesthetic attention (*shenmei zhuyi* 審美注意), it is manifested by focusing on the formal side or structural composition of an object. What differs aesthetic attention from our other attending to objects is that it is free from being subsumed under conceptualization. Li reveals here Kant's influence, especially from the third *Critique*, and continues to describe the logically uncontrolled attention as allowing the subject's imagination and emotion to "enter into the aesthetic activity and permeate the forms of the object."[43] We can see that Kant's interplay of cognitive faculties has been modified by supplanting the understanding with emotion. This replacement can lead to several important implications. First, employing emotion can be taken for depriving the aesthetic of the cognitive dimension. Thus, similarly to Kant's judgment of beauty, we do not achieve cognition as the manifold subsumed under concepts. Nor do we obtain the subsumption of the imagination that "agree[s] with its concepts in general,"[44] which is the case of Kant's judgment of beauty. However, as indicated, this judgment also has a cognitive dimension, if we do not strictly adhere to the idea that only discursive knowledge can be labeled cognition. Aesthetic experience involves the ordering of sensations by sensibility, which recognizes the form and purpose (in dependent beauty). This action is cognitive. One can also admit an interpretation according to which emotion is a nondiscursive cognitive faculty, especially if the cognitive character of appraisals is taken into consideration. Emotion is composed of appraisals that recognize and respond to changes in the environment. The form or structure of an object is responded to in a meaningful way as, on the affective level, the subject enacts adaptively. Considering that aesthetic experience takes place in a new sensuousness, this adaptation is detached from its original "biological drive" and constitutes a variety of adapting on the aesthetic level. In this way, the involvement of emotion can be seen as cognitive.

Second, Li offers a more affective view of experience in comparison to Kant, who operates with a highly theoretical subject. It does not have to imply that aesthetic experiences always have an emotionally intense phenomenology, as many of them certainly do not. However, the involvement of emotion provides a better explanation for the feeling of pleasure, which is founded in an embodied and embedded subject. It emerges in the subject's enactment in environment, and is explainable in terms of the processes that take place in a living being.

Third, including emotion in the interplay supports the importance of affectivity in cognition. As mentioned above, it does not only provide the possibility of explaining the emotional phenomenology in terms of situated subject. The involvement of emotion also opens a possibility of explaining the experience as a process that includes affective appraisals, which do not necessarily have to be conscious.

One should also consider that attention in perception varies and, subsequently, we can differ in our perceptual awareness of the properties of the perceived object. This issue is discussed by Bence Nanay with regard to aesthetic experience. He refers to Arien Mack's[45] subdivision of attention into focused and distributed. The former is encountered when one focuses on some particular part of a perceived object. In this case, only the part attended to is present in our consciousness. However, a more common case of attention is distributed, which consists in embracing the whole object of experience. Nanay remarks that the difference between these two modes of attention lies in the range, for instance, the size of the visual field. This should be complemented by the conceptual feature, which is connected with what is attended to, which is based on the distinction between properties and objects. According to Nanay, the type of attention mostly encountered in aesthetic experiences, referred to as "aesthetics attention," is focused with regard to objects and distributed with regard to properties. He regards this type of attention as disinterested, as opposed to attention that focuses on both the object and its properties.[46] Attention thus conceived complies with Li's idea of aesthetic attention. Despite a disinterestedness that qualifies it as aesthetic, it is not bereft of a cognitive dimension, as it consists in perceiving some object as distinct from the environment. It also embraces the object qualities in the way that they are present within consciousness yet without special focus. The disinterestedness in such perception does not mean that the subject is indifferent in perception, in which case her/his attention would be distributed in two respects. As Nanay remarks, the lack of practical interest does not exclude all interests from experience.[47] The focus that is devoted to the object is a meaningful act. The subject is not merely receptive of, but attends to, the object in a way that is a sense-making enactment without what is regarded as practical interest. One might remark that practical interest is not clearly determined. It is usually understood as of direct or not remotely indirect benefit or importance for the subject. However, the interest in feeling aesthetic pleasure can also be interpreted as practical. Humans do not manifest their indifference by attending performances or listening to music; they do so in order to feel the sophisticated, aesthetic pleasure. Hence, practical interest should be viewed in a conventional rather than absolute way. Considering this, aesthetic attention is interested internally, for aesthetic "gratification," by which it can be interpreted as meaningful, sense-making enactment that adapts the subject to the environment in the way that evokes pleasure. This type of disinterested, or, put in a different way, aesthetically interested, attention in perception complies with Li's aesthetic attention.

The third stage of aesthetic experience is the sense of beauty (*meigan* 美感). It is also referred to as aesthetic pleasure or enjoyment (*shenmei yukuai* 審美愉快) or aesthetic feeling (*shenmei ganshou* 審美感受).[48] At this stage, aesthetic experience reaches fulfillment via the feeling of aesthetic pleasure.

Li does not limit his aesthetic experience to what is strictly sensuous. Although inseparable from sensuousness, aesthetic experience concurrently bears a suprasensuous dimension, because sensuousness has been humanized, as a result of which it is a sedimented social rationality. Li believes that in terms of pure sensuousness, aesthetic experience would be reduced to a sensory response and receptive, physiological feeling of pleasure. The pleasure achieved in aesthetic experience is similar to Kantian in that it involves a dynamic engagement of psychological faculties. Strangely, Li also believes that the judgment of beauty precedes pleasure, a fact that stands as evidence of pleasure not being purely physiological.[49] To make this discussion possible at all, one has to assume that the judgment is nonphysiological and precedes the calibrated, physiological response—pleasure. It is undeniable that the processes in which aesthetic pleasure and purely physiological pleasure come into being are different. Theoretically speaking, however, Li himself admits that the aesthetic sedimentation is different from those of the epistemological and ethical, where reason and will respectively impose themselves on sensuousness.[50] Aesthetic sedimentation is structurally different in that the rational is amalgamated with the sensuous. Thus, the possible interplay of the rational and physiological is unlikely to lead to a judgment that is prior to the physiologically embedded, yet not purely physiological, pleasure. In such a case, considering that the judgment is not in the form of discursive thought, it would be difficult to determine what it actually would be like. It is also essential to notice that pleasure belongs to the account of aesthetic experience phenomenology, and judgment would also have to be included there, as conscious and preceding pleasure. It seems more natural to depart from the amalgamated character of new sensuousness, where the feeling itself is the judgment, from which it follows that judgment cannot precede pleasure. It can be supported by the role of affects in cognition. Based on the structure of the emotional episode, it can be seen that intrinsic pleasure is an immediate response after the novelty appraisal and it emerges from the interaction with the environment rather than intellectual processing of some kind.[51] Also, some affective science studies confirm that affective states, both positive and negative, influence human attitudes and judgments, as can be illustrated by affect-priming, which consists in affective states activating or facilitating the use of affect-consistent information from memory in cognition. This results in judgments that are mood-congruent. Another example comes from mechanisms, where the affects-as-information model holds that temporary affective states serve as a "heuristic cue" in judgment informing, which usually takes place when confronting an unfamiliar object.[52] It can be seen that empirical studies tend to view affects as constitutive in judgment informing.

Structure of Aesthetic Experience

Structure-wise, Li distinguishes between four components of aesthetic experience: sensation, understanding, imagination, and emotion. They are not the building blocks of the experience but rather functional and dynamic elements that configure one another by way of complex psychological processes, which leads to the emergence of aesthetic pleasure. Li describes the nature of this process as intuitive, as "it happens in immediacy and excludes cognition."[53] It seems that, in his description of aesthetic experience, Li remains under Kant's influence not only in that the structure includes the understanding and imagination. In fact, the two new psychological faculties added by Li, from Kant's philosophy perspective, belong to sensibility. Thus, they are more immediate in the sense of processing sensations and preparing them for the understanding. Li also seems to conceptualize the role of understanding in his model similarly to that of Kant in that he does not regard the experience to be cognitive in nature. However, as demonstrated in Kant's aesthetics, the cognitive character of aesthetic experience should not be dismissed merely because it does not finish with the subsumption under determinate concepts. It should also be considered that Li's psychological substance involves the rational molding of emotion in a way that is very similar to Confucianism, where emotion plays an important role in constituting practical knowledge. This aspect seems to have been adopted by Li because humanized emotions are not reducible to reflexes but are meaningful responses. Also, it should be considered that aesthetic experiences accumulate and result in sedimenting new psychological structures, which, even if not strictly cognitive themselves, influence other forms of cognition.

The first element of aesthetic experience is aesthetic sensation (*shenmei ganzhi* 審美感知). The word *ganzhi* (感知) is generally translated in philosophy as "perception," although Li decides to use "sensation" in the English-language version of *Four Essays on Aesthetics*, probably to avoid semantic overlaps with the remaining elements. Aesthetic sensation occurs at the moment when the stage of aesthetic attitude is followed by aesthetic attention. Li understands this in accordance with new sensuousness, which not only entails the physiological-biological processing, as is the case of nonhuman animals. The sensation is in fact interspersed with psychological components, thanks to which it is not confined to strictly sensuous perception. The suprasensuous elements of sensation are unconscious.[54] This implies that the phenomenology of sensation is comprehensively sensuous, without nonsensuous psychological components, which in fact are involved in the perception process. The involvement of processes other than purely physiological is the result of the sedimentation of the sense organs. Li illustrates the humanized perception with a three-dimensional perception of two-dimensional images that is possible thanks to the stereoscopic practice of the eyes. The conversion process of a two-dimensional image into a three-dimensional perception is unconscious. Such an ability is the result of sedimenting the cognitive faculty of understanding, among others, into the human senses.[55] This change in the human sense organs cannot be attributed to a purely biological evolution of organisms but psychological substance sedimentation.

At the same time, Li remarks that despite sedimentation, the sense organs remain deeply informed by their original physiology. This can be seen across the sedimentation layers, by, for instance, some shape or color preferences.[56] Hence, the elements of originally adaptive significance have been imported to aesthetics and they remain meaningful in aesthetic experience. However, one should recognize a shift in meaningfulness. The original importance of, for instance, the color of the percept was a sign that referred to the adaptively important features of the perceived object. In aesthetic experience, the perceived quality is adopted without its original reference. This aesthetic importance, which influences aesthetic preferences, apart from the adaptive origin, can also be influenced by other factors, in which practice has taken place, such as the type of natural environment or how a given society is organized. These factors can shape particular preferences and lead to the origin of diverse aesthetic cultures, which can be showcased by different concepts of and styles in art across history and geography. However, whatever cultural sedimentation takes place, it always acts upon the human physiology. Thus, despite aesthetic sensation being considerably informed by other, psychological and cultural, components, which have been built into sensuousness through practice, it still operates with the sensuous material.

The second element of aesthetic experience is aesthetic understanding (*shenmei lijie* 審美理解). Li distinguishes four implications of understanding for aesthetic experience, the first three of which are "not real aesthetic understanding" and should be treated as prerequisites needed for entering aesthetic experience. The first one is that the subject is always conscious of the situational context of experience. This is particularly referred to experiences that take place in aesthetic situations. For instance, when an actor or spectator of a theatrical performance, the subject is conscious that the situation is fictive rather than from everyday life.[57] However, it should be noticed that it is not context consciousness in general that is particular to aesthetic understanding. Excluding nonstandard situations, such as perceptual and mental disorders, humans are conscious of everyday life situations when they behave accordingly. Li seems to mean that the particular feature of situation consciousness in aesthetic understanding consists in being aware of the conventional or artificial character of situations. However, considering that this type of consciousness is even of a preliminary nature, this characteristic does not seem to hold either, since everyday life also includes situations that are artificial yet unrelated to aesthetic experience. Despite not entering in an "aesthetic situation," humans are equally conscious of their character and respond in a way that complies with the convention of a given situation. Consider psychological assertiveness trainings, which quite often resort to acting out scenes for entraining or explaining assertive behavior. These trainings are also performed in accordance with some script, in a specific context, of which the trainees are fully aware.

Li further characterizes context consciousness as a particular kind of understanding consisting in nonutilitarianism and psychological distance to actual life, which in acting allows integration of oneself with the character and act beyond the practical and ethical motivations.[58] However, the underlying subdivision into real life and the one in the aesthetic experience seems considerably inconsistent. First of all, this would exclude aesthetic experiences in actual life. Second, we can view the realm of everyday life as one with ethically and practically established conventions, and the "aesthetic realm" as an analogous one, governed by its own conventions. Moreover, humans can switch between these two realms and consciously adopt different conventions in their behavior. Third, the distance to life and nonutilitarianism in aesthetic experience is not absolute. In fact, even in the case of artworks, human aesthetic experiences are motivated by the prospect of feeling aesthetic pleasure. For this reason, humans are guided by their aesthetic preferences in selecting from a range of artistic choices in order to maximize the probability of feeling aesthetic pleasure.

It can be seen that the context-consciousness prerequisite in aesthetic and nonaesthetic experiences is not different to the degree that would qualify this type of consciousness as unique for aesthetic experiences.

The second implication of aesthetic understanding is connected with background knowledge. Li believes that it is particularly discernible in art, where the symbols or motifs, which are related to a cultural or historical period, are prerequisites for the correct appreciation of artworks.[59] This prerequisite for aesthetic experience is very similar to the context consciousness in that it prepares for correct understanding. Moreover, it should not be viewed as a distinctive feature of aesthetic understanding, as practically every type of understanding requires background knowledge.

As for the third implication, Li distinguishes the "intellectual cognition of the technical characteristics of the object."[60] This implication has no distinct aesthetic character, as it is present in almost every type of cognition, including scientific.

In comparison to the above three implications, Li regards the fourth as unique for aesthetic understanding. It refers to "a certain indefinite cognition that permeates sensation, imagination, and emotion and blends with them to form an organic unity."[61] In the aesthetic context, Li's understanding is similar to that of Kant, where, in contrast to discursive cognition, it is indefinite in nature. Li explains the indefiniteness in understanding with an example of salt dissolved in water. The salt can be detected by taste but its substance is untraceable. Analogously, understanding, when dissolved by other psychological factors, can be felt yet is impossible to be encapsulated in thought.[62] One can observe a very similar characteristic to Kant in that the experience engages the cognitive faculty and results in a special type of cognition, which orders the experienced material in a certain way that evades discursiveness. In this sense, Li contradicts himself by concurrently stating that aesthetic experience is intuitive and excludes cognition.[63] This tension results from assuming that cognition is tantamount to discursive knowledge production. However, as can be seen, the processes in aesthetic experience do not only involve cognitive faculties but are cognitive in character.

However, Li seems to confirm the cognitive nature of aesthetic experience by depicting it as more comprehensive than the scientific account of the world. According to him, aesthetic comprehension is broader than the scientific approach in that it "attracts people to try to understand its implications and to pursue its truth worth in a spirit of endless pleasure." In comparison to scientific cognition, the aesthetic account of reality is embedded in human sensuousness, the deepest structure of psychological substance, by which it is felt instead of thought, and therefore apprehended in a more direct and comprehensive way. As can be seen, aesthetic experience presents an alternative form of cognition. Li also claims that art, is a "barometer of life preceding theoretical cognition."[64] It suggests that art is not only, by virtue of sensuousness, a more direct account of reality, but it is temporally prior to knowledge, which comes into being only after the analysis and conceptualization of the world. It does not mean that the aesthetic apprehension of reality foreshadows cognition itself. It should be viewed as another form of cognition that embraces reality in a more direct, embedded, and enacted rather than discourse-distanced way.

The third element of aesthetic experience is aesthetic imagination (*shenmei xiangxiang* 審美想象). Li believes that aesthetic sensation and understanding use aesthetic imagination as their medium. Sensation and understanding in perceptual physiology and cognitive processes respectively are constants, and it is imagination that makes them variable and links with the fourth element, emotion.[65] Li endows his concept of the imagination with the power of the imagination from Kant's first and third *Critiques*, where it is responsible for figurative synthesis. The sensations, which Li's philosophy claims to be physiological perceptions, are adjusted for understanding. Imagination also acts upon understanding in a way that does not lead to conceptualization, which also sits well with the Kantian model. By pushing sensation beyond physiology and preventing understanding from conceptualization, the imagination adapts these two cognitive faculties in a way that makes the experience aesthetic. From the point of view of the cognitive process, the imagination is decisive in whether the experience is aesthetic or nonaesthetic. However, it should be noted that this division does not entail whether the experience is cognitive or not. Structurally speaking, the two cognitive faculties are involved and combined with emotion, which is also essential in cognition. Functionally, the experience consists in ordering the sensations, by which an alternative to a discursive cognitive act is completed.

The imagination molds sensations in many ways. One of the formative aspects presented by Li is operation with expectation. It situates sensation in innate and developed perceptual habits, which can also be viewed more literally, as expectations regarding the future. The imagination enables these expectations to be combined with sensations so as to form a cohesive perception. Another way in which the imagination shapes perception is by association, which Li believes can be related or analogical. The related type of association is illustrated by connecting a presented scene in a painting, which in Li's example is the Spring Festival, with the atmosphere that accompanies the event in reality.[66] This shows that the related perception is responsible for connecting the sensation with associated feelings in order to create an aesthetic perception that is enriched with associated components that do not emerge strictly from the senses. Such a phenomenology of perception is significantly different from the one in scientific cognition, where the sensations are conceptualized instead of felt. The analogous association enables more metaphorical types of associations to be associated. In comparison with related association that complements the sensuous, the analogical association consists in conversion.

It can be observed that the imagination is unlikely to be an unchanging cognitive faculty. The above-mentioned functions of expectation and association show that the imagination is situated, as it relies on experiential history and a particular context of aesthetic experience. The situated character of imagination, revealed by its function, makes it an important structure of psychological substance. Forming cohesive and meaningful perceptions depends on these modalities, whose characteristics result from sedimentation. In this context, the functional character of imagination can also be viewed in terms of enactment. It shows that perceptions are not receptive, but meaningful actions that are meant to orient the subject in the environment. The association, and particularly anticipation, imbue the enacted perception with meaning in the sense that the aesthetic feeling and understanding are part of the subject's enactment.

It should be noticed that the imagination, despite not leading to conceptualization by the understanding, should not be regarded as an element that deliberately distorts sensuous experience, which in effect produces aesthetic pleasure. In fact, imagination leads to the aesthetic understanding that, as Li puts it, "can reveal wide and diverse meanings." The special character of aesthetic experience consists in its apprehension of reality being characterized with a greater qualitative plenitude, which cannot be encapsulated in a determinate, conceptual form. Science, for instance, is incapable of grasping the emotional aspect of experience. As Li claims, "scientific imagination is a sensuous structure of concepts," which miss the emotional and generally situated aspects of experience.[67] For this reason, in aesthetic experience, the subsumption under concepts is not sense-fixing but quite the opposite, a dynamic sense-making that deliberately evades particular concepts.

The role of imagination in constructing aesthetic experience can be particularly showcased in art, where the works deliberately leave gaps for interpretational surplus and the subject is usually conscious of her/his association and expectations involved in experiencing a piece of art. This, however, does limit the aesthetic experience and engagement of imagination with art. In fact, aesthetic experiences operate with imagination even in experiences that lead to conceptualization. The Kantian model of experience, on which Li strongly relies, shows that imagination is indispensable for discursive cognition. Aesthetic experience is significantly different from other experiences, but the difference should not, in terms of character, exclude it from cognition, and in terms of object, confine it to art.

The fourth element of aesthetic experience is aesthetic emotion (*shenmei qinggan* 審美情感). Li departs from the common intuition that, contrary to other forms of experience such as scientific, emotion is a distinctive feature of aesthetic experience. Emotion liberates imagination, increases understanding, intensifies sensation, and decides on the pattern of aesthetic experience.[68] Li assumes that aesthetic experience is situated and physiological factors, such as instinctive desires, play an important role in it. However, there should be no misconception that aesthetic experience is tantamount to channeling instinctive desires. The humanization of primitive desires has led to complex emotionality, which is comprised of physiological as well as psychological elements. This is revealed in the outcome of aesthetic experience—aesthetic pleasure (*shenmei yukuai* 審美愉快), or sense of beauty (*meigan* 美感), which is the measure for the complexity of emotion sedimented in the psychological construction.

Aesthetic pleasure reflects the anatomy of aesthetic experience in that it does not result in a determinate conceptualization. It inherits the processual dynamics, and therefore there is no one standard of aesthetic pleasure. The particular phenomenology of pleasure depends on the actual harmonious configuration of the four elements of aesthetic experience.[69] The harmony is processual, and so aesthetic pleasure, due to being part of the process, changes in time. This variable character of aesthetic experience is an important distinctive feature in comparison with other forms of cognition. The experiences that result in conceptualization do not grasp the varied and dynamic character of experience, which is conveyed by aesthetic pleasure. The phenomenology of Li's aesthetic experience is embodied, ensuring that the processes that evade conceptualization because of their indeterminate and changing characteristic are not missed or downplayed. These processes particularly prejudge the aesthetic apprehension in experience.

Li points to two aspects of aesthetic pleasure. First, we can feel the same kind of pleasure in responses within significantly different experiences—for instance, artistic and moral.[70] This shows that the discussion of aesthetic experience should not be confined to experiencing artworks, although Li himself mainly resorts to such examples. It should also be remembered that with regard to emotions, Li remains under the influence of Confucianism, where the aesthetic is connected with the ethical. The propriety that cultivates *ren* is part of the moral system, but at the same time it is the pure aesthetic form whose precise performance also bears an aesthetic dimension. Thus, the feeling of pleasure that emerges in an ethically good action is concurrently aesthetic.

Second, the feeling of pleasure can also vary. Li states that "the kind of pleasurable responses we experience are relative to the different arrangements and organizations of the aesthetic psychological construction."[71] This means that aesthetic experience has many modalities and how specifically pleasure is felt depends not only on what object or what properties are specifically experienced. The experience is also constructed on how the enacted response is configured. This particular configuration includes the psychological processes that cannot be entirely explained as elicited by the object. For instance, mood or experiential history are also formative for the enacted response. This again shows that aesthetic experience does not consist in receiving impressions but is coconstituted by the engagement of subjectality's psychological substance.

Types of Aesthetic Pleasure

Although heavily inspired by Kant in understanding the process of aesthetic experience, Li situates his aesthetics on Marxist foundations. This prevents him from delving into analyses of a purely theoretical character, so instead of differentiating between types of beauty, his interest is shifted to how experience is integral with the situated subjectality and new sensuousness. This involves how aesthetic pleasure emerges in apprehension of reality, with regard to which Li distinguishes three aspects: "pleasures of the ear and eye, pleasures of the mind and heart, and pleasure of one's lofty aspiration and moral integrity." These three aspects not only matter in strictly aesthetic terms but play a great importance in the sedimentation of the psychological substance. They develop human sensuous and mental faculties that contribute to a more fine-grained and qualitatively different perception as well as "mental receptivity and capacity." In aesthetics, outputs of this type of sedimentation include aesthetic tastes, concepts, and ideals.[72]

As for pleasures of the ear and the eye (*yue er yue mu* 悦耳悦目), Li refers to these two senses as having undergone the most evident humanization.[73] However, his discussion of pleasure may also refer to the remaining three senses. Li claims that the origin of auditory and visual pleasure is both physiological and cultural. As for physiology, it is the natural foundation of sensuousness, and therefore senses are inseparable from, and influenced by, physiological processes. One of them is the fatigue of senses that results from a long-term, repetitive exposure to similar stimuli. From the perspective of the biological existence of humans, senses need relaxation to recover in order to maintain fast and fastidious perception. Monotonous exposure to stimuli is also detrimental to developing a more fine-grained, awake, and active perception, which matters adaptively. For this reason, senses search for new and varied stimuli. In aesthetic terms, sensory variation is best observable in art, where we are confronted with different styles, some of which are very unnatural in comparison to perceptions in everyday situations.[74] Humans are usually lured by such encounters with new sensory stimulation, which awakens and activates their senses. The pleasure that emerges in such encounters confirms the need for novelty and freshness in sensory stimulation, which can be traced down to the physiological, phylogenetic underpinning. It should also be noted that confronting a new sensory stimulation is not always initially pleasurable. However, according to Li, this case can also be accommodated in physiological terms. On encountering a strange stimulus, humans have to become acquainted with it, and, once familiarization is completed, pleasure can emerge.[75] This can be illustrated by changes in artistic styles, which are nearly always initially contested even by art theoreticians and art critics. Similar examples can also be found beyond art, especially in fashion, where a new collection is initially accepted by few people, then becomes popular, and is finally played out because it is too common.

The other important factor in developing the sensory pleasure is conditioned externally. The molding of the sense organs that has led to aesthetic pleasure is to a large extent connected with the environment in a way that exceeds the basic sensory stimulation. Li describes this conditioning as social but in fact it can be more comprehensively treated as cultural. It consists in the social conditions in which humans live and the rational choices that they make in these circumstances. Li exemplifies this with the

People's Republic of China in the 1950s, when people developed a taste in realistic painting and revolutionary songs, which were replaced by abstract art and rock music after the Cultural Revolution.[76] This shift in aesthetic taste, and what follows, finding pleasure in aesthetic appreciation illustrates the cultural changes of mainland China throughout several decades. Another, even a more representative example can be found in music trends in Western culture from the 1960s to 1980s. The 1960s was a period of important social change in the West, involving political views, pacifism (mainly as a reaction to the Vietnam War), and liberation from conservative social mores. It was accompanied by compositional and expressive innovations in rock music, performed by, for instance Jimi Hendrix or the Doors, performers with whom the hippie subculture identified. The 1970s continued in this mood with alternative rock forms that can be showcased by Led Zeppelin, to be followed in the late 1970s and early 1980s with a greater dissatisfaction directed at government institutions, reflected in punk rock that openly sided with anarchism. It should be noted that the stylistic changes in rock were parallel with political issues and views, fashion, and lifestyle. In this sense, the sensuous pleasure was not only shaped within auditory sensuousness but also cultural processes.

Li believes that the physiological and social factors blend in sensation, which alters human sensuousness, which is no longer merely a perceptive organ. In this sense, sensuousness enjoys freedom in serving not only cognitive but also aesthetic purposes.[77] In this context, aesthetics is a measure of human cultivation through culture and diverse stimuli. Aesthetic apprehension is not bereft of a cognitive function. It provides a more sense-embedded account of reality, which includes the variable aspects that are usually missed in conceptualization. Enactively speaking, aesthetic apprehension is more direct and not necessarily entangled in mental representations that are only then followed by response. Aesthetic experience is more direct in emotionally responding to affordances.

Pleasures of the mind and heart (*yue xin yue yi* 悦心悦意) expose another layer of aesthetic satisfaction, which is not directly connected to the senses. It is broadly understood by Li as the inner world of a human being. This type of pleasure is related to human emotional desire. Similarly to pleasures of the senses, pleasure of the mind and heart becomes more sophisticated and refined by way of humanization.[78] In order to illustrate this type of humanization, Li alludes to Freud in showing that morality and social conventions can suppress the expression of primitive sexual desires, as a result of which they form the unconscious structure. As for their expression, they emerge in a sublimated form as artistic creativity but also as, for instance love letters. The humanization of desires is an alternative way for such expression. It is particularly discernible in aesthetic experience, which involves emotion and sensation, as well as imagination and understanding, the interaction of which illustrates how humanization processes the instinctive desires to achieve refined emotions.[79]

Li claims that aesthetic experience built on human biological stratum possesses universal necessity or social objectivity.[80] He locates the universality in the objective human existence as biological and social beings. In this sense, Li agrees with Kant's belief about the universality of judgment of taste based on humans having the same cognitive faculties.[81] However, in contrast with Kant, his explanation is more comprehensive in considering the material aspect of human existence. Considering embodiment, Li agrees more here with Confucianism in that raw emotionality is calibrated by social behavior to the degree that it is converted into a sensitivity that enables good action as well as, like in the case of ceremonies, aesthetic appreciation of how it is performed. This results from the sedimentation of rationality into emotions. The universality of aesthetic experience can here also be attributed to the common, instinctive emotionality, initially molded by shamanist rituals, about which Li writes in *The Chinese Aesthetic Tradition*.[82]

It is obvious that Li does not hold that the aestheticization of primitive instincts is fed by their suppression. The humanization of primitive desires releases them from suppression so that they can be properly expressed. Converting the instinctive into the aesthetic in fact marks a liberation from repression that is achieved by molding the instincts into human emotions. New emotionality thus achieved is not meant to prevent the primitive instincts from surfacing in behavior but cultivates humans with a qualitatively new emotional sensitivity. As in the pleasure of senses, likewise aestheticization is tantamount to achieving a new personality determined by sensuousness and emotionality.

The final aspect of the aesthetic apprehension of reality is the pleasure of one's lofty aspiration and moral integrity, or, literally, of will and spirit (*yue zhi yue shen* 悦志悦神). It differs from the previously mentioned aspects of pleasure because of the transcendent character it exhibits. This type of pleasure emerges in experience that goes beyond the order of morality and reaches a higher sense of pleasure. The pleasure of lofty aspiration consists in "pursuing and finding satisfaction in certain purposive ideas of morality, and molding and cultivating human will, fortitude, and high ambitions," whereas the pleasure of moral integrity is connected with "the integrity of a subject and a universal being and . . . a supra-moral mental experience." Li believes that pleasure of this kind is encountered in experiencing the sublime, as conceived of by Kant. Experiencing the sublime exceeds the sense-based aesthetic experiences by being exposed to the extreme, infinite magnitude. The pleasure that emerges in this type of experience participates in apprehension of the infinite universe, which can be exemplified by mystical religious experiences in the West or the cosmic harmony of humans and the world in the Chinese tradition. Li explains this experience by the fact that humans, characterized as individual, sensuous, and living in limited space and time, desire to transcend all these limits. This desire is differently expressed across cultures.[83] In the Chinese tradition, harmony is one of the most fundamental features of the cosmos. At the level of sublime experience, humans by virtue of harmony constitute oneness with the cosmos, which annihilates the spatial, temporary, and psychological confinements of their existence. This aspect is particularly emphasized in the *Zhuangzi*. This transcendence takes place at the level of experience phenomenology, although its particular character is conditioned by human embodiment and embeddedness. This can be illustrated by body cultivation practice that is supposed to elicit meditative mental states.

In the previous two aspects of pleasure, Li shows that physiology is sedimented with sociality and sensuousness with rationality. In the case of pleasures of lofty aspiration and moral integrity, physiology is finally overcome by the rational and social.[84] This shows the most refined stratum of humanization of nature. It should be remembered that the transcendent character of this aesthetic experience, which is very similar to mystical state of mind, is phenomenological and enabled by the humanized "human hardware."

Li's notion of aesthetic experience, although often exemplified by literature and visual arts, is clearly not confined to the artistic domain. Li understands aesthetics in the Kantian and Baumgartenian fashion, as the domain of sensuousness. However, Kant's transcendental aesthetics is not developed too far from the description of sense experience, even when the judgment of taste is subjected to a detailed analysis. Li takes the aesthetic a long step further, thanks to anthropological ontology that shows not only the cognitive architecture of subjectality but also how it has been achieved through social practice. This framework is not only a fastidious explanation of the particular character of human cognitive architecture, which is missing in Kant's philosophical system. The humanization of sensuousness allows the aesthetic to be viewed beyond the usual philosophy of art or axiological discourse. The aesthetic is present in cognition, art appreciation, emotional responses, and apparently detached, transcending senses/mystical feeling experiences. Importantly, Li's account of aesthetic experience also shows how it functions in the situated subjectality. Therefore, we achieve a comprehensive account of aesthetics experience, from its phylogenetic and ontogenetic beginnings with practice to the highly humanized human nature operating with highly refined psychological structures.

Conclusions

Li's concept of aesthetic experience reflects his triple philosophical inspiration. As regards Marxism, it is reflected in the external character of experience, which is part of practice that sediments into the subjectality. The aesthetic in experience reveals the new sensuousness that has been achieved in the long process of human development, relying on the practice of manufacturing and using tools. The Marxist perspective also applies in the other direction, as the aesthetic perception manifests itself in a qualitatively different practice and realization of human aims in nature.

It is equally undeniable that Li remains tremendously influenced by Kant while presenting the structure of aesthetic experience. Although the Kantian model is considerably enriched and set on the foundations of anthropological ontology, it can be seen that the thinking behind the structure of aesthetic experience has been considerably informed by Kant's account of cognitive faculties and transcendental aesthetics. In fact, although Li does not favor pragmatism due to its conception of the fundamentally biological adaptation of humans to the environment as well as its overly broad understanding of tool practice,[85] it should be noticed that the pragmatist account of processes involved in aesthetic experience would be more compatible with Li's whole anthropological ontology project. This will be presented in the next chapter.

Confucianism cannot be treated similarly to the other two philosophical inspirations in that it does not influence Li system-wise. However, it is in aesthetic experience in particular where the indispensable Confucian contribution can be observed. Li understands the Confucian cultivation as a process of molding the primitive emotions, which takes place by way of propriety and music. Confucianism aims at achieving a form of sensitivity that, among other things, is manifested in a type of new sensuousness that allows the world to be perceived through a human prism. This molding of emotions complies with Li's concepts both of practice and of aesthetic perception. Considering this aspect of Confucianism, it contributed to explaining how the psychological substance is molded, and, more importantly, the character of aesthetic perception that extends beyond the realm of art.

We can examine how Li's aesthetic experience refers to the spectrum of other existing notions. As in the case of the other concepts mentioned at the beginning of this chapter, one can similarly view Li's through the prism of the four dimensions proposed by Shusterman. As regards the first, evaluative dimension, Li's aesthetic experience includes both the enjoyable and the valuable character. Similarly to Kant, Li regards pleasure as an integral part of aesthetic experience. However, he endows pleasure with more importance. Pleasure penetrates a humanized sensuous apprehension of reality, reflects the uniquely human sedimented emotionality, and enables experiences of suprasensory phenomenology. Hence, pleasure is an indispensable composite of aesthetic experiences on multiple levels. Importantly, these levels also reflect the cognitive dimension of pleasure, by virtue of being enacted, and, at the same time, their humanized character. As part of the subjectality's interaction with and response to the environment, pleasure (or displeasure) is a measure of how subjectality harmonizes with the environment. This reveals the evaluative character of feeling in Li's experience, which finds support in Li's inspiration in Confucianism.

As far as the second, phenomenological dimension is concerned, Li's aesthetic experience is characterized by a phenomenology that is different from other, workaday life experiences. Aesthetic experiences involve attention and are therefore conscious.[86] On the basis of Li's model of aesthetic experience, which consists of the aesthetic attention stage, it would be difficult to think about, for instance, unconscious perception that would lead to an aesthetic experience, as this is built into conscious experiencing. Also, aesthetic experience involves emotion. This already contrasts it with ordinary cognitive experiences. As regards the difference with other experiences that include emotion, it must be noted that in aesthetic apprehension, emotions are not reducible to instinctive, physiological reactions. They are involved in complex, situated cognition and—along with sensation, understanding, and imagination—coconstitute the psychological processes in which aesthetic pleasure emerges. Importantly, aesthetic experience is not only encountered in the reception of artwork, and thus it does not differ from workaday life experiences in terms of object types (in fact, there are nonaesthetic experiences of artworks, for instance, when they are traded) but more in terms of the attitude, attention, and evaluation put together, which results in a different, aesthetic phenomenology.

The third, semantic dimension mostly corresponds to new sensuousness. The humanization of the sense organs has led to a new perception that cannot be reduced to mere physiological receptiveness. Cultural sedimentation has built psychological and cultural components into sensuousness that enable this transcendence from physiological to aesthetic. Thus, humanization can be regarded as a prerequisite for meaningful experience. Enactivistically speaking, perception is an interaction of subjectality with the environment, and, considering that the whole interaction is meaningful, what is conceptually separated in Shusterman's dimension as aesthetic experience is not merely a sensation.

Finally, as regards the fourth, demarcational-definitional dimension, Li's aesthetic experience cannot be confined to the realm of fine art. Li's aesthetic is not based on the aesthetic propensities of artworks and their reception. It is concerned with experience in which the aesthetic can appear in interaction with any part of the environment, which includes nature and artifacts, both artistic and nonartistic.

One might also pose the question whether aesthetic experience is a separate category of experience. As a result of sedimentation, human sense organs have been converted from being purely physiological to aesthetic. As such, the organs have a permanent disposition for aesthetic perception. The same can be stated about the emotional structure of the psychological substance. In other words, human perceptual capabilities are no longer similar to those in other animals—physiological and instinct-driven—and aesthetic perception can be built into most of human perceptual interactions. This can also be supported by Marx's notion of free expression in material production in accordance with laws of beauty. Humans equipped with new sensuousness, in order to fully affirm their humanity, have to engage themselves aesthetically, also by way of perception. Li's concept of aesthetic experience additionally complies with this line of interpretation, as aesthetics is not a philosophical reflection on art.

Considering the above, the status of aesthetic experience as distinct from other types of experience can be questioned. What prejudges an experience to be aesthetic cannot be ascribed to the cognitive faculties, as these can also be involved in nonaesthetic experiences. It seems that a good justification for the distinction is Kant's subsumption under determinate concepts. Aesthetic experience, by virtue of being inclusive of the variable components that result from the interplay of cognitive faculties, including emotion, is indeterminate cognition. However, even this justification is not entirely satisfactory. The nonaesthetic character of conceptual cognition is questioned by John

Dewey, who shows that intellectual experiences, for instance, realized as mathematical operations, also have an inherent aesthetic component, which is described as "internal integration and fulfillment reached through ordered and organized movement." Without the aesthetic, the intellectual would be incomplete, and therefore cognition would not be achieved.[87]

I believe that a distinctive feature of aesthetic experience is that it involves emotion as a cognitively constitutive component. How it matters in aesthetic experience can be explicated in enactivist terms. We can refer to Ioannis Xenakis and Argyris Arnellos who locate aesthetic experience in the adaptive framework of enactivism, which defines the agent's enactments as adaptations to the environment for the sake of self-maintenance. The authors describe aesthetic experience as "naturally engaged when agents interact both with, in general, uncertain physical and cultural contexts."[88] The definition can be referred to Kant's remark on the consciously felt pleasure in cognitive acts that involve the matching of the contingent and the necessary and have not been habituated.[89] Aesthetic experiences meet this condition. Their apprehension of reality is an enactment that is triggered by a "cognitively puzzling" change in the environment and cannot be accommodated by interactive habits. This can be supported by Li's claim that aesthetic pleasure occurs in fresh perceptual situations, whereas through perceptual recursion, aesthetic pleasure will wane.[90] The habituation of such cognitive act agrees with the adaptive and autopoietic reorganization within the agent.

Within the enactive paradigm, the authors indicate that agents' sense-making enactments are evaluation guided. Aesthetic experience is distinct from other cognitive situations due to being primarily emotional. It consists of enactments with emotional evaluation. These evaluations are based on anticipating the possibility of future goal achievement. As the anticipations are not always correct, the agent's interactions are characterized by uncertainty. In this context, aesthetic experience consists in adaptive, emotional evaluations that are meant to minimize uncertainties and maximize goal achievements.[91] This mechanism underpins aesthetic experiences in that the feeling of aesthetic pleasure (or displeasure) emerges depending on whether the value anticipation of goal achievement is positive (or negative). This type of evaluation can be very complex and entail informed responses of a highly cultural nature.

This interpretation remains consistent with Li's aesthetics. Apart from confirming that aesthetic emotions are cognitive by being goal-oriented, informative responses, the interpretation shows that what is regarded as aesthetic value emerges in enactment. Emotion thus conceived agrees with

Li's aesthetic experience conditions of subjective, purposeful enactment with the objective environment, in which the feeling of beauty emerges.

It should be mentioned that these evaluations also apply to complex emotions and rely on experiential history. Within the autopoietic context, there enactments, apart from adaptation, also cause the internal reorganization of the agent. This complies with molding the psychological substance with recursive emotional enactments. It should also be observed that the plasticity of the psychological substance is manifested by changes in aesthetic taste, which results from the accumulated practice. This agrees with the habituation of old experiences and developing new reorganization and adaptation, which relies on aesthetic experiences in cognitively precarious situations. This can be illustrated well by art that usually constructs perceptually, but also conceptually, precarious cognitive situations.

The enactive interpretation, apart from being consistent with Li's theory of both aesthetic experience and the philosophy of subjectality framework, is beneficial for further aesthetic explorations. For instance, as emotional evaluations result from a particular character of psychological substance, enactivism offers an insight into the idiosyncratic dimension of pleasure. Importantly, enactivism does not limit emotional evaluations to positive ones, whereby it can also provide explanations for other aesthetic feelings of, for instance, ugliness or the sublime. However, most importantly, it offers a comprehensive explanation of how aesthetic, cognitive, and interactive elements are combined in aesthetic experience.

Chapter 8

An Alternative Account of Aesthetic Experience

John Dewey

Introduction

As previously mentioned, Li is generally skeptical about pragmatism. When Li mentions the pragmatist approach to Kant's philosophy, he admits that pragmatism similarly holds that knowledge and concepts are of practical provenance. As a result of pragmatist interpretation of cognition, Kant's transcendental forms are supplanted with practical operations on objects. Li approves of this approach because of a resemblance to Marx's view of humans as part of nature and their becoming that necessarily depends on interaction with the world. However, Li concurrently believes this similarity to be considerably superficial. Admittedly, pragmatism underscores the fact that humans interact with the environment, although the interaction is understood in terms of biological adaptation. Li's Marxism-informed anthropological ontology conceives the becoming of humanity as transcending the biological level and supplanting adaptation with human purposiveness. Li also points to pragmatists attaching importance to tool practice, yet their conception of tools is more capacious and even comprises human mental apparatus. Neither does pragmatism regard practice as a means of discovering objective laws.[1] Li holds that the pragmatist conception misses the fundamental Marxist element of social practice. Therefore, it appears to be not only incompatible with Li's philosophical framework but also reductionist in approach.

However, it should be noticed that despite being dismissive of pragmatism, Li actually appropriates a more incompatible philosophical system to his anthropological ontology framework. On reinterpreting through the lens of historical materialism, a modified version of Kant's interplay of cognitive faculties constitutes the framework for aesthetic experience. In fact, considering Li's overall notion of aesthetic experience and the concept of subjectality, the Deweyan-pragmatist account seems to be a more compatible version by virtue of offering a less "intellectual," emotion-based phenomenology of experiencing the aesthetic. Dewey also proposes a similar, anthropological and adaptive aesthetic and embeddedness of the subject in the environment. It should also be acknowledged that Li clearly distinguishes human purposiveness in interaction with environment from its biologically adaptive counterpart, which he ascribed to pragmatism. However, pragmatists do not necessarily regard adaptive interactions as entirely physiological and abstaining from other than biological complexity. For instance, Dewey assumes a far wider anthropological perspective to reveal how humans developed knowledge and art.[2] As will be shown, the human engagement with the environment presented by Dewey converges considerably with Li's concept.

In this chapter, I will present John Dewey's notion of aesthetics and discuss how it is compatible with Li's philosophical aesthetics project. In my discussion, I will mainly demonstrate that the two conceptions converge considerably in the experiential aspect, which involves the aesthetic in cognitive processes. I will also indicate that Dewey's account of experiencing the aesthetic is not only compatible with Li's philosophical framework of anthropological ontology; it is actually an alternative conceptualization that would provide a comprehensive and cohesive phenomenology and process description within Li's aesthetic. Considering Dewey's conceptualization of aesthetic experience within Li's philosophy of subjectality is philosophically worthwhile for two reasons. First, it could supplant a variety of Kant's account of aesthetic experience that in the context of Li's whole philosophical system gives the impression of being imposed on the actual process of experiencing the aesthetic. Second, it offers a possibility to integrate Li's aesthetics with interdisciplinary research into aesthetics.

Anthropological Argumentation

Dewey proposes a notion of aesthetics that is founded on experience. Apart from the processes and phenomenology of aesthetic experience, it is essential to discover the reason why the aesthetic is located in experience rather than, say, artworks, as well as how it is related to human life. One can observe two ways in which this statement is promoted by Dewey: anthropological and, roughly speaking, adaptive.

Simlarly to Li, Dewey clearly states that the aesthetic is not inherent in objects and must involve experience. The object itself has no independent aesthetic standing that can be traced down to its propensities. In fact, the aesthetic can emerge in the experience of any object. This abandons the demarcation line between art and ordinary life objects, as well as artifacts and nature. Dewey refers to an anthropological explanation that the objects that are now regarded as aesthetic, especially in a gallery or museum space, quite often used to be part of everyday life.[3] Not to mention ready-made art, sculpture and painting used to be part of public space decorations, in the same way are murals are now. Interestingly, Dewey refers to a very similar anthropological argument to Li's in claiming that primitive society dances, cave paintings, and shrine decorations were "part of significant life of an organized community."[4] Dewey intends to show that what is nowadays art originally used to be part of the tissue that constituted even very early forms of social life. The fact that the aesthetic is embedded in everyday life is most constitutive for Dewey's theory. There is a continuity between what can be now described as experiencing art and experiences in work-aday life. Therefore, the establishment of art galleries and museums does not testify to the unique status or independent provenance of art; in fact, Dewey holds that museums tend to showcase some nonaesthetic aspects of collective human life, such as the emergence of new political ideologies or economical relations.[5] For Dewey, aesthetics is about experiencing the world, rather than special object propensities.

Dewey's shift of interest from object to experience can be illustrated by his claim that art should not be identified with its products. What defines art is the experienced completeness in the process of production. Interestingly, Dewey illustrates the experiential importance with utensils that he does not value as beautiful. His negative assessment is based on the production process that he describes in the following way:

> Wherever conditions are such as to prevent the act of production from being an experience in which the whole creature is alive and in which he possesses his living through enjoyment, the product will lack something of being esthetic.[6]

The completeness of experience in which pleasure emerges is crucial for the aesthetic engagement. But there is also another aspect that bears important implications for Li's philosophy. Considering that Dewey was overtly critical of capitalism, we can assume that he located his example in a specific social context.[7] Such contextualization brings him close to Marx's estranged labor, which in capitalism prevents the worker from expressing her/his humanity in the free production in accordance with the laws of beauty. Being aware that Dewey does not represent Marxist philosophy, his view on the importance of production, and the experience of the aesthetic that it involves, departs from a very similar intuition. This in turn also situates Dewey very close to Li's understanding of practice that seeks harmony with the world through aesthetic engagement.

Argument from Adaptation to Dynamic Reality

Both Dewey and Li assume a historical and anthropological perspective with regard to the origin of the aesthetic. Aesthetic apprehension emerges from everyday activities of the human collective and is therefore inseparable from life. The similarity between the two philosophical views can be further illustrated by Dewey situating the aesthetic in human adaptation to the environment.

The necessity of considering life is explained in that the life of humans, like other animals, consists in interaction with the environment. Dewey clearly indicates the fact that human beings, as other living organisms, are not closed systems involved in interchanges with the environment, but they interact "in the most intimate way." A human being forms an independent living system that is built into the environment.[8] Accordingly, experience is not only viewed as a sensuous interaction but a complex participation of the subject in the world. This intuition is very similar to Li's assumption that subjectality is not separated from the world but actively lives it.

Dewey describes the environment as a dynamic system characterized as a flux between extremes. This dynamic consists in incessant changes. The changes interlock and sustain each other, as well as pattern in order. Importantly, the order is not externally imposed but intrinsically arranged. Given this, Dewey assumes an organismic, dynamic reality characterized by the regularity of changes. Humans, as part of the environment, are deeply embedded in interaction that is characterized by adaptive purpose, which consists in achieving "at least a temporary equilibrium"[9] with the environment. Due to being an integral part of the world dynamics, humans inevitably undergo moments of discord to reach an equilibrium state. In other words, humans interact with the intention of maintaining a harmonious relation with the environment.

The attainment and loss of harmony forms a certain life rhythm. Dewey points to the fact that the changes in the world do not form identical repetitive cycles in which humans always achieve identical harmony.[10] The world naturally changes through human intentional interaction, or, enactivistically speaking, through enacting a harmonious world. The dynamic and nonrepetitive character of the processes in the world explains why it is impossible to miss disequilibrium. This further patterns Dewey's model according to autopoietic enactivism, because the sense-making enactments take place in precarious situations.

The inevitable dynamic of loss and achievement of harmonious relation does not only take place on the biological or physiological level of living. Humans are conscious of the interchange and the adjustment takes place on the psychological level as well. Here an important role is played by emotions. The phases of imbalance are emotionally indicated, thanks to which humans can reflect on them and overcome the disunity by restoring a harmonious relation with the environment. Desire for harmony turns emotion into interest in the environment. In the moments of balance, responding to the achievement of temporal order with a harmonious feeling is also a reflection that endows the experienced object with meaning.[11] Here, emotion plays a cognitive role in guiding a human being in her/his harmonizing adaptation. It is also present in more complex psychological enactments, especially in aesthetic experience, where the process of achieving harmony is encapsulated in the emotional dynamic.[12] It should also be noticed that the harmonious state is "gratified" with a harmonious feeling, manifested by "happiness and delight." Dewey distinguishes between pleasure and happiness and delight. Pleasure is viewed more in terms of physiological and occurrent by chance reactions.[13] Happiness is an aesthetic pleasure, a more complex response to the achievement of equilibrium.

Apart from the external character of organismic adaptation to the environment, Dewey clearly points out that humans tend to achieve internal order in terms of their temporally existing identity. He also claims that humans as organisms are dynamic systems that increase their complexity that is manifested by increase in fine-grained apprehension of reality as well as new and complex interaction. As for experiential history, Dewey mentions that past experiences do not form static memory but a guidance concerning one's present actions. Integrity is also achieved with the future perspective in terms of motivation.[14] It can be seen that the Dewey's model in this respect patterns with sedimentation, as the complexity of human living in the world is possible thanks to the forging of psychological substance.

It has to be concurrently observed that the inner harmony is integrated and motivated by external adaptation. The inseparability of the environment agrees with Dewey's observation that the usually assumed subject-object division in experience, although distinguishable, is not stringently demarcated in terms of independence. In fact, we cannot talk about a self-sufficient, disconnected psyche. The psychological aspect constitutes an embedded, continuous, coherent identity, whose dynamic depends on adaptive involvement. This only confirms Dewey's choice to talk about the aesthetic in terms of experience. It should also be noticed that Dewey's model in which humans adapt themselves to the environment and constantly reorganize themselves because of experiential history, and with regard to new anticipations built upon them, converges with enactivist autopoiesis. In this sense, the active aspect of aesthetic experience becomes even more visible. The emotional embracing of the world dynamics is the evaluative basis for confronting new affordances and reorganizing internal self-maintaining processes.

Similarly to Li's anthropological ontology, Dewey acknowledges that humans have progressed throughout history by developing the way in which they are purposively involved in the world. Importantly, he claims that culture has come into being as an accumulation of human interactions with the environment.[15] We can infer that Dewey assumes a phylogenetic process that gradually, through recursive interactions, has led to the emergence of a supraphysiological form of life that, inter alia, manifests itself in culture-informed practice. Hence, Dewey's aesthetic operates with a variety of sedimentation, which is not confined to the practice of manufacturing and using tools, however. This can be exemplified by art, where humans are able to consciously unify their sensuousness, needs, impulses, and action. This consists in a human using "the materials and energies of nature with intent to expand his own life," which is done "in accord with the structure of his organism—brain, sense-organs, and muscular system."[16] Art can be here understood as uniquely human practice that serves both the internal development and constitutes a meaningful expression of humanity by transforming nature.

It can be seen that Dewey has similar intuitions to Li in assuming a model of an inconstant reality, in which humans interactively adjust themselves to changes in the environment. The adjustment involves changes both in humans and the environment, which bears a similarity to Li's social practice that both transforms reality and sediments qualitative changes into humans. It involves, but also transcends, the biological foundation of the interaction. Both philosophies assume that, apart from physiological adaptation, there is also independent human purposefulness, according to which humans harmonize with the world consciously and on their own terms. This makes the aesthetic apprehension of reality and interaction a refined, uniquely human form of active involvement in the world. Analogously, in both Dewey's and Li's philosophies, the achievement of harmony with the world is accompanied with the feeling of pleasure, which cannot be reduced to the primitive instinctive pleasures. Although the aesthetic enactment of harmony can be labeled adaptive, it has to be borne in mind that the adaptation is not motivated by instincts but independent purposiveness and involves complex psychological structures.

Aesthetic Cognition

Considering the above-described character of reality, it is important to understand how Dewey refers experiencing the aesthetic to the world and cognition. He admits that although nature can be precisely rendered in the discourse of science, the formalized description of reality misses the whole dynamic and emotional evaluation of it, as can be illustrated by the juxtaposition of gustatory qualities: sweet and bitter. Despite a precise semantic distinction between the two lexical items, their evaluative connotation, which as Dewey holds, was favorable and hostile opposition, is lost. This as well as other aspects are not missed in direct experience of reality through human interaction with it.[17] This is where one can experience the aesthetic, which emerges from the comprehensive and direct apprehension of reality in its dynamic. This situation of aesthetic experience implies that it is cognitive. This aspect of aesthetic experience converges with Li's concept, where experiencing the aesthetic allows the world to be apprehended in its dynamic richness. It cannot be framed in the receptiveness that is aimed at feeling pleasure. Experiencing the aesthetic emerges in interaction instantiating subjectality's harmonization with the world, which involves direct engagement in reality that uncovers it in plenitude.

Dewey contrastively explains how aesthetic experience differs from a scientific or intellectual one. Intellectual experience is predominantly concerned with a conclusion, which has an independent value or truth. In aesthetic experience, its end cannot matter independently but only by virtue of the whole experience.[18] The aesthetic apprehension consists not only in reaching completion but in experiencing the plenitude of the experience throughout all its stages. In this broad sense, Dewey's concept of aesthetic experience shares with Li, and to some extent with Kant, an intuition that the aesthetic encapsulates the richness of experience rather than a specific stratum of it, say, intellectual. For this reason, aesthetic experience is impossible to encapsulate in confining concepts.

Dewey makes an important claim about how aesthetic experience is related to the world. Objects that are aesthetically appreciated must meet objective conditions. The objectivity of the conditions is understood by Dewey as "belonging to the world of physical materials and energies." Thus, the aesthetic appreciation is anchored in reality, even when experiencing highly artistically processed objects is considered. The characteristic feature of reality that is present in both aesthetic and other experiences are "rhythms of nature." They are understood by Dewey as regularities that have always been present in nature. The rhythms of nature direct and have led to the developing of sophisticated adaptive patterns in human practice, such as, for instance, agriculture. The application of the rhythms of nature became wider, and, apart from strict and practical adaptation, rhythms were also employed in celebration, as a result of which, for instance, dance or sculpture came into being. This was followed by other stages, when the regularity of the rhythms of nature was reflected upon, which led to science as well as philosophy. As can be seen, experiences previously qualified as aesthetic and intellectual are founded on, and perpetuate, natural rhythms, which Dewey refers to as "natural laws."[19] Apart from being set in the same adaptive matrix, both the intellectual and the aesthetic experiences can be treated as different expressions of reality, understood as ordered sense-making processes. Because of the fact that the objective feature of reality lies at the core of the aesthetic, the ordering of experience is necessarily rooted in reality. Thus, aesthetic experience is also a form of cognition, different from science in the way it is formulated.

The connection of the aesthetic with the rhythms of nature brings Dewey's aesthetics close to Li's concept. In fact, natural rhythms and social practice can complement each other. From the perspective of natural rhythms, tool practice had to comply with, and was perfected by, the regularities in nature, which have organized human behavior through recursive practice and sedimented into humans as intellectual and aesthetic apprehension. Dewey also believes that humans have to adapt themselves to nature through their actions by following natural laws.[20] This also agrees with Li's philosophy in that humans express themselves subjectively in objective world in accordance with objective laws, which includes the laws of beauty. In this sense, both philosophers endorse a similar model of expression. However, one must remember that Li's objective expression through practice is specifically determined as tool practice.

Aesthetic Experience

Dewey postulates a concept of "*an* experience" that is contrasted with other, incomplete experiences. Assuming completeness and fulfillment as the key features, Dewey describes how an experience is particularly structured. An experience is processual and thus changes over time. The completeness consists in integration of composite experiences into a smooth stream of subsequent parts that culminate in fulfillment.[21] Experience of this kind is not reserved to any particular activity and can be illustrated by examples from everyday life as well as art. Importantly, these experiences are individualized, composed of specific life elements, making each and every experience qualitatively unique. The fact that an experience is composed of concrete parts is essential for assessing its completeness. Holistically speaking, an experience is continuous without any gaps, whereas, individually speaking, none of the parts should have its identity compromised when forming a complete whole.[22] Dewey's composition is not tantamount to a mere sequence of composite experiences that lead to a compositional conclusion. The unified structure necessarily includes the composites combined in their richness in a unified experiential quality and the end as the fulfillment or consummation. This is the sine qua non for experiencing the aesthetic.

Although Dewey discriminates between intellectual and art experiences, an experience also applies to the intellectual activity of thinking, where premises are combined in a way that leads to conclusion, making an experience complete. Dewey also draws attention to the fact that despite the nearly self-evident structural completeness, intellectual experiences also contain an aesthetic composite. The difference between intellectual activity and its opposition, art, consists in the material of which they are constituted. Art works are made of material that consists of qualities, whereas intellectual activity consists of symbols that do not have intrinsic quality. Despite this discrepancy, intellectual actions are also aesthetic, thanks to their internal integration and fulfillment reached in conclusion. Dewey makes a very important claim at this point, namely, that an intellectual experience would be inconclusive without the aesthetic element that is responsible for the unity of experience.[23] This implies that the aesthetic is indispensable in cognition. Otherwise, intellectual actions would be procedures of connecting experienced elements followed mechanically, which is not tantamount to the completeness of experience and, in turn, does not result in conclusion.

Dewey further characterizes the unifying and bringing to completion of an experience as emotional. Aesthetic emotion can be built upon both pleasure and pain. Despite that, emotion is conceptually distinguishable and is not literally a building block of experience. Similarly to Li's structure of aesthetic experience, emotion should be understood instead as a unifying function of experience. It is responsible for selecting appropriate experiential material and adjusting it qualitatively for the sake of experiential unity.[24] Emotion is indispensable in experiencing the aesthetic but also, by virtue of its unifying function, plays an essential role in intellectual activity, which otherwise would not be conclusive. We can characterize emotion as stretching over the whole experience and unifying it with all the dynamics or dramaturgy. Thus, emotion is not only a compositional frame; it adheres to every single event in an experience. Because of the encapsulation of every moment in one, cohesive, and varied feeling, experience does not break down into separate emotions but is rather characterized as a dynamic aspect of the whole experience. This bears an important implication. Emotion is characteristic of the whole experience, not only the subject. Dewey describes emotion as referring to "events and objects in their movement," which additionally emphasizes that the emotional character of experience is a record of its dynamics. Importantly, emotions are not to be mistaken for reflexes, as these are physiological reactions with no unifying faculty, and can be unconscious.[25] This notion of emotion converges with Li's sedimented emotional substance. It enables aesthetic perception, which is particularly understood by Dewey as unifying and making an experience complete. In both cases, emotion is not merely a refined instinctive response but it emerges in the interaction of the subject and the environment. The emergence of emotion makes the interaction meaningful.

Dewey characterizes every experience as interaction that aims toward a feeling of harmony.[26] Thus, an experience can be interpreted as a meaningful enactment of harmony that contains the conscious feeling of unity and completion, manifested by pleasure. This shows the cognitive aspect of an experience that consists in uncovering the intrinsic order of the experienced object.

Structure of Aesthetic Experience

Dewey claims that in aesthetic experience, the various parts mutually adapt to one another to constitute a whole. This is evidently true of artwork reception but also in perceiving nonartistic objects such as an urban landscape. The aesthetic quality of every perceived part, as well as the whole that they constitute, is calibrated by all other parts. This leads to an implication that perception consists in acts that arrange the sensible data into a unified form. Dewey defines the form as "the operation of forces that carry the experience of an event, object, scene, and situation to its own integral fulfillment."[27] What is additionally important here is that the unifying of perception is not an action of imposing some external structure on the object of perception. Quite the contrary, perception helps to arrange the parts into their own form, which emerges from the mutual configuration of the constituent parts. Hence, aesthetic experience uncovers the intrinsic form that dynamically unites the composite experiences into a whole and brings them to fulfillment. In this sense, aesthetic experience is a cognitive act.

Aesthetic form is characterized by the conditions of continuity, cumulation, conservation, tension, and anticipation. They outline the movement toward the consummation of aesthetic experience. During experience, our evaluation cumulates and is conserved for the sake of apprehending the whole object. To constitute an aesthetic experience, the sequence of acts must be in a continuity that is determined by the anticipation of resolution. The experience is additionally characterized by intrinsic tension that fuels development and fulfillment of aesthetic apprehension. The constitution of a unified form requires the engagement of the perceiver, who has to struggle to unify the aesthetic experience. This involves integrating experiential history with the new perception, which requires realignment with the new experience.[28] In aesthetic experience, the result is only as important as the culmination of all the composite, preceding processes, and therefore the perceiver has to remain engaged in the experience throughout every stage. It does not mean that in an intellectual experience one can "jump to conclusions," but since intellectual actions operate with symbols, the emotional engagement in every stage of aesthetic experience is qualitatively different and more direct and intense. In fact, unlike intellectual experience, it can be stated that in Deweyan aesthetic experience, the completion is not the concluding result in the literal sense of the word. It is where the experience finishes, and although it can be distinguished as a separate part in experiential phenomenology, aesthetic experience in fact consists in holistic consummation throughout all stages. This fact also has an important cognitive implication, as the aesthetic cognitive uncovering of aesthetic form is distributed over the whole experience. Considering this stretched location, in comparison to intellectual cognition, where the cognitive moment is final, aesthetic apprehension cannot be intellectually, or therefore conceptually, encapsulated.

Dewey also points to a distinctive feature of the structurally final consummation phase that is especially particular in experiencing art—presenting something new, which reveals itself through unexpectedness or strangeness.[29] Considering that aesthetic experience is not only confined to art, we can interpret strangeness more widely as experiencing something that has not been exactly anticipated. It can be mapped onto enactivism, where a precarious situation entails an adaptive enactment of an autopoietic agent, who has to adjust to new circumstances in the environment. When Dewey introduces strangeness in consummation, he intends to show that art is not merely mechanical and requires a special type of apprehension and consummation. This type of consummation is present in every aesthetic experience, which is not standardized; it is always a unique process in which a human being cannot solely rely on her/his experiential history and actively adapts in the uncovering of a new form. This can also be said of enactivist adaptations, which require an engagement that concurrently changes the intrinsic autopoietic processes.

A More Compatible Alternative?

It can be stated that Dewey's and Li's accounts of aesthetic experience differ considerably at the level of description. Although Li's aesthetic is significantly different from that of Kant, he still refers to viewing aesthetic experience in terms of an interplay of cognitive faculties. However, on closer look, Li's and Dewey's conceptualizations of aesthetic experience are not completely at odds in how the aesthetic is experienced in dynamic reality.

Li's aesthetic experience would be impossible without new sensuousness, which operates with humanized sense organs and emotions that make transcending the physiological and instinctive responses to environment possible. Although Dewey does present a precise corresponding assumption for his aesthetic, it can also be inferred from his anthropological argument that artistic activity and appreciation have developed from the human collective practice of living. The growing sophistication of artistic forms must have been paired with adequate perceptual faculties that have gradually become independent from their instinctive and physiological underpinning. This historical aspect of human perception, which includes sensuousness and emotion, can be more evidently confirmed by internalizing the rhythms of nature. Dewey not only demonstrates that the process involves the recognition of regularities in nature and developing scientific cognition that operates with abstraction. Internalizing the rhythms of nature has also taken place in a more sense-embedded way. It can be exemplified by music, whose perception is possible thanks to developing auditory perception through, for instance, rhythmic accompaniment. This process can be labeled in Li's theory as humanization of the sense organs. The deeply sense-embedded apprehension of reality in a musical way, for instance, was integrated with an appropriate development of emotion, which enabled supra-instinctive attention to, interest in, and response to the world. Like Li, Dewey in using the anthropological argument and proposing the natural rhythms assumes the plasticity of the senses and emotions, which can be molded by recursive practice and experience.

As for the particular stages of aesthetic experience, despite Li's precision manifested by the distribution of functions among cognitive faculties, it can be said that Dewey's account is equally good at capturing the processual character of experience in a dynamic form that reflects human interaction with the environment. The first element in Li's aesthetic experience—sensation—is responsible for humanized sense perception. It can be, for instance, seeing things in processing a two-dimensional image into three-dimensional perception. This aspect of sensuousness has been considered by Dewey in internalizing natural rhythms. The recursive perceptual acts have led to the uncovering of regularities, which has been built into the senses and become an unconscious disposition.

The main function of the understanding in Li's aesthetic experience structure consists in molding an experience into an organic unity, which results in an indefinite cognition. Here it is particularly visible how strong Li's conceptualization is formatted by Kant. Dewey's theory approaches the organization of sensations into an organic unity with emotion, which enables the sensuous plenitude of sensations to be absorbed and encapsulates their dynamic in a complete unity. When compared with Li's conceptualization, Dewey does not try to conform to conceptualization as fulfillment. Aesthetic experience, by virtue of being embodied and wholly embracing sensuousness, is internally unified in emotion. Dewey presents a more direct account of experience as it is, so to speak, constituted on a more fundamental level of sensuousness rather than the result of an interplay of the sensuous and the intellectual. In fact, this element of Dewey's theory appears to be an interesting alternative within Li's account of aesthetic experience, in contrast to the one Li builds on Kant's cognitive faculties. This can be additionally supported by the importance of emotional response in the two philosophies. It is more likely to assume that an emotional experience is concurrently a response to the environment rather than an experience that leads to an indeterminate conceptualization that causes a feeling.

The imagination is an element in Li's aesthetic experience responsible for shaping sensations so that they are "aesthetically processed" by the understanding. Such molding of sensations involves being situated in perceptual habits such as expectations or associations. Dewey's aesthetic experience does not presuppose any specific faculty or function for this. The processing of sensations is viewed more as their mutual configuration and the influence of one's experiential history.

Finally, emotion makes it possible to experience the aesthetic as pleasure. Similarly to Dewey's, aesthetic pleasure in Li's model reflects the dynamic anatomy of the whole aesthetic experience. In this respect, the two philosophers converge in their understanding of emotion. However, in Dewey's aesthetic experience, emotion is largely responsible for constituting the whole aesthetic experience (unifying and pleasure), whereas in Li's concept this is achieved by different faculties.

Comparing the two accounts of aesthetic experience, it can be stated that Li presents a more elaborate conceptualization of the processes that underlie experiencing the aesthetic. However, on considering that in both concepts aesthetics is a form of cognition, and that the aesthetic is closely connected with life and confined to the realm of art, one can express a doubt concerning Li's conceptualization. It is based on the fact that Li, perhaps unnecessarily, distributes the process among four functions, which give the impression of an imposed theoretic construction. This doubt can be supported by the fact that Li, in formulating his account of aesthetic experience, is strongly influenced by Kantian interplay of cognitive faculties—the imagination and the understanding. Transplanting this concept into Li's philosophical framework may not be a perfect match. Although the two faculties are complemented by sensation and emotion, the overall account remains a theoretical construction that may give the impression of being imposed on the very process rather than growing from it. In contrast, Dewey's account offers an emotion-based process, which encapsulates what is governed by the four faculties in Li's theory. It can be stated that Dewey's account is therefore less detailed, but, considering the intangibility of aesthetic experience, it offers several advantages over Li's conceptualization.

One such advantage in Dewey's conceptualization is that aesthetic experience is more emotional than intellectual. Experiencing the aesthetic is founded on sensuousness and emotional response. Although conceptualization of interplay that involves the sensible and intellectual faculties is comprehensive, it can be questioned if it applies to the process that actually takes place. The interplay leads to indeterminate conceptualization, but in fact it is difficult to determine what the actual indeterminacy consists in. Li certainly does not mean a cognitive act that is impossible to conceptualize by virtue of being a perceptual confrontation with something that we have never encountered—for example, an unknown species of plant, which does not fit any concept. Emotional capturing of the experience dynamic is not suitable for conceptualization and attempts to force it into concepts does not result in aesthetic pleasure but is instead a cognitive mistake.

The emotional character of aesthetic experience is not only more convincing in terms of phenomenology. In the perspective of process, aesthetic experience description as an emotional response to the environment is more compatible with scientific accounts of experience. For instance, in affective sciences, the dynamic emotional episode is composed of appraisals.[30] Appraisal theories are founded on the assumption that the organism's evaluation of circumstances is crucial in the elicitation and differentiation of emotions. Appraisals can indicate novelty, pleasantness, certainty or predictability, coping potential, or even compatibility with social and cultural standards.[31] The experiential dynamic can be interpreted as an emotional episode. Hence, the complexity and changes in emotion over time would depend on the constituent appraisals. This may explain how aesthetic experience changes its dynamic and reaches fulfillment. Appraisals also emphasize that the dynamic of emotion is not preset. The appraisals trigger evaluations that can affect the sensorimotor system and conditions of experience (which in fact is an enactment). Thus, emotion is lived and develops in each and every moment. This is compatible with aesthetic experience phenomenology, where the agent is not a witness but a participant in the experience.

Appraisal theory combined with enactivism shows that aesthetic experience can also be viewed as a complex cognitive process that is not intended to reach any type of determinate or indeterminate conceptualization. Enactment includes evaluation, response, and the feeling of pleasure. We should additionally consider the result of the experience that is the emotional consummation felt rather than thought. From this perspective, resorting to an interaction of intellectual faculties appears to be empirically challenging and redundant.

Both Dewey's and Li's aesthetic concepts presuppose a situated subject. Without embodiment and embeddedness, the practice of manufacturing and using tools, as well as internalization of natural rhythms would lose their foothold. The intellectual components in aesthetic experience structure weaken the integral character of aesthetics within the philosophy of subjectality. It ought to be noted that the intellectual is involved at the level of sensibility, where sensations are processed by humanized sense organs and emotion. Considering that the process performed by them is not receptive and is a concurrent interaction with the environment, the integral participation of intellectual faculties is no less problematic than in the first and third *Critiques*. It should also be taken into consideration that the perceptual enactment that is based on the senses and emotions, as well as their cognitive dimension, are more verifiable than intellectual activity in the empirical study of experience.

Conclusion

Dewey's account of aesthetic experience is an interesting alternative to the adapted and converted Kant's interplay of cognitive faculties implanted in Li's aesthetics. It can be summarized by two reasons. First, Dewey's emotional character of experience matches anthropological ontology well. It inclines more toward the interpretation that complex experiences of nonphysiological and noninstinctive motivation can be handled by humanized sensuousness and emotions. In other words, the humanization of these two aspects can be better explored in an emotion-based account of aesthetic experience.

Second, considering that perception, including emotions, is embodied, Dewey's conceptualization opens aesthetic experience for interdisciplinary, and especially psychological, research. Since Li seeks development and explanation of his psychological substance conception in neurosciences and psychology,[32] a reconceptualization of experience in a way that focuses less on dualism, would be more compatible for further research.

Chapter 9

Contemporary Experience-Based Aesthetics

Introduction

This chapter is devoted to analyzing how Li's aesthetic can be situated in contemporary philosophical aesthetics research. At the outset, one must acknowledge that research into aesthetics covers a vast area and is represented by various approaches. For obvious reasons, Li's aesthetic, as every particular theory, can only refer to part of it. Therefore, the discussion will take place within the branch demarcated by shared assumptions and approaches.

I regard Li's aesthetic as particularly compatible with the family of aesthetic theories that can be determined by means of three shared features. First and foremost, it is focus on experience, which can be treated as the departure point for further theoretical development. This entails that the main field of concern is how one experiences the aesthetic or what constitutes aesthetic experience. Such a scope naturally puts emphasis on the processes and conditions of experiencing the aesthetic. This orientation is naturally connected with the question of the objects or events involved in experience, which leads to the second feature that can be described as not being tantamount to philosophy of art. This qualification does not exclude art from aesthetic experience or aesthetic study. The feature only indicates that aesthetics is not to be conceived as a philosophical reflection on art. This means that aesthetics does not presuppose art as its only or central object of study and offers a wider scope. Finally, the third feature, similarly to the previous one, presented in the form of a negative characteristic, situates aesthetics beyond axiology. This emphasizes the focus on aesthetic experience as an account of processes that lead to experiencing the aesthetic rather than, for instance, concept-based discussion on the nature of beauty or other aesthetic values.

Considering the character of aesthetics determined by these three features, I will focus on theories proposed by Bence Nanay and Wolfgang Welsch. However, my choice of these two particular theories is not only dictated by the fact that they endorse an experience-oriented concept. Apart from philosophizing in this particular vein, both Nanay and Welsch clearly discuss how aesthetics as a discipline should be conceptualized in particular, and, accordingly, what aesthetic research should focus on. More generally, they try to determine how aesthetics is located in, and refers to, other philosophical disciplines. The two proposed conceptualizations also considerably differ from each other, which allows experience-based aesthetics to be presented from varying standpoints.

I will mainly focus on how Nanay and Welsch conceptualize aesthetics as a philosophical discipline and demonstrate how Li's notion of aesthetics can be viewed from this particular angle. I will start from discussing the concepts of aesthetics proposed by Nanay and Welsch and show where their intuitions overlap with Li's. Next, I will proceed to present how Li's idea can enter the discussion about the shape of aesthetics in this particular branch and discuss what possible contribution it can make toward conceptualizing contemporary aesthetics.

Bence Nanay's Aesthetics in a Perceptual Paradigm

Although Nanay's construction of aesthetics is founded on experience, at the very outset we must state that he opposes recognizing aesthetic experience as a separate category of experience. Nanay believes that aesthetic experiences that are usually referred to as "aesthetic" are of high intensity or emotional significance. However, many particular experiences of different kinds can meet these criteria, and, therefore, it is difficult to define aesthetic experience in a distinctive and exhaustive way.[1] Nevertheless, dismissing the uniqueness of aesthetic experience does not prevent Nanay from remaining within the general experiential framework and proposing his concept of aesthetics as a philosophy of perception.

To this end, Nanay first contrasts his concept with philosophy of art. This discipline is defined as a philosophical inquiry into art.[2] Such an understanding entails a variety of philosophical approaches to art, which can include epistemological, metaphysical, and axiological ones. Despite a wide scope in terms of approach, focusing exclusively on art would not exhaust all the issues that belong to the discipline of aesthetics. It should also be noted that not all aesthetic issues necessarily apply to art,[3] as well as the fact that art can function very well beyond the aesthetic framework.

Nanay claims that aesthetics can be viewed in terms of philosophy of perception. This claim has two provisos. The first one is that aesthetics is not to be viewed as a subdiscipline of the philosophy of perception. What is actually meant is that there are many problems in aesthetics that can be effectively investigated from a philosophy of perception perspective. Thus, aesthetics remains an independent discipline. The latter proviso supplements the former in that philosophy of perception does not address all issues that can be found in aesthetics.[4] Considering this explication, Nanay does not actually argue for identifying aesthetics as philosophy of perception. What is intended is actually offering a philosophy of perception framework that is supposed to address the problems present in what is regarded as aesthetic research.

The philosophy of perception that addresses aesthetics is construed broadly. It comprises of a variety of questions relevant to perception, as well as those related to it. Accordingly, some issues, such as the difference between perception and belief or rationality in perception can be equally well encountered in the philosophy of mind. The very concept of perception is conceived equally broadly. Perception is not meant here as what takes place in sensibility, but is also intertwined with—for instance—conceptualization, attention, sensory imagination, and influences from top-down processes that are not perceptual.[5] It can be said that perception encapsulates the processes involved in both sensory and mental perception. Thus, the philosophy of perception can also be viewed as a study of perception integrated with some philosophy of mind. On one hand, assuming such an approach to aesthetics can lead to the statement that it is mainly process-oriented, which might be regarded as confinement. However, on the other hand, the approach is highly comprehensive with regard to the wide range of processes that are related to perception and the production of imagery.[6]

As for the motivation to apply philosophy of perception thus construed to aesthetics, Nanay claims that it offers a promising research opportunity to investigate problems and debates that belong to aesthetics. He further claims that "some of the most productive and relevant debates in aesthetics have been and are about the philosophy of perception and the ones that are not particularly productive or relevant are not," as well as that "the success of this research direction in the present and recent past gives us some (not overwhelming) reason to follow this research direction in the future."[7] It can be seen that the perspective of philosophy of perception has not been proposed for theoretical reasons only. Nanay considers the recent and present state of the art in the discipline that in turn makes him propose this particular conceptualization of aesthetics.

By referring to Imre Lakatos's view that in the long run progressive research programs (understood as "temporal sequence[s] of a set of various different theories") should supplant the degenerative ones,[8] Nanay argues that the state of the art in aesthetics creates the possibility to consider the philosophy of perception. The change is beneficial by virtue of including new or downplayed directions of research that would be incompatible or considered unlikely to develop if they were to remain within the confines of the old research program. Considering this, one can state that the motivation behind this proposal is dictated by pragmatic reason in the sense that it optimizes the current and future research in the field.

To justify a new turn in aesthetics research, Nanay has to prove that we can really observe a tendency toward the research that can be thoroughly and insightfully explored in terms of philosophy of perception. To illustrate this, he refers to a fundamental debate on the nature of aesthetic experience, where he distinguishes three kinds of theories. The first one defines aesthetic experiences in terms of properties represented in experience, while the second deals with the role that experiences play in mental processing, and the third examines the intrinsic properties of experiences. First, it can be seen that all three determine the difference between aesthetic and nonaesthetic with regard to the aspects that belong to the philosophy of perception. Second, the question of properties representation sits among the most important issues in the philosophy of perception. The question of the role of aesthetic experience in mental life is mostly discussed by aestheticians in perceptual terms. Finally, as regards the intrinsic distinctive properties of aesthetic experience, one of the most discussed properties—aesthetic attention belongs to the core of perception-related issues. Importantly, Nanay does not intend to show that all experiences are necessarily perceptual but that they can be explored by the philosophy of perception.[9]

Another example of a fundamental debate in aesthetics is connected with the nature of depiction. Here one can also distinguish between three main trends: that only pictures have syntactic properties and semantic properties, or that they elicit a certain perceptual state in particular observers. Considering the state of the art, Nanay concludes that the third approach is progressive, whereas the remaining two, which are not related to perception, are degenerative.[10]

It appears that this line of argumentation could be debunked with another, long-standing aesthetic debate of an axiological nature, connected with aesthetic values. However, Nanay points to the important fact that aesthetic values discussion used to be connected with the philosophy of art, not aesthetics. He also believes that on the ground of aesthetics, value can be viewed more in terms of experiential properties, which redirects the discussion to philosophy of perception.[11]

These three examples show that the argument for philosophy of perception is based on the contemporary productive and progressive issues in aesthetics being within the scope of a broadly construed philosophy of perception. The argument for philosophy of perception is also based on the premise that progressive programs should be promoted.

Apart from being problematized within the philosophy of perception paradigm, aesthetics can also benefit the methodological front, mainly because the philosophy of perception research is often supported by evidence from empirical sciences.[12] Considering this, aesthetics viewed in terms of the philosophy of perception can also refer to methodologies that are empirically informed. The possibility of referring to empirical research can enrich aesthetics by investigating some problems that have been so far viewed only from a theoretical standpoint. One such example is how patients with brain lesions, such as optic ataxia or visual agnosia, perceive pictures differently.[13] On the level of purely theoretical research, aesthetics does not consider, for instance, special cases or peripheral factors. By operating with empirically informed methodologies, cases of nonstandard perception in subjects and the conditions under which it takes place may also be considered.

Nanay's concept of aesthetics as a discipline agrees with the three features that determine a group of theories that are convergent with Li's. It would be difficult to think about proposing a philosophy of perception paradigm without contextualizing it in experience. This connection is natural in terms of both concept and methodology. Neither is this concept tantamount to philosophy of art or axiology. Nanay's proposal emerges from the state of the art in aesthetics, not only aiming to accommodate the widest possible spectrum of research in the field but also concentrating particularly on its most dynamic and promising research directions. One of the benefits of such an approach is opening aesthetics to empirically informed methodologies that can test aesthetic theory.

As previously mentioned, this motivation is pragmatic in character, as it aims at optimizing the progressive fronts of aesthetic research. This could lead to the interpretation that conceptualizations of aesthetics, and, more generally, other philosophical disciplines, are temporal. Aesthetics, along with other disciplines, needs reconceptualization, owing to the occurrence of directions of research that require entirely new paradigms. From a wider perspective, this can be viewed in terms of Li's sedimentation and humanization of nature theory. Social practice leads to the emergence of new tools, which concurrently determine an entirely new world constituted in interaction with subjectality. With regard to aesthetics, this is particularly apparent in the case of visual media technologies that allow unprecedented image mediation. This in turn affects our perception of the world. For instance, the use of icons instead of real objects and descriptions in computer interfaces and mobile devices entails a different and new perceptual and sensorimotor processing. The recursive practice of using such technologically advanced tools results in sedimenting into the subjectality psychological structures that are responsible for qualitatively new perceptual processes. This in turn also results in a new theoretical reflection on human practice in the world reflected, inter alia, in aesthetics. In this sense, the temporal status of aesthetic conceptions and the need to "upgrade them" to a new reality reflects the dynamic process of humanizing nature.

It should also be observed that, in the context of Li's aesthetics, Nanay's postulated concept converges with the core of the aesthetic. Aesthetics begins with a specific apprehension of reality, which would not be possible without the new sensuousness. Hence, the fundamental aspect of Li's aesthetics can be attributed to philosophy of perception.

Wolfgang Welsch's Transdiciplinarity of Aesthetics

Welsch is a proponent of a wide and inclusive view on aesthetics as a discipline. His concept is indispensably connected with the experiential paradigm, and it can in fact be said that his multifaceted discussion of aesthetics illustrates that a large part of contemporary research in this discipline may be viewed in terms of how humans apprehend reality.

In Welsch's discussion, the aesthetic is free from philosophy of art and axiological confinements. Welsch clearly points to the fact that, historically speaking, most of what has been referred to as aesthetic research is in fact philosophy of art. To differentiate this research from aesthetics, he coins the term "artistics." Instead of following the artistics interpretation of aesthetics, Welsch returns to the etymological source of the word "aesthetics" in ancient Greek—*aisthesis*, which denotes sensation and perception.[14] It can be seen that, on a general level, Welsch inclines toward Baumgarten's, and to some extent Kant's, understanding of aesthetics as the study of sensuous perception.

However, it would also be incorrect to understand aesthetics solely as the study of sensuousness and perception. Welsch proposes that aesthetics should not be conceptualized in a monolithic and categorical way, but in terms of pluralistic paradigms. This postulate is motivated by two reasons. The first is a thorough aestheticization of human life and environment on an unprecedented global scale. As for humans, not only do they undergo aestheticization of their appearance, but also of their behavior and what can be roughly referred to as spiritual life. The intensity of the aesthetic formatting of these aspects of human life has led to an aesthetic lifestyle. As regards the environment, aestheticization has seized both urban landscape and nature. Aesthetics is also prevalent in some areas with which it is not usually associated. For instance, in the economy one can observe not simply the sale of goods but also a lifestyle attached to it.[15] Interestingly, one can also observe shifting emphasis from the former to the latter, which mirrors the aestheticization process. The global character and intensity of aestheticization exerts an influence on aesthetics as a discipline, which has never operated on such a large scale. This can be particularly well contrasted with art-centered aesthetics, which has not considered extending to everyday life. In fact, aesthetics as such faces a new type of the aesthetic that is deeply present in human identity by means of lifestyle, which makes humans perceive and respond to the world in an aesthetic way. These conditions, as Welsch believes, require an entirely new reorganization of aesthetics, which is unlikely to retain a theoretically monolithic shape.

The second reason is connected with aesthetic apprehension of reality. Whereas in the aestheticization of the world we are confronted with what is largely external to humans, apprehension is an intrinsic process. It is connected with electronic mediation of reality. Like every mediation, it constitutes a selection from the part of reality that it presents. Another important feature relates to the very character of mediation, which in comparison to reality and other media is pictorially dominated.[16] As a result, the object of apprehension is already ordered and converted into a particular medium and thus molds certain perceptual habits.

Another and more specific dimension of the aesthetic apprehension is epistemological aestheticization connected with Baumgarten's claim that, for humans, every truth possesses an aesthetic component, and that conceptual truth "cannot do justice" to individual reality. This can be accomplished by aesthetics (understood in Baumgartenian terms). For this reason, cognition should comprise the logical merged with the aesthetic.[17] Considering this, human cognitive processes are not detached from aesthetic processing of reality, which is built into the human cognitive structures. As a result, knowledge, including scientific, is to some degree determined by aesthetic factors. The aesthetic dimension of cognitive structures paired with the mediation of reality further amplifies the overall character of the aesthetic apprehension of reality.

There are also two important outcomes connected with electronic mediation. The first is named by Welsch as a "derealization of reality"—reality in electronic mediation loses its constancy and can be freely processed. As a result, although being aware of the molding of reality in the media, we do not know the verity of the representations.[18] This epistemological situation resembles being confronted with phenomena and concurrently being unable to verify what they represent from their corresponding noumena. This gradually leads to epistemic indifference and shifting apprehension of the world from reality to its electronic representation.

The epistemological consequences are paralleled with a metaphysical one. It consists in the melting of metaphysical foundations by shifting cognition from things to phenomena.[19] This leads to a redefinition of cognition in aesthetic terms. The cognitive objective is no longer located in reality but how a mediated object is configured in our cognition. This attitude also involves describing reality in entirely new terms. The ontological categories, which refer to being, are replaced with aesthetic ones referring to state. Hence, according to Welsch, the classical ontological categories such as being, reality, constancy, or actuality have been supplanted with appearance, mobility, baselessness, and suspension.[20] In this sense, the main objective of metaphysics—the account of reality—has been exchanged for an aesthetic one, which does not refer to "hard metaphysics" for the sake of depicting the reality constituted in the experience of mediation.

Melting the metaphysical foundations of reality is also connected with human basic cognitive structures that contain aesthetic components. They function similarly to Kant's a priori intuitions that constitute the experienced reality in space and time. Thus, our cognition of reality somehow preordained in a particular way inevitably disconnects us from the metaphysical foundations. In such a case, the foundations are no longer of metaphysical importance in the sense that we are concerned with how the existential and essential representations are dependent on them.

The second phenomenon is described by Welsch as anaestheticization. It is an outcome of two processes, the global aestheticization and electronic mediation. The omnipresent aestheticization, both within and without humans, causes loss of the original aesthetic sensitivity.[21] As a result, we are literally plunged into an aesthetically organized life and world, concurrently unable to experience them in an aesthetic way.

The above processes mean that aesthetics as discipline has to confront these processes and the aesthetic problems that they generate must assume the experiential paradigm. Focus on the aesthetic propensities of objects as an inappropriate approach can be dismissed by the complicated status mediated by the propensities of objects. The experiential paradigm also allows for a more determinate observation, namely, that aesthetic problems can and should be viewed in the perception and action perspective, which here must constitute aesthetic experience.

The character of the two processes confirms Welsch's observation that aesthetics cannot be monolithically determined. Contrary to artistics or axiological conceptualizations, contemporary aesthetics embraces a wider range of phenomena, whereby it generates different theoretical problems that need to be addressed with varied methodologies. Considering this, Welsch proposes a Wittgensteinian family resemblance–based understanding of aesthetics. Accordingly, the aesthetic is characterized by several semantic elements that interact with each other. They refer to the expected sensuousness, hedonistic, artistic, phenomenalistic, but also less obvious semantic fields, such as the cosmetic (related to the formal arrangement of experienced material), poietic (connected with the production of aesthetic objects), or elevatory (pointing to transcending the usual).[22] Considering that the aesthetic is distributed among a number of different meanings, it constitutes a sematic field rather than a clear-cut definition. Therefore, aesthetics should be understood as a capacious and diverse field of study that should not be constrained to some single area that it covers. It can also be stated that the polysemous character of aesthetics does not only imply that it evades a precise definition. Experience-wise, such a diverse and unconstrained understanding of aesthetics suggests that it is present and matters in many aspects of human life. With regard to this, Welsch believes that the aesthetic has not only penetrated our environment, but also changes and organizes our widely understood life in many dimensions, ranging from physical to intellectual.

The family resemblance encapsulation of aesthetics described above also entails a diverse interdisciplinary approach, which, according to Welsch, should be composed of philosophy, sociology, art history, psychology, anthropology, and neurosciences, among others.[23] It can be observed that aesthetics thus conceived is an interdisciplinary study that involves not only philosophical disciplines. Reference to social, cultural, historical, and biological sciences is necessitated by the scope of Welsch's aesthetics and promotes an integrated approach. His concept of aesthetics, by adjusting methodology to the changing object of study reveals concern with comprehensiveness and inclusion of the whole aesthetic domain.

Welsch's proposal can be summed up as highly comprehensive. Not only does it consider the new phenomena that necessitate a redefinition of aesthetics but it also embraces the past and contemporary traditional theories. It can also be seen that Welsch inclines toward the experiential paradigm as the new aesthetic phenomena that make the difference are related to apprehension of reality. It should also be noted that the need for redefinition can be interpreted as an indicator of another progress in Li's humanization of nature, which invites a few further observations.

As regards the aestheticization and apprehension of the world,[24] they can be viewed as underscoring the importance of tool practice. On the grounds of the reality described by Welsch, tools are various technological means of producing aesthetic objects, which can be electronically mediated. They bring a new quality to the world, often thanks to requiring interaction. The global prevalence and intensity of interaction can be exemplified with smartphone applications, computer games, and social media, which emphasize the active character of perception. At least on the phenomenological level, perception is simultaneous with action. Hence, in Welsch's aestheticization, experiences should be viewed in a paradigm where perceptions are also actions.

As for one of the side effects of aestheticization, namely, anaestheticization, in terms of anthropological ontology, it shows the effect of recursive, accumulated perceptual practice and molding of the material world. In the course of this practice, humans have habituated the aesthetic perception, which has lost its distinctive character of aesthetic apprehension. Under such circumstances, aesthetic pleasure is no longer felt.[25] This shows that in the context of social practice and sedimentation of new psychological structures, aestheticization entails anaestheticization.

Social practice is also compatible with epistemological aestheticization. Cognition is not a receptive process but rather an enactment of a world, particularly in this case, which is shaped by human aesthetic needs. For this reason, the concern for metaphysical reality becomes nullified and shifted to how it is aesthetically organized in experience. The cognitive structures that organize cognition in this fashion have been sedimented into humans through long social practice that has developed needs in human life other than physiological and instinctive. The new aesthetic-cognitive structures enable a comprehensive apprehension and practice in the aesthetically humanized nature.

It should also be noted that apprehension of reality thus conceived is performed by a particular psychological substance, in a given time in the history of human practice. This has special implications for scientific practice. Welsch points out that, for many scientists, cognition is more of production than reproduction, as it involves imaginative abilities in research, by which it also involves an aesthetic component.[26] Scientific, but also philosophical, theories are temporal, as they accompany the dynamic, progressive reality as a reflection upon it. Aesthetic apprehension of reality, as the cognitive capacity of psychological substance, is also highly sensitive to the changes in social practice that lead to a new aesthetic configuration of reality. The aesthetic component organizes the experienced material in a certain way, which also informs the theories that explain them. Welsch provides examples of scientists who used certain aesthetic formats to construct their theories. One of them was deciphering the DNA structure by James Dewey Watson, who admitted assuming at the outset of his research that the result would be of "utmost elegance." This shows that scientists include aesthetic premises in their research. They can also aesthetically pattern or illustrate their theories. One of such examples in astronomy is presenting the origin of the universe in the convention of the Big Bang.[27] These aesthetic components are not only conducive to explaining but also producing scientific theories. They are included in the premises concerning the character of potential discovery or format the whole narration of a scientific theory.

One might also note some important anthropological implications. Welsch believes that the aestheticization of reality and apprehension results in *homo aestheticus*, who is a role model characterized by being hedonistic, sensitive, educated, and discerning in taste, manifested by certain physical looks, spirituality, and behavior.[28] Electronic media, especially social media, have become a real anthropological habitat of *homo aestheticus*. The intense merging of life with the media has resulted in adapting the former to the conventions produced by the latter. One such instance may be patterns of self-expression in accordance with the poetics of online communicators.

The determinants of *homo aestheticus* are temporal, which can be explained by the plasticity of psychological substance that is molded by recursive experiences and actions, which are in fact enactments of an aesthetically meaningful world. It consists in human practice with the use of new technologies that are integrated with new, aesthetically adapted sensorimotor processes. This results in developing particular aspects of *homo aestheticus*, who can be understood as an aesthetic dimension of subjectality.

It should be noted that aesthetics is not only an indicator of a new sedimentation and a new *homo aestheticus*. It also indicates habituations that are tantamount to completing particular sedimentations of psychological structures. It can be said that aesthetics thriving on new experiential challenges and habituations moves subjectality to new and cognitively uncertain situations. In this sense, anaesthetics, which results from a lack of unexpected phenomena, is integral and indirectly stimulates the progress of aesthetics.

Conclusions

The redefinitions of aesthetics in Nanay's and Welsch's proposals can be characterized as inclusivist with regard to the range as well as new directions of aesthetic research. Both theories regard the aesthetic as an aspect of experience that stretches beyond the beaten track of artwork appreciation and discussing aesthetic values. Although Nanay and Welsch clearly abstain from being associated with philosophy of art, they are not dismissive of the art realm as an area where the aesthetic matters. The two concepts also reveal flexibility in methodology, which allows aesthetic problems to be approached from an interdisciplinary perspective.

It should also be noted that the two contemporary aesthetic paradigms presented above do not separate aesthetics from cognition. Conceptualizing aesthetics in an experiential paradigm, as well as in terms of sensuousness and perception, inevitably involves cognitive processes. The connection of the aesthetic and the cognitive illustrates a more widely held, especially in naturalized approaches such as neuroaesthetics, conviction that aesthetics is a form of cognition.[29]

The openness in terms of thematic range as well as methodology is broadly dictated by the concern for new and promising research directions. As previously mentioned, Nanay and Welsch assume the temporal aspect of research that necessitates a reorganization of aesthetics as a discipline. Hence, it can be stated that the solutions proposed by the two philosophers are still relevant, but also temporal, as it can be justifiably assumed that future research will need further theoretical adjustments. In this respect, Li's concept of aesthetics offers a solution that can be characterized with a stronger temporal durability. The two proposals, by virtue of being actual solutions, are aesthetic formations at a given time in the history of human practice, from the perspective of Li's theory. Thus, it can be said that Li's aesthetics is metatheoretical with regard to time-particular conceptualizations of aesthetics. In this sense, Li's theory persists through different stages of human practice that entails the inevitability of modifying the conceptions of aesthetics.

Li's historical understanding of aesthetics does not only provide a universal framework that explains the occurrence of new aesthetic conceptualizations (and, subsequently, conceptions). As the historical materialist perspective attributes the changes to the result of social practice, it reveals an explanatory potential of why particular aesthetic conceptualizations occur in a definite historical time. Social practice views the transformation of humanity and the world as meaningful, and thus the changes in the human apprehension of reality are not accidental. Humans become equipped with a new sensuousness that is relative to the stage of their practice, manifested by the use of tools and technologies. In this sense, the particular changes in human apprehension of the world as well as reflection upon it from an aesthetic angle are explainable on the grounds of the dynamic concept of Li's aesthetic.

The historical character of Li's aesthetic entails flexibility in interdisciplinary approaches, which result from progressive human reflection upon a dynamically changing reality. At the historical level, Li's theory already refers to anthropology, cognitive psychology, evolutionary psychology, sociology, history of culture, literature, and art, which are indispensable in explaining the trajectory of aesthetic apprehension of the world, as well as transforming the world in accordance with the laws of beauty. It must be remembered that, in this respect, Li's aesthetics constitutes a dynamic system and the configuration of disciplines it refers to changes according to the progress of social practice. Hence, Li's concept of aesthetics should not be identified with a particular approach configuration. This flexibility constitutes an advantage within the family of experience-based aesthetic theories, as its assumptions already consider methodological adjustment to the dynamic reality.

Li's aesthetic can also be characterized as compatible with the 4E contextualization of aesthetic experience, which allows resorting to research conducted at the intersections of, for instance, naturalized epistemology, philosophy of mind, philosophy of perception, cognitive psychology, and neurosciences. The compatibility with such interdisciplinary methodology enables further exploration of the role of psychological substance in aesthetic apprehension as well as naturalized aesthetic research. This can be seen as another actual paradigm of aesthetic research.

Finally, Li is very consistent in determining social practice in terms of tool manufacturing and use, in opposition to a more inclusive understanding of Western Marxists. However, this confinement may seem to be an interesting problem to be investigated by aesthetics. This invites research into how the manual practice of tool use has molded the human mind in a way that has led to the emergence of an "aesthetic mindset." This problem seems to be particularly worth exploring in connection with artistic practice, where artists think through the material in which they work and experience of the aesthetic strongly depends on the medium in which they work.

Afterword

My intention throughout the book has been to reveal the implicit cognitive dimension of Li Zehou's aesthetics. I believe that offering attention to this aspect underscores the importance of aesthetics not only as a separate concept but an integral part of Li's entire philosophical system. The cognitive perspective allows aesthetics to be viewed as a novel form of apprehending reality that, by transcending physiology and instincts, is an integral part of a human being who purposively interacts with the world.

Li's aesthetics constitutes a form of cognition that provides an insight into the dynamic of experience. As such, it involves interaction with the world within the framework of situated processes. In this respect, Li's aesthetics dovetails with the perspective of situated cognition and contemporary aesthetic research that is characterized by an interdisciplinary and naturalized approach. Considering the compatibility that Li's theory reveals, one may consider whether it can contribute to the contemporary aesthetic research conducted globally.

One of the possible areas of contribution could be the historical perspective of Li's aesthetics. Although the historical approach entails the temporal nature of aesthetic conceptions, it tries to determine the conditions that have led to a particular theory. In light of such an approach, aesthetics, by being dependent on psychological as well as anthropological and social dimensions of human life, can be conceptualized as a study of a continuously changing apprehension of reality. Such an approach could possibly complement research into particular processes involved in aesthetic experience with a special focus on the transformation of these processes through time. Accordingly, particular aesthetic approaches could be systematized and explained in terms of their emergence at a particular time in history, determined by a particular culture. Obviously, culture should not be associated merely with "high culture," such as fine art, but also technology and everyday life, as all of them intertwine in the complex tissue of human practice. This opens an interesting path to investigate how aesthetic cognition is interspersed with multiple social and cultural processes that are seldom included in philosophical research.

Another possible contribution that follows from the historical character of Li's aesthetics is methodological openness, or, to be more precise, methodological flexibility. The integration of aesthetics with empirical sciences naturally entails continuous configuration of methodologies that are most suitable for examining the transforming world and cognitive structures. The reconfiguration does not only consist in updating but is also open to radical reconstructions of methodologies. In this sense, Li's aesthetics offers a framework for aesthetics that is not prone to methodological stagnation. Such a conceptualization of aesthetics could ensure the continuity of aesthetic research, which would resemble sailing the ship of Theseus.

The interconnection of aesthetics with other disciplines in the historical framework can also be conducive to other types of philosophical investigation. For instance, it can explain the origin and formation of particular epistemological theories as well as different conceptions of ethics. All of these emerge in the history of human practice and are interconnected with the aesthetic apprehension of reality, believed by Li to best reflect the becoming of humans.

From a more practical perspective, one characteristic of Li's theory is the assumption of a dynamic reality in which humans are actively engaged. This model of reality entails human engagement, which involves idiosyncratic adjustment in accordance with objective and concurrently dynamic laws. Importantly, humans as part of the world are also subject to the transformation of the world, which continuously influences their cognitive structures. The aesthetic apprehension of reality would appear to be optimal in making the world meaningful in multiple aspects. This is necessary for a practical understanding of the world through living it meaningfully. This interactive character of aesthetic apprehension brings Li's theory alongside not only Dewey's concept but also a wide range of contemporary aesthetic research that considers the complexity of situated experience. Complementing it with the dynamic character of reality paired with the plasticity of psychological structures may offer another insight into how the aesthetic reflects the interrelation between cognition and the world.

Human practice is built into this interactive model. Considering that the world of aesthetic apprehension consists of a qualitatively novel perceptual layer, which is integrated with interaction, the practice of manufacturing and using tools can offer an interesting conceptualization of the constituting sensorimotor processes that underpin the new aesthetic perception. Additionally, tool practice brings an anthropological perspective that allows particular types of apprehension to be traced and explained in a wider, phylogenetic context.

As can be seen, Li's aesthetics reveals its potential for further development on several fronts. Thanks to being an open system in a methodological respect, it lends itself to extension within an interdisciplinary approach that operates with diverse methodologies, which is one of the most promising and progressive directions of research in contemporary aesthetics.

Notes

Introduction

1. For instance, research on this front is made by Alfonsina Scarinzi, "Enactive Literariness and Aesthetic Experience: From Mental Schemata to Anti-representationalism," in *Aesthetics and the Embodied Mind: Beyond Art Theory and the Cartesian Mind-Body Dichotomy*, ed. Alfonsina Scarinzi (Dordrecht: Springer, 2015), 261–80; Mark Johnson, *The Aesthetics of Meaning and Thought: The Bodily Roots of Philosophy, Science, Morality, and Art* (Chicago: University of Chicago Press, 2018); and Vittorio Gallese, "The Aesthetic World in the Digital Era: A Call to Arms for Experimental Aesthetics," *Reti, Saperi, Linguaggi*, no. 1 (2020): 55–84.

2. Theories of this kind are proposed by, for instance, Wolfang Welsch, *Undoing Aesthetics*, trans. Andrew Inkpin (London: Sage, 1997), and Bence Nanay, "Philosophy of Perception as a Guide to Aesthetics," in *Aesthetics and the Sciences of Mind*, ed. Greg Currie, Matthew Kieran, Aaron Meskin, and Jon Robson (New York: Oxford University Press, 2014), 101–20.

3. Jerrold Levinson, "Philosophical Aesthetics: An Overview," in *The Oxford Handbook of Aesthetics*, ed. Jerrold Levinson (Oxford: Oxford University Press, 2005), 3.

4. Richard Shusterman, *Pragmatist Aesthetics. Living Beauty, Rethinking Art* (Lanham, MD: Rowman and Littlefield, 2000), 264.

5. Wolfgang Welsch, *Undoing Aesthetics*, 40.

Chapter 1

1. Zaifu Liu, *Li Zehou Meixue Gailun* [The outline of Li Zehou's aesthetics] (Beijing: San Lian Shudian, 2009), 82.

2. There is both phenomenological and neuroscientific research that supports the thesis that emotions are not only a form of reaction to the world but also a way

of evaluating it. See, for instance, Giovanna Colombetti, *The Feeling Body: Affective Science Meets the Enactive Mind* (Cambridge, MA: MIT Press, 2014), 83–112.

3. Although Li does not relate it directly to aesthetics, he holds that Confucianism is a philosophy that puts human nature in its center and also discusses it inwardly, allowing psychological follow-up terms. Zehou Li, *A New Approach to Kant: A Confucian-Marxist's Viewpoint* (Singapore: Springer, 2018), vii.

4. Zehou Li, *Zhongguo Meixue Shi* [History of Chinese aesthetics] (Hefei: Anhui Wenyi Chubanshe, 1999), 110.

5. Zehou Li, *The Chinese Aesthetic Tradition*, trans. Maija Bell Samei (Honolulu: University of Hawai'i Press, 2010), 47.

6. Confucius, *Analects, with Selections from Traditional Commentaries*, trans. Edward Slingerland (Indianapolis: Hackett, 2003), 17.

7. In fact, Liu Zaifu mentions that Li has his ranking of top ten Chinese philosophers. They are (in order of appearance) Confucius, Zhuangzi, Laozi, Mencius, Xunzi, Hanfei, Wang Bi, Hui Neng, Zhu Xi, and Wang Yangming. Liu, *Li Zehou Meixue Gailun* [The outline of Li Zehou's aesthetics], 62.

8. The trigrams were allegedly compiled by the mythical figure and legendary ruler Fu Xi, from the second millennium BCE.

9. During the early Western Zhou dynasty period, approximately between the eleventh and eighth century BCE, the *Book of Changes* was used for divination.

10. Nowadays it is believed that the Confucius-authored commentaries were in fact added later, at the beginning of the Han dynasty, in the third century BCE.

11. The elements of correlative thinking distinguished by Lai are the primacy of observation, a holistic, all-encompassing perspective, a dialectical and complementary approach to dualisms, correlative thinking and resonance, an interpretive approach to the meanings of the hexagrams and correspondences, constant movement marked by the inevitability of change, and the action-guiding nature of the judgments. Karyn L. Lai, *An Introduction to Chinese Philosophy* (New York: Cambridge University Press, 2008), 213.

12. *The Classic of Changes: A New Translation of the I Ching as Interpreted by Wang Bi*, trans. Richard John Lynn (New York: Columbia University Press, 1994), 47.

13. The ontic status of *qi* is s a very complex issue and my referring to it as "substance" is for the sake of brevity only.

14. *The Classic of Changes*, 47.

15. This statement may be arguable but we can agree that Confucius was the most important philosopher among his contemporaries who focused on the human world.

16. Liu, *Li Zehou Meixue Gailun* [The outline of Li Zehou's aesthetics], 62.

17. Liu, *Li Zehou Meixue Gailun* [The outline of Li Zehou's aesthetics], 62.

18. This extension is particular of most ethically orientated systems in Chinese philosophy, and does not apply to the Western tradition.

19. Julia Diver, "Normative Ethics," in *The Oxford Handbook of Contemporary Philosophy*, ed. Frank Jackson and Michael Smith (Oxford: Oxford University Press, 2007), 32.

20. Walter Sinnott-Armstrong, "Consequentialism," in *The Stanford Encyclopedia of Philosophy*, ed. Edward N. Zalta, Summer 2019 ed., https://plato.stanford.edu/archives/sum2019/entries/consequentialism/.

21. Rosalind Hursthouse and Glen Pettigrove, "Virtue Ethics," in *The Stanford Encyclopedia of Philosophy*, ed. Edward N. Zalta, Winter 2018 ed., https://plato.stanford.edu/archives/win2018/entries/ethics-virtue/.

22. Hursthouse and Pettigrove, "Virtue Ethics."

23. For instance, in fragments 1.7, 2.10, and 5.16.

24. Hursthouse and Pettigrove, "Virtue Ethics."

25. The word can be translated in many ways—for instance D. C. Lau and James Legge in their translations of the *Mencius*, translate *ren* as "benevolence." Din-cheuk Lau, trans., *Mencius* (Middlesex: Penguin, 1984); James Legge, trans., *The Works of Mencius* (New York: Clarendon Press, 1985). Translations of the *Analects* by Arthur Waley and Edward Slingerland use "goodness." See Bryan Van Norden, trans., *Mengzi, with Selections from Traditional Commentaries* (Indianapolis and Cambridge: Hackett, 2008), 202. As regards Bryan Van Norden's translation of the *Mencius*, he uses "benevolence," but in the appended glossary he makes a remark that *ren* in the fragment 7B16 has a wider meaning, with a shade of "humaneness" (202). A completely different understanding is proposed by Roger T. Ames and Henry Rosemont in their translation of the *Analects*. In the introduction, they propose the following translations of *ren*: "authoritative conduct," "to act authoritatively," "authoritative person," and compare them to other existing renderings of *ren* into English. Roger T. Ames and Henry Rosemont, trans., *The Analects of Confucius: A Philosophical Translation* (New York: Ballantine, 1998), 48–51. There is no one exact equivalence encapsulating all the semantic content of the word, and probably the best solution would be either to resort to a given translation depending on the occurrence in a given co(n)text, or to view *ren* as semantically spread between several equivalence variants. For this reason, I choose to leave it untranslated.

26. The assumption of good human nature is characteristic of the "Confucian mainstream." An important Confucian philosopher beyond this mainstream, who held a view that human nature is bad, was Xunzi (c. 310–235 BCE).

27. Mencius, *Mengzi: With Selections from Traditional Commentaries*, trans. Bryan Van Norden (Indianapolis: Hackett, 2008), 46.

28. Rafal Banka, "Li Zehou's Aesthetics as a Form of Cognition," in *Li Zehou and Confucian Philosophy*, ed. Roger T. Ames and Jinhua Jia (Honolulu: University of Hawai'i Press, 2018), 358.

29. Confucius, *Analects*, 3.

30. Banka, "Li Zehou's Aesthetics," 358.

31. Banka, "Li Zehou's Aesthetics," 358.

32. Banka, "Li Zehou's Aesthetics," 358–59.

33. Banka, "Li Zehou's Aesthetics," 359.

34. Jean-Paul Sartre, *Existentialism is a Humanism*, trans. Carol Macomber (New Haven, CT: Yale University Press, 2007), 20.

35. René Descartes, *Meditations on First Philosophy*, in *Discourse on Method and Meditations on First Philosophy*, ed. David Weissman, trans. Donald A. Cress (New Haven, CT: Yale University Press, 1996), 63–64.

36. Banka, "Li Zehou's Aesthetics," 359.

37. Cf. Zehou Li and Jane Cauvel, *Four Essays on Aesthetics: Toward a Global View* (Lanham, MD: Lexington Books, 2006), 24–25.

38. For instance, fragments 3.23 and 8.8.

39. Banka, "Li Zehou's Aesthetics," 359.

40. Confucius, *Analects*, 80.

41. Li, *History of Chinese Aesthetics*, 112.

42. Li, *History of Chinese Aesthetics*, 112–13.

43. Li, *Chinese Aesthetic Tradition*, 49–50.

44. Li, *Chinese Aesthetic Tradition*, 50.

45. Confucius, *Analects*, 59.

46. Slingerland in his commentary sees the fragment as a description of the increasing level of unselfconsciousness and ease particular of the Confucian exemplary person, which suggests the progress is measured by fluency in one's following the Confucian way. See Confucius, *Analects*, 59.

47. Li, *Chinese Aesthetic Tradition*, 54.

48. Li, *Chinese Aesthetic Tradition*, 56–57.

49. Li, *Chinese Aesthetic Tradition*, 43.

50. Li, *History of Chinese Aesthetics*, 123.

51. Confucius, *Analects*, 204.

52. Li, *History of Chinese Aesthetics*, 124.

53. Li, *History of Chinese Aesthetics*, 128.

Chapter 2

1. Eva Kit Wah Man, *Issues of Contemporary Art and Aesthetics in Chinese Context* (Berlin: Springer, 2015), 23.

2. Man, *Issues of Contemporary Art*, 23.

3. Kang Liu, *Aesthetics and Marxism: Chinese Aesthetic Marxists and Their Western Contemporaries* (Durham, NC: Duke University Press, 2000), 128.

4. Liu, *Aesthetics and Marxism*, 124, 125.

5. These are two of the four statements formulated by Zhu. The remaining ones say that because aesthetic experience stems from art and literature, they

should remain the main issue of aesthetics, as well as that art and literature are ideological forms, and thus aesthetic experience is also ideological. Liu, *Aesthetics and Marxism*, 128.

6. Liu, *Aesthetics and Marxism*, 129.

7. It should be noted that, whereas alienation was one of the most important issues in Western Marxism, humanization of nature, as tabled in the *Manuscripts*, was of great interest among Chinese Marxists, especially in aesthetics. Liu, *Aesthetics and Marxism*, xv.

8. Man, *Issues of Contemporary Art*, 24.

9. Man, *Issues of Contemporary Art*, 24.

10. To compare, the first volume of Marx's probably most influential work, *Capital*, was published in 1967, whereas the second and third volumes came out in 1893 and 1894 respectively.

11. However, judging by the cross-outs in the manuscript, it might have been that Marx was considering the editor's comments while preparing a final draft. Robert E. Tucker's footnote in Karl Marx, *Economic and Philosophic Manuscripts*, in *The Marx-Engels Reader*, trans. Martin Milligan, ed. Robert E. Tucker (New York: Norton, 1978), 66.

12. Robert E. Tucker in Marx, *Manuscripts*, 66.

13. The Chinese translation of the *Manuscripts* was published in 1940. Liu, *Aesthetics and Marxism*, 134.

14. Liu, *Aesthetics and Marxism*, 134.

15. For instance, in the *Manuscripts*, Marx does not trace the cause of the alienation of labor.

16. Leszek Kołakowski, *Main Currents of Marxism: Its Rise, Growth, and Dissolution*, vol. 1, *The Founders*, trans. Paul Stephen Falla (Oxford: Clarendon Press, 1978), 132.

17. This revolutionary commitment of art, which concurrently involved ideologically molded aesthetics, is usually historically marked by Mao's famous Yan'an Talk on May 2, 1942, which defined the "official" aesthetics of the People's Republic of China until the end of the 1970s.

18. In terms of aesthetics, it resulted in considerable pluralism, manifested mainly beyond institutions in art but also daily life. That period is often referred to as the "aesthetic fever" (*meixue re* 美學熱). Rafal Banka, "Contemporary Chinese Art as a Product and Reflection of Globalisation in Culture," *Journal of East-West Thought* 7, no. 3 (2017): 41–42.

19. Liu, *Aesthetics and Marxism*, xv.

20. See Mao Zedong, "On Practice," in *On Practice and Contradiction* (London: Verso, 2007), 53.

21. Donglan Chen and Jianping Gao, "*Zhexue Dawen*," in *Li Zehou Zhexue Wencun* (Hefei: Anhui Wenyi Chubanshe, 1999), 2:459; Li, *A New Approach to Kant*, 286.

22. Kołakowski, *Main Currents of Marxism*, 134.
23. Kołakowski, *Main Currents of Marxism*, 136–37.
24. Kołakowski, *Main Currents of Marxism*, 134.
25. Kołakowski, *Main Currents of Marxism*, 137.
26. Marx, *Manuscripts*, 85.
27. Marx, *Manuscripts*, 86.
28. Marx, *Manuscripts*, 86.
29. Marx, *Manuscripts*, 88.
30. Marx, *Manuscripts*, 87.
31. Marx, *Manuscripts*, 88.
32. Kołakowski, *Main Currents of Marxism*, 142.
33. Marx expresses this view in a very precise way in the first thesis from *Theses on Feuerbach*. He claims that in cognition, the object cannot be "conceived only in the form of the *object or of contemplation*, but not as *sensuous human activity, practice*." Karl Marx, "Theses on Feuerbach," in *Karl Marx Selected Works*, trans. William Lough (New York: International Publishers, n.d.), 1:471–72.
34. Marx, *Manuscripts*, 88.
35. Marx, *Manuscripts*, 89.
36. Marx, *Manuscripts*, 89.
37. Marx, *Manuscripts*, 72.
38. Marx, *Manuscripts*, 72–73.
39. Marx, *Manuscripts*, 73–74.
40. Marx, *Manuscripts*, 75.
41. Kołakowski, *Main Currents of* Marxism, 138–39.
42. Kołakowski, *Main Currents of Marxism*, 130.
43. Kazimierz Ajdukiewicz, *Problems and Theories of Philosophy*, trans. Henryk Skolimowski and Anthony Quinton (London: Cambridge University Press, 1973), 106.
44. This is consistent with one of the four dialectical laws—the law of the transformation of the quantitative changes into qualitative ones. It explains that the developmental processes in nature, including those that involve humans, take place when some qualitative changes, in reaching a given point of intensity, undergo a sudden transformation into qualitative changes. Ajdukiewicz, *Problems and Theories of Philosophy*, 107. In this law, human consciousness can be seen as a result of accumulation of physical, chemical, and biological processes in matter.
45. Kołakowski, *Main Currents of Marxism*, 130.
46. Marx, *Manuscripts*, 76.
47. This belief reverberated later in some twentieth-century approaches to Marxist aesthetics, for instance within a broader trend of the so-called "vulgar sociologism," among others represented by the Russian philosopher Alexander Bogdanov (1873–1928). The point of view departed from the assumption that aesthetics should remain in a direct relation with production instead of producing objects that are separated from the real world (of labor) and meant to be passive, bourgeois

contemplation of their content. Labor is the foundation of social life as well as the ideology that supervenes on it, and therefore labor is where the aesthetic should stem from. Stefan Morawski, "O marksistowskiej myśli estetycznej" [On Marxist aesthetic thought], in *Estetyki filozoficzne XX wieku* [Philosophical aesthetics of the twentieth century], ed. Krystyna Wilkoszewska (Kraków: Universitas, 2000), 134.

48. Marx, *Manuscripts*, 76–77.

Chapter 3

1. Kang Liu, *Aesthetics and Marxism*, 165.

2. The book was written down by Li during the second half of the Cultural Revolution in 1972–76, and published in China in 1979.

3. Li, *A New Approach to Kant*, v.

4. Immanuel Kant, *Critique of Pure Reason*, trans. Norman Kemp Smith (Basingstoke, UK: Palgrave Macmillan, 2007), A6–8/B10–12.

5. Kant, *Critique of Pure Reason*, A9–10/B13–14.

6. Li, *A New Approach to Kant*, 48.

7. Li, *A New Approach to Kant*, 50.

8. Kant, *Critique of Pure Reason*, B17–18.

9. Karl Marx, "Theses on Feuerbach," 1:472–473.

10. Li, *A New Approach to Kant*, 56–58.

11. Li, *A New Approach to Kant*, 56.

12. Li, *A New Approach to Kant*, 56.

13. Li, *A New Approach to Kant*, 57–58.

14. Kant, *Critique of Pure Reason*, A68/B93.

15. Kant, *Critique of Pure Reason*, A19/B33.

16. Kant, *Critique of Pure Reason*, A51/B75.

17. Kant, *Critique of Pure Reason*, A20/B34.

18. Brigitte Sassen, "18th Century German Philosophy Prior to Kant," in *The Stanford Encyclopedia of Philosophy*, ed. Edward N. Zalta, Summer 2015 ed., https://plato.stanford.edu/archives/sum2015/entries/18thGerman-preKant/.

19. Andrew Janiak, "Kant's Views on Space and Time," in *The Stanford Encyclopedia of Philosophy*, ed. Edward N. Zalta, Spring 2020 ed., https://plato.stanford.edu/archives/spr2020/entries/kant-spacetime/.

20. Kant, *Critique of Pure Reason*, A23/B37–38.

21. Li, *A New Approach to Kant*, 75.

22. For a comprehensive discussion of time perception, see Robin Le Poidevin, "The Experience and Perception of Time," in *The Stanford Encyclopedia of Philosophy*, ed. Edward N. Zalta, Summer 2019 ed., https://plato.stanford.edu/archives/sum2019/entries/time-experience/.

23. Li, *A New Approach to Kant*, 75.

24. Li, *A New Approach to Kant*, 75.

25. Kant, *Critique of Pure Reason*, A20–21/B34–35.

26. Kant, *Critique of Pure Reason*, A21/B35.

27. Li, *A New Approach to Kant*, 79–80.

28. Li, *A New Approach to Kant*, 84–86.

29. John Locke, *An Essay concerning Human Understanding* (Kitchener, ON: Batoche Books, 2001), 99–100.

30. Li, *A New Approach to Kant*, 87.

31. Li, *A New Approach to Kant*, 86.

32. Li, *A New Approach to Kant*, 88.

33. Li, *A New Approach to Kant*, 88.

34. Li, *A New Approach to Kant*, 88–89.

35. Li, *A New Approach to Kant*, 88–89.

36. Li, *A New Approach to Kant*, 89.

37. Karl Marx, *Economic and Philosophic Manuscripts*, 75.

38. Li, *A New Approach to Kant*, 91.

39. Kant, *Critique of Pure Reason*, A79–80/B104.

40. Kant, *Critique of Pure Reason*, B151.

41. Kant, *Critique of Pure Reason*, B151.

42. Kant, *Critique of Pure Reason*, A137–139/B176–178.

43. Kant, *Critique of Pure Reason*, A140/B179.

44. Kant, *Critique of Pure Reason*, A140–142/B179–181.

45. Li, *A New Approach to Kant*, 128–129.

46. Li, *A New Approach to Kant*, 129–131.

47. Immanuel Kant, *Critique of the Power of Judgment*, trans. Paul Guyer (New York: Cambridge University Press, 2002), 5:180–81.

48. Kant, *Critique of the Power of Judgment*, 5:184.

49. Kant, *Critique of Pure Reason*, B151.

50. Kant, *Critique of the Power of Judgment*, 5:187.

51. Kant, *Critique of the Power of Judgment*, 5:184.

52. Kant, *Critique of the Power of Judgment*, 5:187.

53. In contrast, aesthetic empirical judgment asserts agreeableness (*das Angenehme*) or disagreeableness, and is named the judgment of sense. Kant, *Critique of the Power of Judgment*, 5:223.

54. The other type of beauty is adherent, and it presupposes the concept of the object and "perfection of the object in accordance with it."

55. Kant, *Critique of the Power of Judgment*, 5:230.

56. Kant, *Critique of the Power of Judgment*, 5:217.

57. In another translation into English by Werner S. Pluhar, we have the same meaning: "Which concepts they are is left indeterminate." Immanuel Kant, *Critique of Judgment*, trans. Werner S. Pluhar (Indianapolis: Hackett, 1987), 5:256.

58. Kant, *Critique of the Power of Judgment*, 5:209.

59. Kant, *Critique of the Power of Judgment*, 5:238.

60. Kant, *Critique of the Power of Judgment*, 5:295.

61. Kant, *Critique of the Power of Judgment*, 5:297.

62. Kant, *Critique of the Power of Judgment*, 5:297.

63. I have already partly reconstructed Kant's argumentation in this respect when describing the judgment of taste as pure, so here I will focus only on other features important for our discussion.

64. Kant, *Critique of the Power of Judgment*, 5:205.

65. Kant points to an important distinction between the agreeable, beautiful, and good, all of which are related to the feeling of pleasure (*Lust*). As for the agreeable (*das Angenehme*), this is what mainly gratifies one's senses and can even be found in animals. Good, on the contrary, can be found only in humans, as they are rational, but it is what gratifies reason and the basis for establishing an objective value. It is only the beautiful that is connected with free satisfaction, and disconnected from interest, which according to Kant always involves attachment to the object of satisfaction rather than merely playing with it. Kant, *Critique of the Power of Judgment*, 5:210.

66. Kant, *Critique of the Power of Judgment*, 5:209.

67. Kant, *Critique of the Power of Judgment*, 5:256.

68. Li, *A New Approach to Kant*, 298–99.

69. Kant, *Critique of the Power of Judgment*, 5:211.

70. Kant, *Critique of the Power of Judgment*, 5:216.

71. Kant, *Critique of the Power of Judgment*, 5:218.

72. Kant, *Critique of the Power of Judgment*, 5:220–21.

73. Kant, *Critique of the Power of Judgment*, 5:237–38.

74. Kant, *Critique of Judgment*, 5:219. In Paul Guyer's translation, *Zusammenstimmung* is rendered into English as "agreement." See Kant, *Critique of the Power of Judgment*, 5:219.

75. Kant, *Critique of Judgment*, 5:219.

76. Li, *A New Approach to Kant*, 329.

77. Li, *A New Approach to Kant*, 329.

78. Li, *A New Approach to Kant*, 330.

79. Marx, *Manuscripts*, 72–73.

80. Marx, *Manuscripts*, 76.

81. Marx, *Manuscripts*, 75.

82. Kant, *Critique of the Power of Judgment*, 5:229.

83. Kant, *Critique of the Power of Judgment*, 5:230.

84. Kant refers to the example of finding an average personal appearance that can be taken as the standard of beauty and concludes that it is community- or ethnicity-specific. Kant, *Critique of the Power of Judgment*, 5:234.

85. Kant, *Critique of the Power of Judgment*, 5:233.

86. Kant, *Critique of the Power of Judgment*, 5:299.

87. Li, *A New Approach to Kant*, 308.

88. Kant, *Critique of the Power of Judgment*, 5:356.

89. After Li, *A New Approach to Kant*, 308.

90. Kant, *Critique of the Power of Judgment*, 5:314.

91. Li, *A New Approach to Kant*, 309.

92. Kant, *Critique of the Power of Judgment*, 5:309.

93. Kant, *Critique of the Power of Judgment*, 5:318.

94. Kant, *Critique of the Power of Judgment*, 5:371.

95. After Li, *A New Approach to Kant*, 315.

96. Kant, *Critique of Pure Judgment*, 5:431.

97. Kant, *Critique of Pure Judgment*, 5:442–43.

98. Kant, *Critique of Pure Judgment*, 5:431.

99. Kant, *Critique of Pure Judgment*, 5:432.

100. Kant, *Critique of Pure Judgment*, 5:433. On the other hand, Kant does not accept art and science unconditionally. He considers a case in which humans can indulge in them for the sake of their own vanity. However, this is ascribed to the inclinations of human animality, which are not conducive to the proper development of humans through culture. See Kant, *Critique of Pure Judgment*, 5:433.

101. Li, *A New Approach to Kant*, 324.

102. Li, *A New Approach to Kant*, v.

103. Kant, *Critique of the Power of Judgment*, 5:187.

104. Kant, *Critique of the Power of Judgment*, 5:297.

105. Zehou Li, *The Chinese Aesthetic Tradition*, 5–7.

Chapter 4

1. Zehou Li and Jane Cauvel, *Four Essays on Aesthetics*, 170–71.

2. It should be remembered that there are also other types of semantic modification of the suffix "*xing*" than the "property" one.

3. This English translation also appears in the original Chinese text.

4. Fragment of an interview with Li Zehou: Lian Zhou, Anying Chen, and Huayin Yu, "Lishi Yanjie yu Lilun de 'Du,'" *Tianya* 2 (1999): 130. Quoted English translation from John Zijiang Ding, "Li Zehou: Chinese Aesthetics from a Post-Marxist and Confucian Perspective," in *Contemporary Chinese Philosophy*, ed. Nicholas Bunnin and Chung-ying Cheng (Malden, MA: Blackwell,2 002), 247.

5. In Li's later writings translated into English, "subjectality" has been accepted as a "standard" equivalence.

6. Li, *A New Approach to Kant*, 165.

7. Li, *A New Approach to Kant*, 70.

8. It has to be admitted that *benti* is not always translated as "substance" in Li's English publications. For instance, John Zijiang Ding uses "noumenon" as an

English equivalence. However, in a recent translation project of Li's most important works into English, coordinated by Roger T. Ames and Jinhua Jia, "substance" is the recommended standard equivalent.

9. Li and Cauvel, *Four Essays on Aesthetics*, 40.

10. Unless otherwise stated, all quotations translated from Chinese in this chapter are my translation.

11. Zehou Li, *Wo de Zhexue Tigang* [The outline of my philosophy], in *Li Zehou Shi Nian Ji* 1979–1989 [The decade of Li Zehou's collected works, 1979–1989] (Hefei: Anhui Yishu Chubanshe, 1994), 2:499.

12. Li, *Wo de Zhexue Tigang* [The outline of my philosophy], 499.

13. Li, *Wo de Zhexue Tigang* [The outline of my philosophy], 499.

14. Li, *Wo de Zhexue Tigang* [The outline of my philosophy], 499.

15. Thomas Hobbes, *Leviathan* (Minneapolis: Learner, 2018), 120–31.

16. Mo Tzu, *Basic Writings* (New York: Columbia University Press, 1966), 34–35.

17. Ludwig Wittgenstein, *Philosophical Investigations*, trans. G. E. M. Anscombe (Oxford: Blackwell, 1986), 48e, 200* (*sic*).

18. Martin Heidegger, *Being and Time*, trans. John Macquarrie and Edward Robinson (Oxford: Blackwell, 1962), 154–55.

19. Li, *Wo de Zhexue Tigang* [The outline of my philosophy], 500.

20. Sartre, *Existentialism Is a Humanism*, 20.

21. Li, *Wo de Zhexue Tigang* [The outline of my philosophy], 500.

22. Li, *Wo de Zhexue Tigang* [The outline of my philosophy], 500.

23. Wittgenstein, *Philosophical Investigations*, n>> (23) (*sic*).

24. See fragments 23, 66, 206. Wittgenstein, *Philosophical Investigations*, n>>-128, 31?–32e, 826 (*sic*).

25. Li, *Wo de Zhexue Tigang* [The outline of my philosophy], 500.

26. Li, *Wo de Zhexue Tigang* [The outline of my philosophy], 502–3.

27. Li, *A New Approach to* Kant, 36–37.

28. After Philip Zimbardo, *Psychologia i życie* (*Psychology and Life*) (Warsaw: Wydawnictwo Naukowe PWN, 1999), 172–76.

29. Li, *Wo de Zhexue Tigang* [The outline of my philosophy], 501.

30. Li, *Wo de Zhexue Tigang* [The outline of my philosophy], 501.

31. Other theories attribute the emergence of speech to, for instance, the changes in the cranial structure. See Daniel E. Lieberman, "Sphenoid shortening and the evolution of modern cranial shape," *Nature* 393 (1998): 158–62.

32. Michael C. Corballis, "The Evolution of Consciousness," in *The Cambridge Handbook of Consiousness*, ed. Philip David Zelazo, Morris Moscovitch, and Evan Thompson (New York: Cambridge University Press, 2007), 589.

33. See, for instance, Michael C. Corballis, *From Hand to Mouth: The Origins of Language* (Princeton, NJ: Princeton University Press, 2002).

34. Corballis, "The Evolution of Consciousness," 587.

35. Li, *Wo de Zhexue Tigang* [The outline of my philosophy], 501.

36. Michael Wheeler, "Martin Heidegger," in *The Stanford Encyclopedia of Philosophy*, ed. Edward N. Zalta, Winter 2018 ed., https://plato.stanford.edu/archives/win2018/entries/heidegger/.

37. Vladimir Illich Lenin, *Philosophical Notebooks*, trans. C. Dutt, ed. S. Smith, vol. 38 of *Collected Works* (Moscow: Progress Publishers, 1965), 213.

38. Li, *A New Approach to Kant*, 159; Zehou Li, "Kangde Zhexue yu Jianli Zhutixing Lungang" [The outline of Kant's philosophy and establishing subjectality], in *Zhexue Meixue Wenxuan* (Changsha: Hunan Renmin Chubanshe, 1985), 156.

39. Li, *A New Approach to Kant*, 160–161.

40. Li, *A New Approach to Kant*, 160.

41. See Andy Clark and David Chalmers, "The Extended Mind," *Analysis* 58, no. 1 (1998): 9–10.

42. Li, *Wo de Zhexue Tigang* [The outline of my philosophy], 501.

43. Li, *Wo de Zhexue Tigang* [The outline of my philosophy], 501.

44. Li, *A New Approach to Kant*, vii.

45. Zehou Li, *The Chinese Aesthetic Tradition*, 6–7.

46. Li parallels this statement with an allusion to Heidegger in that nonbeing is needed to reveal being. Martin Heidegger, "What Is Metaphysics?," trans. David Farrell Krell, in *Pathmarks*, ed. William McNeill (Cambridge: Cambridge University Press, 1998), 94.

47. Ajdukiewicz, *Problems and Theories of Philosophy*, 106–7.

48. Li, *Wo de Zhexue Tigang* [The outline of my philosophy], 502.

49. Li, *A New Approach to Kant*, 158.

50. Li, *A New Approach to Kant*, 157.

51. Li, *Wo de Zhexue Tigang* [The outline of my philosophy], 502.

52. Anjan Chatterjee, *The Aesthetic Brain: How We Evolved to Desire Beauty and Enjoy Art* (New York: Oxford University Press, 2013), 13, 14.

53. For full experiment description, see John D. Balling and John H. Falk, "Development of visual preference for natural environments," *Environment and Behavior* 14, no. 1 (1982): 11–17.

54. Chatterjee, *The Aesthetic Brain*, 48–49.

55. Chatterjee, *The Aesthetic Brain*, 52–53.

56. Li, *Wo de Zhexue Tigang* [The outline of my philosophy], 502–3.

57. Other works that continue research on this front are, for instance, *A History of Pre-Modern Chinese Thought* and *A History of Pre-Modern Chinese Thought*, published in Chinese in 1979 and 1987 respectively.

58. Li, *A New Approach to Kant*, vii.

59. Li and Cauvel, *Four Essays on Aesthetics*, 66.

60. Confucius, *Analects*, 80.

61. Karl Marx, *Economic and Philosophic Manuscripts*, 76.

62. Zhuangzi, *Zhuangzi Jinzhu Jinyi*, ed. Chen Guying (Beijing: Zhonghua Shuju, 1985), 855–56.

63. Li, *Wo de Zhexue Tigang* [The outline of my philosophy], 502.

64. Li, *Wo de Zhexue Tigang* [The outline of my philosophy], 502.

65. Li, *Wo de Zhexue Tigang* [The outline of my philosophy], 503.

66. Hans Küng and Julia Ching, *Christianity and Chinese Religions* (New York: Doubleday, 1989), xi.

67. Li, *Wo de Zhexue Tigang* [The outline of my philosophy], 503.

68. Li, *A New Approach to Kant*, vii.

69. Studies in this area, with regard to Chinese culture are run by Shihui Han at Peking University. For an example of such research, see Shuhui Han and Georg Northoff, "Culture-Sensitive Neural Substrates of Human Cognition: A Transcultural Neuroimaging Approach," *Nature* 9 (2008): 646–54.

70. The name was first used by Levine in 1983. See Joseph Levine, "Materialism and Qualia: The Explanatory Gap," *Pacific Philosophical Quarterly* 64, no. 4 (1983): 354–61.

71. Martine Nida-Rümelin, "Dualist Emergentism," *Contemporary Debates in Philosophy of Mind*, eds. Brian P. McLaughlin and Jonathan Cohen (Malden, MA: Blackwell, 2007), 270–71.

72. Ajdukiewicz, *Problems and Theories of Philosophy*, 107.

Chapter 5

1. Daniel Dennett, "Where Am I?," in *The Mind's I: Fantasies and Reflections on Mind and Soul*, ed. Douglas R. Hofstadter and Daniel C. Dennett (New York: Basic Books, 1981), 225.

2. Shaun Gallagher and Dan Zahavi, *The Phenomenological Mind: An Introduction to Philosophy of Mind and Cognitive Science* (Oxford: Routledge, 2008), 131.

3. Quoted in Gallagher and Zahavi, *The Phenomenological Mind*, 132.

4. Quoted in Gallagher and Zahavi, *The Phenomenological Mind*, 132.

5. Robert D. Rupert, "Challenges to the Hypothesis of Extended Cognition," *Journal of Philosophy* 101, no. 8 (2004): 393.

6. Robert A. Wilson, Lucia Foglia, "Embodied Cognition," in *The Stanford Encyclopedia of Philosophy*, ed. Edward N. Zalta, Spring 2017 ed., https://plato.stanford.edu/archives/spr2017/entries/embodied-cognition/.

7. Distinction originally introduced by David Kirsh and Paul Maglio. The authors additionally determine epistemic actions as "physical actions that make mental computation easier, faster, or more reliable." In addition to the action presented in the Tetris example, epistemic actions can also be more stretched in time, such as, for instance, time-saving preparing workspace. See David Kirsh and Paul Maglio,

"On Distinguishing Epistemic from Pragmatic Action," *Cognitive Science* 18, no. 4 (1994): 513–14, 515.

8. Andy Clark and David Chalmers, "The Extended Mind," 8–9.

9. Clark and Chalmers, "The Extended Mind," 9.

10. Clark and Chalmers, "The Extended Mind," 11–12.

11. Francisco J. Varela, Evan Thompson, and Eleanor Rosch, *The Embodied Mind: Cognitive Science and Human Experience* (Cambridge, MA: MIT Press, 1993), 172–73.

12. Varela, Thompson, and Rosch, *The Embodied Mind*, 9.

13. For presentation of different views within enactivism, see Wilson and Foglia, "Embodied Cognition," and Richard Menary, "What Is Radical Enactivism?," in *Radical Enactivism: Intentionality, Phenomenology and Narrative: Focus on the Philosophy of Daniel D. Hutto*, ed. Richard Menary (Amsterdam: John Benjamins, 2006), 1–13.

14. Richard Menary, "What Is Radical Enactivism?," 2, 3.

15. Evan Thompson, "Living Ways of Sense Making," *Philosophy Today* 55, suppl. (2011): 114–15.

16. Ezequiel Di Paolo, "Autopoiesis, Adaptivity, Teleology, Agency," *Phenomenology and the Cognitive Sciences* 4 (2005): 430.

17. Thompson, "Living Ways of Sense Making," 115.

18. Thompson, "Living Ways of Sense Making," 116.

19. Thompson, "Living Ways of Sense Making," 119.

20. Evan Thompson, "Life and Mind: From Autopoiesis to Neurophenomenology. A Tribute to Francisco Varela," *Phenomenology and the Cognitive Sciences* 3 (2004): 387.

21. Varela, Thompson, and Rosch, *The Embodied Mind*, 173.

22. Varela, Thompson, and Rosch, *The Embodied Mind*, 173.

23. Varela, Thompson, and Rosch, *The Embodied Mind*, 176.

24. See, for instance, Li, *A New Approach to Kant*, vii.

25. Colombetti, *The Feeling Body*, xiii.

26. Colombetti, *The Feeling Body*, 1–2.

27. Colombetti, *The Feeling Body*, 2.

28. Colombetti, *The Feeling Body*, 15–17.

29. In fact, such a rule of composition for mereological objects is proposed by Peter van Inwagen. See Peter van Inwagen, *Material Beings* (Ithaca, NY: Cornell University Press, 1990), 81–97.

30. Evan Thompson, *Mind in Life: Biology, Phenomenology, and the Sciences of Mind* (Cambridge MA: Harvard University Press, 2007), 126.

31. Colombetti, *The Feeling Body*, 19.

32. Klaus R. Scherer, "Introduction: Cognitive Components of Emotion," in *Handbook of Affective Sciences*, ed. Richard J. Davidson, Klaus R. Scherer, and H. Hill Goldsmith (New York: Oxford University Press, 2003), 564.

33. Phoebe C. Ellsworth and Klaus R. Scherer, "Appraisal Processes in Emotion," in *Handbook of Affective Sciences*, ed. Richard J. Davidson, Klaus R. Scherer, H. Hill Goldsmith (New York: Oxford University Press, 2003), 572.

34. Ellsworth and Scherer, "Appraisal Processes in Emotion," 573–74.

35. In my discussion, I follow the interpretation that emotional episodes are composed of appraisals. There is also a competing standpoint that appraisals antecede the episodes. Ellsworth and Scherer, "Appraisal Processes in Emotion," 575.

36. For discussion concerning the possible origin of emotion from bodily and subjective feelings, see, for instance, William James, "What Is Emotion?" *Mind* 9, no. 2 (1884), 188–205; Robert B. Zajonc, "Thinking and Feeling: Preferences Need No Inferences," *American Psychologist* 35, no. 2 (1980): 151–75.

37. Ellsworth and Scherer, "Appraisal Processes in Emotion," 577–78.

38. Li, *A New Approach to Kant*, 329.

Chapter 6

1. One must note that *Explaining Graphs* is not a linguistic work in the contemporary, scholarly sense. Li himself refers to the explanation as pseudo-etymological. Li, *The Chinese Aesthetic Tradition*, 1.

2. Li, *The Chinese Aesthetic Tradition*, 1.

3. Li, *The Chinese Aesthetic Tradition*, 2.

4. Li, *The Chinese Aesthetic Tradition*, 3.

5. Li, *The Chinese Aesthetic Tradition*, 7–8.

6. Li and Cauvel, *Four Essays on Aesthetics*, 49–50.

7. Plato, *Symposium*, ed. and trans. Robin Waterfield (Oxford: Oxford University Press, 1998), 54.

8. This form of participation is achieved by the reflection of the form of beauty in a material object. Since forms and matter are disjunct in terms of ontic status and they cannot amalgamate, beauty is not ontically part of material objects.

9. Li and Cauvel, *Four Essays on Aesthetics*, 50–51.

10. Li and Cauvel, *Four Essays on Aesthetics*, 51.

11. Tomasz Maruszewski, *Psychologia poznania* [Cognitive psychology] (Gdańsk: Gdańskie Wydawnictwo Psychologiczne, 2002), 41–49.

12. This theory seems highly improbable, for instance, due to shape perception not being able to cause in the brain a stimulation of a given shape, because the shape information is encoded not by brain stimulation but special nerve cells the impulses from which are interpreted as a given shape. For details, see Maruszewski, *Psychologia poznania* [Cognitive psychology], 49.

13. Li and Cauvel, *Four Essays on Aesthetics*, 51–52.

14. Immanuel Kant, *Critique of the Power of Judgment*, 5:184.

15. For discussion on aesthetic supervenience, see Nick Zangwill, "Beauty," in *The Oxford Handbook of Aesthetics*, ed. Jerrold Levinson (Oxford: Oxford University Press, 2005), 328–29.

16. Li and Cauvel, *Four Essays on Aesthetics*, 51.

17. Li and Cauvel, *Four Essays on Aesthetics*, 52–53.

18. Li and Cauvel, *Four Essays on Aesthetics*, 53.

19. The full Chinese name for subjectivism is "*zhuguanzhuyi* 主觀主義," whereas for objectivism "*keguanzhuyi* 客觀主義."

20. Li and Cauvel, *Four Essays on Aesthetics*, 53–54.

21. Li and Cauvel, *Four Essays on Aesthetics*, 54.

22. Li and Cauvel, *Four Essays on Aesthetics*, 54.

23. Li and Cauvel, *Four Essays on Aesthetics*, 54–55.

24. Marx, *Economic and Philosophic Manuscripts*, 76.

25. Li and Cauvel, *Four Essays on Aesthetics*, 56.

26. Zehou Li, *Wo de Zhexue Tigang* [The outline of my philosophy], 2:499.

27. Li and Cauvel, *Four Essays on Aesthetics*, 57.

28. Zhuangzi, *Zhuangzi Jinzhu Jinyi*, 94–95.

29. Li and Cauvel, *Four Essays on Aesthetics*, 62–64.

30. Li and Cauvel, *Four Essays on Aesthetics*, 68–69.

31. Li and Cauvel, *Four Essays on Aesthetics*, 71–72.

32. Li and Cauvel, *Four Essays on Aesthetics*, 72.

Chapter 7

1. James Shelley, "The Concept of the Aesthetic," in *The Stanford Encyclopedia of Philosophy*, ed. Edward N. Zalta, Winter 2017 ed., https://plato.stanford.edu/archives/win2017/entries/aesthetic-concept/.

2. Gary Iseminger, "Aesthetic Experience," in *The Oxford Handbook of Aesthetics*, ed. Jerrold Levinson (Oxford: Oxford University Press, 2005), 100.

3. Richard Shusterman, "The End of Aesthetic Experience," *Journal of Aesthetics and Art Criticism* 55, no. 1 (1997): 30.

4. Shusterman, "The End of Aesthetic Experience," 30.

5. We must remember that Beardsley in *Aesthetics* from 1958 proposed a concept of internalist aesthetic experience, and later in *The Aesthetic Point of View* from 1982 formulated an externalist one. This example is based on the earlier, internalist concept. Monroe Beardsley, *Aesthetics* (Indianapolis: Hackett, 1958); *The Aesthetic Point of View* (Ithaca, NY: Cornell University Press, 1982).

6. Monroe Beardsley, *Aesthetics*, 527.

7. George Dickie, "Beardsley's Phantom Aesthetic Experience," *Journal of Philosophy* 62, no. 5 (1965): 131–32.

8. Bence Nanay, *Aesthetics as Philosophy of Perception* (New York: Oxford University Press, 2016), 10, 12.

9. Li and Cauvel, *Four Essays on Aesthetics*, 83.

10. Li and Cauvel, *Four Essays on Aesthetics*, 85–86.

11. See, for instance Balling and Falk. "Development of Visual Preference for Natural Environments," 5–28; Chatterjee, *The Aesthetic Brain*, 13–14, 48–53.

12. The experiment was conducted by Frédéric Brochet. Discussed in Matthew Kieran, "The Fragility of Aesthetic Knowledge: Aesthetic Psychology and Appreciative Virtues," in *The Aesthetic Mind. Philosophy & Psychology*, ed. Elisabeth Schellekens and Peter Goldie (New York: Oxford University Press, 2011), 34–35.

13. Li and Cauvel, *Four Essays on Aesthetics*, 86.

14. Li and Cauvel, *Four Essays on Aesthetics*, 87.

15. Carl Gustav Jung, "The Significance of Constitution and Heredity in Psychology," in *The Collected Works of C. G. Jung*, vol. 8, *Structure and Dynamics of the Psyche*, ed. and trans. Gerhard Adler and Richard Francis Carrington Hull (Princeton, NJ: Princeton University Press, 1975), 110–11.

16. Li and Cauvel, *Four Essays on Aesthetics*, 87.

17. Interestingly, this aspect of Kant's philosophy is one of the most consistent with Li's anthropological ontology. In his interpretation of Kant, Li usually underpins his concepts with historical materialism, but it seems that common sense already includes a kind of social practice genesis.

18. Kant, *Critique of the Power of Judgment*, 5:295–96.

19. Li and Cauvel, *Four Essays on Aesthetics*, 88–89.

20. Li and Cauvel, *Four Essays on Aesthetics*, 89.

21. Li and Cauvel, *Four Essays on Aesthetics*, 89.

22. Li and Cauvel, *Four Essays on Aesthetics*, 89.

23. Li and Cauvel, *Four Essays on Aesthetics*, 89.

24. Karl Marx, *Economic and Philosophic Manuscripts*, 87–88.

25. Li and Cauvel, *Four Essays on Aesthetics*, 90.

26. Li, *Wo de Zhexue Tigang* [The outline of my philosophy], 2:502.

27. Li and Cauvel, *Four Essays on Aesthetics*, 91–92.

28. Li and Cauvel, *Four Essays on Aesthetics*, 92.

29. Li and Cauvel, *Four Essays on Aesthetics*, 92.

30. Li, *A New Approach to Kant*, 329.

31. Li and Cauvel, *Four Essays on Aesthetics*, 93.

32. Jesse J. Prinz, "Constructive Sentimentalism: Legal and Political Implications," *Nomos* 53 (2013): 3, 6–7, 13.

33. Li and Cauvel, *Four Essays on Aesthetics*, 97.

34. Ellsworth and Scherer, "Appraisal Processes in Emotion," 574.

35. Li and Cauvel, *Four Essays on Aesthetics*, 97.

36. Experiment by Yoram S. Bonneh, Alexander Cooperman, and Dov Sagi, "Motion-Induced Blindness in Normal Observers," *Nature* 411 (2001): 798–801.

37. Experiment by Steven J. Luck, Geoffrey F. Woodman, Edward K. Vogel, "Event-Related Potential Studies of Attention," *Trends in Cognitive Sciences* 4, no. 11 (2000): 432–40.

38. Experiment by Irvin Rock, Christopher M. Linnett, Paul Grant, and Arien Mack, "Perception without Attention: Results of a New Method," *Cognitive Psychology* 24, no. 4 (1992): 502–34.

39. Daniel J. Simmons and Christopher F. Chabris, "Gorillas in Our Midst: Sustained Inattentional Blindness for Dynamic Events," *Perception* 28, no. 9 (1999): 1059–74.

40. Jesse J. Prinz, *The Conscious Brain: How Attention Engenders Experience* (New York, Oxford University Press, 2012), 83–87.

41. Piotr Winkielman, Kent C. Berridge, and Julia J. Wilbarger, "Unconscious Affective Reactions to Masked Happy versus Angry Faces Influence Consumption Behavior and Judgments of Value," *Personality and Social Psychology Bulletin* 31, no. 1 (2005): 121–35.

42. Prinz, *The Conscious Brain*, 81.

43. Li and Cauvel, *Four Essays on Aesthetics*, 97–98.

44. Kant, *Critique of the Power of Judgment*, 5:256.

45. Arien Mack, "Is the Visual World a Grand Illusion?" *Journal of Consciousness Studies* 9, nos. 5–6 (2002): 105.

46. Nanay, *Aesthetics as Philosophy of Perception*, 21–25.

47. Nanay, *Aesthetics as Philosophy of Perception*, 26.

48. Li and Cauvel, *Four Essays on Aesthetics*, 98.

49. Li and Cauvel, *Four Essays on Aesthetics*, 99.

50. Li and Cauvel, *Four Essays on Aesthetics*, 93.

51. Ellsworth and Scherer, "Appraisal Processes in Emotion," 574.

52. Joseph P. Forgas, "Affective Influences on Attitudes and Judgments," in *Handbook of Affective Sciences*, ed. Richard J. Davidson, Klaus R. Scherer, H. Hill Goldsmith (New York: Oxford University Press, 2003), 599–600.

53. Li and Cauvel, *Four Essays on Aesthetics*, 100.

54. Li and Cauvel, *Four Essays on Aesthetics*, 100–101.

55. Li and Cauvel, *Four Essays on Aesthetics*, 101.

56. Li and Cauvel, *Four Essays on Aesthetics*, 101.

57. Li and Cauvel, *Four Essays on Aesthetics*, 103–4.

58. Li and Cauvel, *Four Essays on Aesthetics*, 104.

59. Li and Cauvel, *Four Essays on Aesthetics*, 104.

60. Li and Cauvel, *Four Essays on Aesthetics*, 104.

61. Li and Cauvel, Four *Essays on Aesthetics*, 104.

62. Li and Cauvel, *Four Essays on Aesthetics*, 105.

63. Li and Cauvel, *Four Essays on Aesthetics*, 100.

64. Li and Cauvel, *Four Essays on Aesthetics*, 105.

65. Li and Cauvel, *Four Essays on Aesthetics*, 106.

66. Li and Cauvel, *Four Essays on Aesthetics*, 106.

67. Li and Cauvel, *Four Essays on Aesthetics*, 107.

68. Li and Cauvel, *Four Essays on Aesthetics*, 107–8.

69. Li and Cauvel, *Four Essays on Aesthetics*, 108.

70. Li and Cauvel, *Four Essays on Aesthetics*, 110.
71. Li and Cauvel, *Four Essays on Aesthetics*, 111.
72. Li and Cauvel, *Four Essays on Aesthetics*, 115.
73. Li and Cauvel, *Four Essays on Aesthetics*, 91–92.
74. Li and Cauvel, *Four Essays on Aesthetics*, 116–17.
75. Li and Cauvel, *Four Essays on Aesthetics*, 117.
76. Li and Cauvel, *Four Essays on Aesthetics*, 117.
77. Li and Cauvel, *Four Essays on Aesthetics*, 118.
78. Li and Cauvel, *Four Essays on Aesthetics*, 118–19.
79. Li and Cauvel, *Four Essays on Aesthetics*, 119.
80. Li and Cauvel, *Four Essays on Aesthetics*, 119.
81. Kant, *Critique of Judgment*, 5:219.
82. Li, *The Chinese Aesthetic Tradition*, 5–7.
83. Li and Cauvel, *Four Essays on Aesthetics*, 120–21.
84. Li and Cauvel, *Four Essays on Aesthetics*, 121–22.
85. Li, *A New Approach to Kant*, 68.
86. One can also treat priming as an unconscious aesthetic experience, in which some visual features (such as symmetry, proportion, etc.) evoke a percipient's response (here pleasure). However, Li's idea of aesthetic experience excludes such character of aesthetic experience as a whole. Alternatively, priming can be included in aesthetic attitude.
87. John Dewey, *Art as Experience* (New York: Milton, Balch, 1934), 38.
88. Ioannis Xenakis and Argyris Arnellos, "Aesthetics as an Emotional Activity That Facilitates Sense-Making: Towards an Enactive Approach to Aesthetic Experience," in *Aesthetics and the Embodied Mind: Beyond Art Theory and the Cartesian Mind-Body Dichotomy*, ed. Alfonsina Scarinzi (Dordrecht: Springer, 2015), 247.
89. Kant, *Critique of the Power of Judgment*, 5:187.
90. Li and Cauvel, *Four Essays on Aesthetics*, 116.
91. Xenakis and Arnellos, "Aesthetics as an Emotional Activity," 249.

Chapter 8

1. Li, *A New Approach to Kant*, 68–69.
2. Dewey, *Art as Experience*, 147–48.
3. Dewey, *Art as Experience*, 5–6.
4. Dewey, *Art as Experience*, 7.
5. Dewey, *Art as Experience*, 8.
6. Dewey, *Art as Experience*, 28.
7. In fact, Dewey is more explicitly critical of capitalism in other examples, for instance, when discussing private collectors, who gather artworks in order to confirm their wealth. See Dewey, *Art as Experience*, 8.
8. Dewey, *Art as Experience*, 13, 22.

9. Dewey, *Art as Experience*, 14.
10. Dewey, *Art as Experience*, 14.
11. Dewey, *Art as Experience*, 14–16.
12. Dewey, *Art as Experience*, 15.
13. Dewey, *Art as Experience*, 17.
14. Dewey, *Art as Experience*, 18, 23.
15. Dewey, *Art as Experience*, 28.
16. Dewey, *Art as Experience*, 25.
17. Dewey, *Art as Experience*, 16.
18. Dewey, *Art as Experience*, 55.
19. Dewey, *Art as Experience*, 147–49.
20. Dewey, *Art as Experience*, 150.
21. Dewey, *Art as Experience*, 35.
22. Dewey, *Art as Experience*, 36.
23. Dewey, *Art as Experience*, 38.
24. Dewey, *Art as Experience*, 41–42.
25. Dewey, *Art as Experience*, 42.
26. Dewey, *Art as Experience*, 43–44.
27. Dewey, *Art as Experience*, 135–36.
28. Dewey, *Art as Experience*, 137–38.
29. Dewey, *Art as Experience*, 139.
30. There are also theories that regard that appraisals antecede emotions. This entails that separating emotion from cognition. Ellsworth and Scherer, "Appraisal Processes in Emotion," 575.
31. Ellsworth and Scherer, "Appraisal Processes in Emotion," 573.
32. Li, *A New Approach to Kant*, vii.

Chapter 9

1. Nanay, *Aesthetics as Philosophy of Perception*, 12.
2. Nanay, *Aesthetics as Philosophy of Perception*, 4.
3. Nanay, "Philosophy of Perception as a Guide to Aesthetics," 102.
4. Nanay, "Philosophy of Perception as a Guide to Aesthetics," 101.
5. Nanay, "Philosophy of Perception as a Guide to Aesthetics," 104.
6. Nanay, confines the imagery to visual, but in fact it can be produced as bearing characteristics of other sense, or several senses.
7. Nanay, "Philosophy of Perception as a Guide to Aesthetics," 105–6.
8. Nanay, "Philosophy of Perception as a Guide to Aesthetics," 106.
9. Nanay, "Philosophy of Perception as a Guide to Aesthetics," 108.
10. Nanay, "Philosophy of Perception as a Guide to Aesthetics," 110.
11. Nanay, "Philosophy of Perception as a Guide to Aesthetics," 110–11.

12. Nanay, "Philosophy of Perception as a Guide to Aesthetics," 112.
13. Nanay, "Philosophy of Perception as a Guide to Aesthetics," 113.
14. Welsch, *Undoing Aesthetics*, 78.
15. Welsch, *Undoing Aesthetics*, 81–82.
16. Welsch, *Undoing Aesthetics*, 85.
17. After Welsch, *Undoing Aesthetics*, 40–41.
18. Welsch, *Undoing Aesthetics*, 85.
19. Welsch, *Undoing Aesthetics*, 15.
20. Welsch, *Undoing Aesthetics*, 37.
21. Welsch, *Undoing Aesthetics*, 83.
22. Welsch, *Undoing Aesthetics*, 9–16.
23. Welsch, *Undoing Aesthetics*, 98.
24. Welsch, *Undoing Aesthetics*, 3–4.
25. This resembles Kant's third *Critique*, matching the natural and theoretical laws, which after becoming a habit shifted the accompanying pleasure to the unconscious. Kant, *Critique of the Power of Judgment*, 5:184.
26. Welsch, *Undoing Aesthetics*, 45.
27. Welsch, *Undoing Aesthetics*, 45.
28. Welsch, *Undoing Aesthetics*, 6, 81.
29. See Gallese, "The Aesthetic World in the Digital Era," 57.

Bibliography

Ajdukiewicz, Kazimierz. *Problems and Theories of Philosophy*. Translated by Henryk Skolimowski and Anthony Quinton. London: Cambridge University Press, 1973.

Balling, John D., and John H. Falk. "Development of Visual Preference for Natural Environments." *Environment and Behavior* 14, no. 1 (1982): 5–28.

Banka, Rafal. "Contemporary Chinese Art as a Product and Reflection of Globalisation in Culture." *Journal of East-West Thought* 7, no. 3 (2017): 41–55.

———. "Li Zehou's Aesthetics as a Form of Cognition." In *Li Zehou and Confucian Philosophy*, edited by Roger T. Ames and Jinhua Jia, 356–73. Honolulu: University of Hawai'i Press, 2018.

Beardsley, Monroe. *The Aesthetic Point of View*. Ithaca, NY: Cornell University Press, 1982.

———. *Aesthetics*. Indianapolis: Hackett, 1958.

Bonneh, Yoram S., Alexander Cooperman, and Dov Sagi. "Motion-Induced Blindness in Normal Observers." *Nature* 411 (2001): 798–801.

Cai, Yi (蔡儀). *Wenxue Gailun* (文學概論) [Outlines of literature]. Beijing: Renmin Wenxue Chubanshe, 1981.

———. *Xin Meixue* (新美學) [New aesthetics]. Shanghai: Shanghai Qunyi Chubanshe, 1942.

Chatterjee, Anjan. *The Aesthetic Brain: How We Evolved to Desire Beauty and Enjoy Art*. New York: Oxford University Press, 2013.

Chen, Donglan, and Jianping Gao (陳冬蘭, 高建平). "*Zhexue Dawen*" (哲學答問). In *Li Zehou Zhexue Wencun* (李澤厚哲學文存), 2:457–98. Hefei: Anhui Wenyi Chubanshe, 1999.

Clark, Andy, and David Chalmers. "The Extended Mind." *Analysis* 58, no. 1 (1998): 7–19.

The Classic of Changes: A New Translation of the I Ching as Interpreted by Wang Bi. Translated by Richard John Lynn. New York: Columbia University Press, 1994.

Colombetti, Giovanna. *The Feeling Body: Affective Science Meets the Enactive Mind*. Cambridge, MA: MIT Press, 2014.

Confucius (孔子). *The Analects of Confucius: A Philosophical Translation*. Translated by Roger T. Ames and Henry Rosemont. New York: Ballantine, 1998.

———. *Analects, with Selections from Traditional Commentaries*. Translated by Edward Slingerland. Indianapolis: Hackett, 2003.

———. *Baihua Lunyu Duben* (白話論語讀本). Translated and edited by Si Liu. Shanghai: Shanghai Guangyi Shuju, 2017.

Corballis, Michael C. "The Evolution of Consciousness." In *The Cambridge Handbook of Consciousness*. Edited by Philip David Zelazo, Morris Moscovitch, Evan Thompson, 271–95. New York: Cambridge University Press, 2007.

———. *From Hand to Mouth: The Gestural Origins of Language*. Princeton, NJ: Princeton University Press, 2002.

Dennett, Daniel. "Where Am I?" In *The Mind's I: Fantasies and Reflections on Mind and Soul*, edited by Douglas R. Hofstadter and Daniel C. Dennett, 217–29. New York: Basic Books, 1981.

Descartes, René. *Meditations on First Philosophy*. In *Discourse on Method and Meditations on First Philosophy*, edited by David Weissman. Translated by Donald A. Cress. New Haven, CT: Yale University Press, 1996.

Dewey, John. *Art as Experience*. New York: Milton, Balch, 1934.

Dickie, George. "Beardsley's Phantom Aesthetic Experience." *Journal of Philosophy* 62, no. 5 (1965): 129–36.

Ding, John Zijiang. "Li Zehou: Chinese Aesthetics from a Post-Marxist and Confucian Perspective." In *Contemporary Chinese Philosophy*, edited by Nicholas Bunnin and Chung-ying Cheng, 246–59. Malden, MA: Blackwell, 2002.

Di Paolo, Ezequiel. "Autopoiesis, Adaptivity, Teleology, Agency." *Phenomenology and the Cognitive Sciences* 4 (2005): 429–52.

Diver, Julia. "Normative Ethics." In *The Oxford Handbook of Contemporary Philosophy*, edited by Frank Jackson and Michael Smith, 31–62. Oxford: Oxford University Press, 2007.

Ellsworth, Phoebe C., and Klaus R. Scherer. "Appraisal Processes in Emotion." In *Handbook of Affective Sciences*, edited by Richard J. Davidson, Klaus R. Scherer, and H. Hill Goldsmith, 572–95. New York: Oxford University Press, 2003.

Forgas, Joseph P. "Affective Influences on Attitudes and Judgments." In *Handbook of Affective Sciences*, edited by Richard J. Davidson, Klaus R. Scherer, and H. Hill Goldsmith, 596–618. New York: Oxford University Press, 2003.

Gallagher, Shaun, and Dan Zahavi. *The Phenomenological Mind: An Introduction to Philosophy of Mind and Cognitive Science*. Oxford: Routledge, 2008.

Gallese, Vittorio. "The Aesthetic World in the Digital Era: A Call to Arms for Experimental Aesthetics." *Reti, Saperi, Linguaggi*, no. 1 (2020): 55–84.

Han, Shihui, and Georg Northoff. "Culture-Sensitive Neural Substrates of Human Cognition: A Transcultural Neuroimaging Approach." *Nature* 9 (2008): 646–54.

Heidegger, Martin. *Being and Time*. Translated by John Macquarrie and Edward Robinson. Oxford: Blackwell, 1962.

———. "What Is Metaphysics?" Translated by David Farrell Krell. In *Pathmarks*, edited by William McNeill, 82–96. Cambridge: Cambridge University Press, 1998.

Hobbes, Thomas. *Leviathan*. Minneapolis: Learner, 2018.

Hursthouse, Rosalind, and Glen Pettigrove. "Virtue Ethics." In *The Stanford Encyclopedia of Philosophy*, edited by Edward N. Zalta. Winter 2018 ed. https://plato.stanford.edu/archives/win2018/entries/ethics-virtue/.

Iseminger, Gary. "Aesthetic Experience." In *The Oxford Handbook of Aesthetics*, edited by Jerrold Levinson, 99–117. Oxford: Oxford University Press, 2005.

Janiak, Andrew. "Kant's Views on Space and Time." In *The Stanford Encyclopedia of Philosophy*, edited by Edward N. Zalta. Spring 2020 ed. https://plato.stanford.edu/archives/spr2020/entries/kant-spacetime/.

Johnson, Mark. *The Aesthetics of Meaning and Thought: The Bodily Roots of Philosophy, Science, Morality, and Art*. Chicago: University of Chicago Press, 2018.

Jung, Carl Gustav. "The Significance of Constitution and Heredity in Psychology." In *The Collected Works of C. G. Jung*. Vol. 8, *Structure and Dynamics of the Psyche*, edited and translated by Gerhard Adler and Richard Francis Carrington Hull, 107–13. Princeton, NJ: Princeton University Press, 1975.

Kant, Immanuel. *Critique of Judgment*. Translated by Werner S. Pluhar. Indianapolis: Hackett, 1987.

———. *Critique of Pure Reason*. Translated by Norman Kemp Smith. Rev. 2nd ed. Basingstoke, UK: Palgrave Macmillan, 2007.

———. *Critique of the Power of Judgment*. Translated by Paul Guyer. New York: Cambridge University Press, 2002.

Kieran, Matthew. "The Fragility of Aesthetic Knowledge: Aesthetic Psychology and Appreciative Virtues." In *The Aesthetic Mind: Philosophy and Psychology*, edited by Elisabeth Schellekens and Peter Goldie, 32–43. New York: Oxford University Press, 2011.

Kirsh, David, and Paul Maglio. "On Distinguishing Epistemic from Pragmatic Action." *Cognitive Science* 18, no. 4 (1994): 513–49.

Kołakowski, Leszek. *Main Currents of Marxism: Its Rise, Growth, and Dissolution*. Vol. 1, *The Founders*, translated by Paul Stephen Falla. Oxford: Clarendon Press, 1978.

Küng, Hans, and Julia Ching. *Christianity and Chinese Religions*. New York: Doubleday, 1989.

Lai, Karyn L. *An Introduction to Chinese Philosophy*. New York: Cambridge University Press, 2008.

Lenin, Vladimir Illich. *Philosophical Notebooks*. Translated by Clemens Dutt. Edited by Stewart Smith. Vol. 38 of *Collected Works*. Moscow: Progress Publishers, 1965.

Le Poidevin, Robin. "The Experience and Perception of Time." In *The Stanford Encyclopedia of Philosophy*, edited by Edward N. Zalta. Summer 2019 ed. https://plato.stanford.edu/archives/sum2019/entries/time-experience/.

Levine, Joseph. "Materialism and Qualia: The Explanatory Gap." *Pacific Philosophical Quarterly* 64, no. 4 (1983): 354–61.

Levinson, Jerrold. "Philosophical Aesthetics: An Overview." In *The Oxford Handbook of Aesthetics*, edited by Jerrold Levinson, 3–24. Oxford: Oxford University Press, 2005.

Li, Zehou (李澤厚). *The Chinese Aesthetic Tradition*. Translated by Maija Bell Samei. Honolulu: University of Hawai'i Press, 2010.

———. *A History of Classical Chinese Thought*. Translated by Andrew Lambert. New York: Routledge, 2020.

———. "Kangde Zhexue yu Jianli Zhutixing Lungang"(康德哲學與建立主體性論綱) [The outline of Kant's philosophy and establishing subjectality]. In *Zhexue Meixue Wenxuan* (哲學美學文選), 148–63. Changsha: Hunan Renmin Chubanshe, 1985.

———. "Lun Meigan, Mei yu Yishu" (論美感, 美與藝術). *Zhexue Yanjiu* 5 (1956): 43–73.

———. *Meixue Si Jiang* (美學四講) [Four essays on aesthetics]. Beijing: San Lian Shudian,1989.

———. *A New Approach to Kant: A Confucian-Marxist's Viewpoint*. Translated by Jeanne Haizhen Allen and Christopher Ahn. Singapore: Springer, 2018.

———. *The Path of Beauty: A Study of Chinese Aesthetics*. Translated by Lizeng Gong. Hong Kong: Oxford University Press, 1994.

———. *Wo de Zhexue Tigang* (我的哲學提綱) [The outline of my philosophy]. In *Li Zehou Shi Nian Ji 1979–1989* (李澤厚十年集 1979–1989) [The decade of Li Zehou's collected works, 1979–1989], 2:449–533. Hefei: Anhui Yishu Chubanshe, 1994.

———. *Zhongguo Jindai Sixiang Shilun* (中國近代思想史論) [A history of premodern Chinese thought]. Beijing: Renmin Chubanshe, 1979.

———. *Zhongguo Meixue Shi* (中國美學史) [History of Chinese aesthetics]. Hefei: Anhui Wenyi Chubanshe, 1999.

———. *Zhongguo Xiandai Sixiang Shilun* (中國現代思想史論) [A history of modern Chinese thought]. Beijing: Dongfang Chubanshe, 1987.

Li, Zehou, and Jane Cauvel. *Four Essays on Aesthetics: Toward a Global View*. Lanham, MD: Lexington Books, 2006.

Lieberman, Daniel E. "Sphenoid Shortening and the Evolution of Modern Cranial Shape." *Nature* 393 (1998): 158–62.

Liu, Kang. *Aesthetics and Marxism: Chinese Aesthetic Marxists and Their Western Contemporaries*. Durham, NC: Duke University Press, 2000.

Liu, Zaifu (劉再復). *Li Zehou Meixue Gailun* (李澤厚美學概論) [The outline of Li Zehou's aesthetics]. Beijing: San Lian Shudian, 2009.

Locke, John. *An Essay concerning Human Understanding*. Kitchener, ON: Batoche Books, 2001.

Luck, Steven J., Geoffrey F. Woodman, and Edward K. Vogel. "Event-Related Potential Studies of Attention." *Trends in Cognitive Sciences* 4, no. 11 (2000): 432–40.

Mack, Arien. "Is the Visual World a Grand Illusion?" *Journal of Consciousness Studies* 9, nos. 5–6 (2002): 102–10.

Man, Eva Kit Wah. *Issues of Contemporary Art and Aesthetics in Chinese Context*. Berlin: Springer, 2015.

Mao, Zedong. "On Practice." In *On Practice and Contradiction*, 52–66. London: Verso, 2007.

Maruszewski, Tomasz. *Psychologia poznania* [Cognitive psychology]. Gdańsk: Gdańskie Wydawnictwo Psychologiczne, 2002.

Marx, Karl. *Economic and Philosophic Manuscripts*. In *The Marx-Engels Reader*, edited by Robert E. Tucker, 66–125. Translated by Martin Milligan. New York: W. W. Norton and Company, 1978.

———. "Theses on Feuerbach." In *Karl Marx Selected Works*, translated by Clemens Dutt, 1:471–73. New York: International Publishers, n.d.

Menary, Richard. "What Is Radical Enactivism?" In *Radical Enactivism: Intentionality, Phenomenology and Narrative: Focus on the Philosophy of Daniel D. Hutto*, edited by Richard Menary, 1–13. Amsterdam: John Benjamins, 2006.

Mencius (孟子). *Mencius*. Translated by Din-cheuk Lau. Middlesex: Penguin, 1984.

———. *Mengzi* (孟子). Beijing: Zhonghua Shuju, 2007.

———. *Mengzi: With Selections from Traditional Commentaries*. Translated by Bryan Van Norden. Indianapolis: Hackett, 2008.

———. *The Works of Mencius*. Translated by James Legge. New York: Clarendon Press, 1985.

Mo Tzu (Mozi). *Basic Writings*. New York: Columbia University Press, 1966.

Morawski, Stefan. "O marksistowskiej myśli estetycznej" [On Marxist aesthetic thought]. In *Estetyki filozoficzne XX wieku* [Philosophical aesthetics of the twentieth century], edited by Krystyna Wilkoszewska, 133–58. Kraków: Universitas, 2000.

Nanay, Bence. *Aesthetics as Philosophy of Perception*. New York: Oxford University Press, 2016.

———. "Philosophy of Perception as a Guide to Aesthetics." In *Aesthetics and the Sciences of Mind*, edited by Greg Currie, Matthew Kieran, Aaron Meskin, and Jon Robson, 101–20. New York: Oxford University Press, 2014.

Nida-Rümelin, Martine. "Dualist Emergentism." In *Contemporary Debates in Philosophy of Mind*, edited by Brian P. McLaughlin and Jonathan Cohen, 269–86. Malden, MA: Blackwell, 2007.

Plato. *Symposium*. Edited and translated by Robin Waterfield. Oxford: Oxford University Press, 1998.

Prinz, Jesse J. *The Conscious Brain: How Attention Engenders Experience*. New York: Oxford University Press, 2012.

———. "Constructive Sentimentalism: Legal and Political Implications." *Nomos* 53 (2013): 3–18.

Rock, Irvin, Christopher M. Linnett, Paul Grant, and Arien Mack. "Perception without Attention: Results of a New Method." *Cognitive Psychology* 24, no. 4 (1992): 502–34.

Rupert, Robert D. "Challenges to the Hypothesis of Extended Cognition." *Journal of Philosophy* 101, no. 8 (2004), 389–428.

Sartre, Jean-Paul. *Existentialism Is a Humanism*. Translated by Carol Macomber. New Haven, CT: Yale University Press, 2007.

Sassen, Brigitte. "18th Century German Philosophy Prior to Kant." In *The Stanford Encyclopedia of Philosophy*, edited by Edward N. Zalta. Summer 2015 ed. https://plato.stanford.edu/archives/sum2015/entries/18thGerman-preKant/.

Scarinzi, Alfonsina. "Enactive Literariness and Aesthetic Experience: From Mental Schemata to Anti-representationalism." In *Aesthetics and the Embodied Mind: Beyond Art Theory and the Cartesian Mind-Body Dichotomy*, edited by Alfonsina Scarinzi, 261–280. Dordrecht: Springer, 2015.

Scherer, Klaus R. "Introduction: Cognitive Components of Emotion." In *Handbook of Affective Sciences*, edited by Richard J. Davidson, Klaus R. Scherer, and H. Hill Goldsmith, 563–71. New York: Oxford University Press, 2003.

Shelley, James. "The Concept of the Aesthetic." In *The Stanford Encyclopedia of Philosophy*, edited by N. Zalta. Winter 2017 ed. https://plato.stanford.edu/archives/win2017/entries/aesthetic-concept/.

Shusterman, Richard. "The End of Aesthetic Experience." *Journal of Aesthetics and Art Criticism* 55, no. 1 (1997): 29–41.

———. *Pragmatist Aesthetics: Living Beauty, Rethinking Art*. Lanham, MD: Rowman and Littlefield, 2000.

Simmons, Daniel J., and Christopher F. Chabris. "Gorillas in Our Midst: Sustained Inattentional Blindness for Dynamic Events." *Perception* 28, no. 9 (1999): 1059–74.

Sinnott-Armstrong, Walter. "Consequentialism." In *The Stanford Encyclopedia of Philosophy*, edited by Edward N. Zalta. Summer 2019 ed. https://plato.stanford.edu/archives/sum2019/entries/consequentialism/.

Thompson, Evan. "Life and Mind: From Autopoiesis to Neurophenomenology. A Tribute to Francisco Varela." *Phenomenology and the Cognitive Sciences* 3 (2004): 381–98.

———. "Living Ways of Sense Making." *Philosophy Today* 55, suppl. (2011): 114–23.

———. *Mind in Life: Biology, Phenomenology, and the Sciences of Mind*. Cambridge MA: Harvard University Press, 2007.

van Inwagen, Peter. *Material Beings*. Ithaca, NY: Cornell University Press, 1990.

Varela, Francisco J., Evan Thompson, Eleanor Rosch. *The Embodied Mind: Cognitive Science and Human Experience*. Cambridge, MA: MIT Press, 1993.

Welsch, Wolfgang. *Undoing Aesthetics*. Translated by Andrew Inkpin. London: Sage, 1997.

Wheeler, Michael. "Martin Heidegger." In *The Stanford Encyclopedia of Philosophy*, edited by Edward N. Zalta. Winter 2018 ed. https://plato.stanford.edu/archives/win2018/entries/heidegger/.

Wilson, Robert A., and Lucia Foglia. "Embodied Cognition." In *The Stanford Encyclopedia of Philosophy*, edited by Edward N. Zalta. Spring 2017 ed. https://plato.stanford.edu/archives/spr2017/entries/embodied-cognition/.

Winkielman, Piotr, Kent C. Berridge, and Julia J. Wilbarger. "Unconscious Affective Reactions to Masked Happy versus Angry Faces Influence Consumption Behavior and Judgments of Value." *Personality and Social Psychology Bulletin* 31, no. 1 (2005): 121–35.

Wittgenstein, Ludwig. *Philosophical Investigations*. Translated by G. E. M. Anscombe. Oxford: Blackwell, 1986.

Xenakis, Ioannis, and Argyris Arnellos. "Aesthetics as an Emotional Activity That Facilitates Sense-Making: Towards an Enactive Approach to Aesthetic Experience." In *Aesthetics and the Embodied Mind: Beyond Art Theory and the Cartesian Mind-Body Dichotomy*, edited by Alfonsina Scarinzi, 245–59. Dordrecht: Springer, 2015.

Zajonc, Robert B. "Thinking and Feeling: Preferences Need No Inferences." *American Psychologist* 35, no. 2 (1980): 151–75.

Zangwill, Nick. "Beauty." In *The Oxford Handbook of Aesthetics*, edited by Jerrold Levinson, 325–44. Oxford: Oxford University Press, 2005.

Zhou, Lian, Anying Chen, and Huayin Yu (周濂, 陳岸瑛, 於華音). "Lishi Yanjie yu Lilun de 'Du' " (歷史眼界與理論的 "度") [Historical vision and theoretical measure]. *Tianya* (天涯) 2 (1999): 128–35.

Zhu, Guangqian (朱光潛). *Shilun* (詩論) [On poetry]. Shanghai: Huadong Shifan Daxue Chubanshe, 2018.

———. *Yishu Xinlixue* (藝術心理學) [The psychology of art]. Hefei: Anhui Jiaoyu Chubanshe, [1930] 2006.

Zhuangzi (莊子). *Zhuangzi Jinzhu Jinyi* (莊子今注今譯) [Zhuangzi: contemporary translation and commentaries]. Edited by Chen Guying. Beijing: Zhonghua Shuju, 1985.

Zimbardo, Philip. *Psychologia i życie* [Psychology and life]. Warsaw: Wydawnictwo Naukowe PWN, 1999.

Index

adaptation: and appraisal, 108–109; Dewey on, 165; 168; in enactivism, 158–59, 172; and new sensuousness, 133, 140; phylogenetic, 131; and practice, 64, 87; pragmatist, 155, 161; and sedimentation, 50, 66, 130; and sense-making, 103, 106–107

aesthetic, the, 154–155, 157, 167, 174, 182, 188, 190; and cognition, 140; and cognition according to Dewey, 158, 162–63, 164, 166–70, 175; and cognition according to Kant, 42–43, 63–64; in Confucianism 20–22, 150; and emotion, 110; and freedom, 57, 88–89, 153; in Marxism, 34–35; and practice, 58; and sedimentation, 57; and subjectality, 71; according to Welsch, 185

aesthetic apprehension of reality, 152, 153, 156, 164, 167, 168, 171, 189, 192; Welsch, 183–84, 186, 187

aesthetic attention (*shenmei zhuyi* 審美注意), 138, 140–42, 156, 180

aesthetic attitude (*shenmei taidu* 審美態度), 114, 138–39, 144, 213n86

aesthetic emotion (*shenmei qinggan* 審美情感), 149–50

aesthetic enjoyment. *See* sense of beauty

aesthetic experience, 70, 71, 104, 105, 108, 110, 115; conceptualization of, 128–29; and experimental research, 129–30; and humanization of senses, 136–37; Nanay, 178; stages of according to Li, 138–43; structure of according to Dewey, 171–72; structure according to Li, 143–150; typology, 125–27; Zhu Guangqian, 24–25, 198–99n5

aesthetic feeling. *See* sense of beauty

aesthetic fever, the (*meixue re* 美學熱), 1, 199n18

aestheticization, 153; Welsch, 183–187 passim

aesthetic pleasure: Kant, 66, 67; Li, 57, 149–50; types of, 151–54. *See also* sense of beauty

aesthetic imagination (*shenmei xiangxiang* 審美想象), 147–49

aesthetic judgment: Kant, 52–56

aesthetic preferences: dependence of, 130, 144; origin of, 83–84

aesthetics 3–4; Confucianism, 22; Dewey, 162–63; Kant, 42–43, 63; Marxism, 34–35; Nanay, 178–82 passim; and philosophy of art, 178–79; Welsch, 182–85 passim

aesthetic sensation (*shenmei ganzhi* 審美感知), 143–45
aesthetic understanding (*shenmei lijie* 審美理解), 145–47
affective science, 105, 107, 142–43
affectivity, 105–106
alienation. *See* estrangement of labor
Althusser, Louis, 27
anaestheticization, 184, 186
Analects, The (Confucius), 15, 18
appraisal, 108–09. *See also* appraisal theory
appraisal theory, 107, 175. *See also* appraisal
anthropological ontology, 1, 46, 72, 87. *See also* subjectality
a priori: Kant, 39–40, 95; Li, 41, 47, 65, 69, 88
a posteriori judgment, 40
Arnellos, Argyris, 158
art, 90, 147, 149, 151; Confucianism 18–20 passim, 89; Dewey, 163, 166, 169, 172; Kant, 58–60; as practice, 21, 91, 121
artistics, 182, 185
attention: in consciousness, 139; distributed and focused, 14. *See also* aesthetic attention
autopoiesis. 103, 166. *See also* autopoietic enactivism
autopoietic enactivism, 96, 102–103, 110, 165. *See also* autopoiesis

Baumgarten, Alexander Gottlieb, 4, 43, 154, 183
Beardsley, Monroe, 127, 210n5
beauty: in art according to Kant, 54–55; Chinese etymology of, 112–13; Confucianism, 8, 13; enactive approach to, 119; Kant's adherent (*pulchritudo adhaerens*) 58–59, 202n54; Kant's free (*pulchritudo vaga*), 58; Marxism, 34–35; objectivism and subjectivism of, 113–14; objectivism of through practice, 117–19; as practice, 119
Book of Changes, The, 9–10, 12, 13, 90, 196n9
brain in the vat, 96–97
Brochet, Frédéric, 130

Cai, Yi, 24, 25
Cartesian cogito, 28, 80
Chalmers, David, 99, 100
Chinese Aesthetic Tradition, The (Li), 67, 153
Ching, Julia, 90
Clark, Andy, 99, 100
cognition and the aesthetic, 4, 146–47, 149, 159; Confucianism, 20; Dewey, 167–70, 172; Kant, 43, 50, 52–53, 55, 56, 63–64; Marxism, 35; Welsch, 183–84
cognition and practice, 47, 79–80, 88, 100, 104, 121–22, 186; Confucianism, 17; Marxism, 28, 30, 200n33
Colombetti, Giovanna, 105, 106
common sense (*sensus communis*), 53, 54, 56, 64, 133, 211n17
Confucian aesthetics, 21–22
Confucianism: and emotions, 13, 21, 81–82; and social practice, 86; and virtue ethics, 16–18
Confucius, 7, 8, 10, 13, 16
consciousness: in emergentism, 93; Li, 82–83; Marxism, 28, 32–33, 200n44
cosmological thinking. *See* cosmology
cosmology, 10–12; Confucianism, 12; influence on Li, 86. See also *Book of* Changes; *qi*
Critique of the Critical Philosophy: A Study of Kant (Li). See *A New*

Approach to Kant: A Confucian-Marxist's Viewpoint, 38
Critique of Judgment. See *Critique of the Power of Judgment*
Critique of the Power of Judgment (Kant), 52, 63, 115, 133, 140, 215n25
Critique of Pure Reason (Kant), 42, 52, 63, 176

Danto, Arthur, 126
Dennett, Daniel C., 96
Descartes, René, 18
destiny, 90–91
Dewey, John, 126, 127, 158, 192
dialectical laws, 200n44
Dickie, George, 127
Di Paolo, Ezequiel, 102

Economic and Philosophic Manuscripts (Marx), 25–26, 35, 37, 38, 57–58, 91, 135, 199n7
Ellsworth, Phoebe C., 108, 139
embedded cognition, 98–99
embodied cognition, 96–98
emergentism, 93
emotion: in affective science, 107–108; Confucianism, 13, 21; in Dewey's concept of aesthetic experience, 170. *See also* aesthetic emotion; emotional substance
emotional substance (*qinggan benti* 情感本體), 81–82, 85, 105, 108
enactivism, 100–102, 115–16, 158, 159, 172
Engels, Friedrich, 26, 27, 40, 46, 80
estrangement of labor (*die entfremdete Arbeit*), 26, 31–32, 34–35, 57, 199n7. *See also* labor
explanatory gap, 93–94
extended cognition, 81, 98–99

Feuerbach, Ludwig, 80
figurative synthesis (*synthesis speciosa*), 48–49, 63, 65, 147
First Critique, The. See *Critique of Pure Reason*
4E, 96, 110, 189
Four Essays on Aesthetics (Li), 144
Frankfurt School, the, 27, 28, 92
free beauty. *See* beauty

Gallagher, Shaun, 97
Gao, Ertai, 24
gestalt, 114–16, 130–32 passim

Hegel, Georg Wilhelm Friedrich, 80
Heidegger, Martin, 74; readiness-at hand and presence-at hand, 79
historical ontology. *See* subjectality
History of Classical Chinese Thought, A (Li), 86
Hobbes, Thomas, 74
humanization of nature (*ziran de renhua* 自然的人化), 13, 26, 57–58, 61, 62, 113, 117, 118, 122, 133, 182, 186, 199n7
Hursthouse, Rosalind, 14, 16

imagination, the: Kant, 48–49; in Li's concept of aesthetic experience, 174; and understanding, 49, 63–64. *See also* aesthetic imagination
Iseminger, Gary, 126
isomorphic structures, 114–15, 116, 118, 130, 131

joy (*le* 樂), 8, 20, 22
Jung, Carl Gustav, 131, 132

Kant, Immanuel, 71, 76, 80, 91, 95, 115, 133, 134, 140, 143, 150. See also *Critique of the Power of Judgment*; *Critique of Pure Reason*
Kirsh, David, 99, 207–208n7

Kołakowski, Leszek, 26, 28, 32, 33
Küng, Hans, 90

labor, 26. *See also* estrangement of labor; practice; practice of making and using tools; sedimentation
Lai, Karyn L., 10
Lakatos, Imre, 180
language: development from manual gesture, 78–79; as practice according to Li and Wittgenstein, 78
Leibniz, Gottfried Wilhelm, 43, 44
Lenin, Vladimir Illich, 79–80
Levinson, Jerrold, 3
Liu, Kang, 37–38
Liu, Zaifu, 196n7
Locke, John, 45, 80

Mack, Arien, 141
Maglio, Paul, 99, 207–208n7
Man, Eva Kit Wah, 24
Manuscripts, The. See *Economic and Philosophic Manuscripts*
Mao, Zedong, 199n17; on practice, 27–28
Marx, Karl, 27, 28, 34, 35, 57, 199n11; social existence according to, 74–75
Mencius, 16, 196n7
music: Confucianism, 8, 18, 19–21, 89, 155; and humanization of sense organs, 136, 173

Nanay, Bence, 128, 141, 188
nature: Confucian human, 16; and cosmos, 11; and humans, 82–84, 119–120; and humans in Marxism, 28–29, 32; necessity of, 41; and practice, 87; purposiveness of, 61. *See also* humanization of nature
New Approach to Kant: A Confucian-Marxist's Viewpoint, A (Li), 38, 64, 69, 72, 80, 82, 86, 91
new sensuousness (*xin ganxing* 新感性), 125, 133–138 passim, 142, 144, 155, 157, 172, 182, 189
Newton, Isaac: mechanics laws, 40, 41
Nida-Rümelin, Martine, 93

ontogenesis, 134
Outline of My Philosophy, The (Li), 72, 119, 136

Paris Manuscripts. See *Economic and Philosophic Manuscripts*
Path of Beauty: A Study of Chinese Aesthetics, The (Li), 91
Pettigrove, Glen, 14, 16
philosophy of art: and aesthetics, 3, 110, 126, 155, 177, 181, 182; Kant, 58–60
philosophy of subjectality. *See* anthropological ontology; subjectality
phylogenesis, 134
Piaget, Jean, 77; theory of development, 77–78, 91
Plato, 114
pleasures of the ear and the eye (*yue er yue mu* 悦耳悦目), 151–152. *See also* aesthetic pleasure: types of
pleasures of the mind and heart (*yue xin yue yi* 悦心悦意), 152–153. *See also* aesthetic pleasure: types of
pleasure of one's lofty aspiration and moral integrity (*yue zhi yue shen* 悦志悦神), 153–154. *See also* aesthetic pleasure: types of
practice, 76, 80; Confucian 16–18; Marxist, 27–29, 32–35 passim. *See also* practice of making and using tools; sedimentation
practice of making and using tools, 27, 46, 66, 73, 99

practice of tool manufacturing and use. *See* practice of making and using tools
pragmatism, 155, 161–62
Prinz, Jesse J., 138, 139
psychological substance (*xinlibenti* 心裡本體), 72, 73, 77; and emotional substance, 81–82, 92, 143; humanization of, 136–137; and individual life, 85; and practice, 83, 88, 99
purposiveness of nature: and humans according to Kant, 51–52, 60–62

qi (氣), 11, 196n13

ren (仁), 15, 16; and music, 19, 20; as sensitivity, 17, 21, 88; translation of, 197n25
representationism, 101
rhythms of nature, 168, 173, 176
Rosch, Eleanor, 101, 103, 104
Rupert, Rob, 98

Sartre, Jean-Paul, 18, 75
schemata: Kant, 49–50; Li, 50
Scherer, Klaus R., 107, 108
scientific laws: Li, 41
sedimentation (*jidian* 積澱), 46; and the aesthetic, 57, 62, 142; and affectivity, 105; and embodiment, 97–98; and extended cognition, 99; rational, 81–82; 86; and self-maintenance, 107; and sense organs, 62, 144, 157
self-maintenance, 102, 103, 107, 119, 158
sense-making, 102–103, 106–107, 118, 119, 14; in aesthetic experience, 148–49, 158
sense of beauty (*meigan* 美感), 142, 149
sense organs: humanization of, 136; Marxism, 30. *See also under* sedimentation
Shelley, James, 125
Shusterman, Richard, 126, 127, 156, 157
situated cognition, 96, 101, 105, 107, 156, 191
social existence, 25, 29, 74, 75, 83
space and time: Kant, 43–45; Leibniz, 44; Newton, 43–44; Li, 45–46, 47, 76–77
Straus, Edwin, 97
subject, 38; Cartesian, 18; in Chinese cosmology, 11–12; Confucianism, 17, 20, 22; in enactivism, 103; in extended cognition, 99; Kant, 42, 62, 63, 64; Marxism, 28, 30; and subjectality, 81
subjectality 1, 81; historical context of, 71; substances of, 72; translation of, 69–70. *See also* emotional substance; psychological substance; techno-social substance
substance (*benti* 本體): and emotion, 21–22; and practice, 27, 32; Li's understanding of, 73; *qi* as, 196n13; translation of, 204–05n8; *yin* and *yang*, 11. *See also* emotional substance; psychological substance; techno-social substance

technology, 41, 121, 122, 192
techno-social substance (*gongjubenti* 工具本體), 72–76 passim, 81, 85
Theses on Feuerbach (Marx), 200n33
Third Critique, The. See *Critique of Judgment*
Thompson, Evan, 101, 102, 103, 106
tool making and using practice. *See* practice of making and using tools

tool manufacturing and use. *See* practice of making and using tools
tool practice. *See* practice of making and using tools
tool usage and production. *See* practice of making and using tools

understanding, the, 47, 153, 156; Kant, 42–45, 49–56 passim, 63, 65, 66, 140; in Li's aesthetics, 143–50 passim, 173–74

Varela, Francisco J., 101, 103, 104, 106
virtue ethics, 14–16; Confucian ethics as, 16–17

Welsch, Wolfgang, 178, 188
Williams, Raymond, 27
Wittgenstein, Ludwig, 74; family resemblance, 128, 185; on language, 76, 78

Xenakis, Ioannis, 158

Yijing, The. See *Book of Changes*
yinyang (陰陽). *See* cosmology

Zahavi, Dan, 97
Zhu, Guangqian, 24–25, 37, 118
Zhuangzi, The, 89, 120, 154
zhutixing (主體性). *See* subjectality

www.ingramcontent.com/pod-product-compliance
Lightning Source LLC
LaVergne TN
LVHW050151080826
844660LV00002B/167

* 9 7 8 1 4 3 8 4 8 9 2 3 0 *